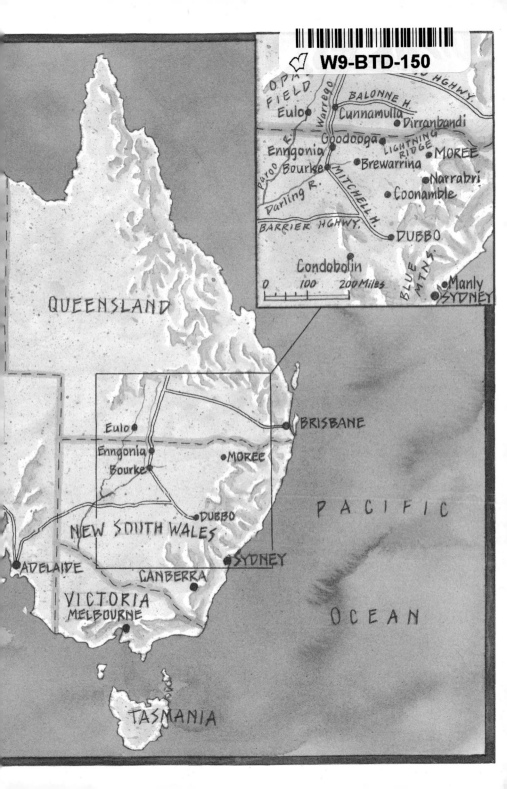

QUEENSLAND

O.P... FIELD

Eulo

Warrego

BALONNE H.

Cunnamulla

Dirranbandi

...O HGHWY.

Goodooga

LIGHTNING RIDGE

MOREE

Enngonia

Payoo

Bourke

Brewarrina

Narrabri

Darling R.

MITCHELL H.

Coonamble

BARRIER HGHWY.

DUBBO

Condobolin

BLUE MTNS.

Manly
SYDNEY

0    100    200 Miles

Eulo

Enngonia
Bourke

MOREE

BRISBANE

DUBBO

NEW SOUTH WALES

SYDNEY

PACIFIC

ADELAIDE

CANBERRA

VICTORIA
MELBOURNE

OCEAN

TASMANIA

WHEN YOU SEE THE EMU IN THE SKY

# WHEN YOU SEE
# THE EMU IN THE SKY

*My Journey
of Self-Discovery
in the Outback*

ELIZABETH FULLER

WILLIAM MORROW AND COMPANY, INC.
NEW YORK

Copyright © 1997 by Elizabeth Fuller

Endpaper map copyright © by David Cain

It is the policy of William Morrow and Company, Inc., and its imprints
and affiliates, recognizing the importance of preserving what has been written,
to print the books we publish on acid-free paper,
and we exert our best efforts to that end.

Library of Congress Cataloging-in-Publication Data

Fuller, Elizabeth (Elizabeth L.)
    When you see the emu in the sky : my journey of self-discovery in
the Outback / Elizabeth Fuller
    p.  cm.
    ISBN 0-688-14895-6 (hardcover)
    1. Fuller, Elizabeth (Elizabeth L.) —Journeys—Australia.
2. Women authors, American—20th century—Biography.   3. Self-
actualization (Psychology).   3. Americans—Travel—Australia.
5. Women—Travel—Australia.   6. Australian aborigines.   I. Title.
PS3556.U43Z474   1997
818'.5403—dc21                                                                97-16194
[B]                                                                                    CIP

Printed in the United States of America

First Edition

1   2   3   4   5   6   7   8   9   10

FRONTISPIECE ILLUSTRATION BY JO ANNE METSCH

BOOK DESIGN BY OKSANA KUSHNIR

FOR REUEL

and in memory of
Randy Allen (1957–1995)
and
for Max Eulo and all my friends
in Enngonia

---

## ACKNOWLEDGMENTS

My deepest thanks to Father Ted Kennedy, Sister Dorothy, and Sister Pat for all the kindness they showed me during my Australian stay.

In addition, three other Down Under friends have my gratitude—Joan and Tony Kenrick, and Anthony Gaha, who tirelessly checked and rechecked the spelling of Aborigine words in the manuscript.

On this side of the globe, I'd like to thank Gerald and John Dorman, my two delightful stepsons. Gerald for giving me his laptop computer after mine crashed, and John, whenever he was around, for good-naturedly driving Chris to and from golf courses so I could write without interruption. I don't want to forget my friend Mary Ann Roehm for doing more than her fair share of driving too.

Thanks to my literary agent, Roberta Pryor, who had the inspired idea of sending the story proposal to Liza Dawson. And thanks to Liza for liking it, buying it, and passing it along to Elmer Luke, my brilliant, wise, and patient editor, who guided this story, which is so close to my heart, to its completion. Last, but not least, I want to thank my son, Christopher, for having the trust in me—well, sort of—to accompany me deep into the Outback. And, oh yes, thanks, Christopher, for refraining from using my office as a putting green during my writing hours!

WHEN YOU SEE THE EMU IN THE SKY

# O N E

The sun had just begun to set, turning the skies that canopied the vast, flat western horizon into a surrealistic red. It was the most beautiful but the most dangerous time of the day to be driving in the Australian Outback. At dusk and dawn, kangaroo go on the move. They aren't dangerous, but they will leap into the road as if they own it. A Big Gray roo can weigh as much as two hundred pounds and can do as much damage to any moving car as the other way around.

In Australia's immense interior it's not uncommon to drive for hundreds of miles without seeing another car or house or service station. Travelers are cautioned to bring plenty of bottled water and make the trip in a caravan. Even the massive trailer trucks travel four, five, six in a row. They're called road trains—a cross between a truck and a train. Each is about thirty-five or forty feet long and will have another trailer hitched on called a "dog." Sometimes six dogs are hitched on. And when you see the rigs barreling down the highway, the only thing to do is to get off the road, fast. The roads are so dead straight that you can see the trucks coming for miles. They're usually hauling cattle on three-tiered tractor-trailers. When the road trains approach, kicking up dust, rocks, and cattle droppings, the earthy drivers, like the Big Grays, don't make the weakest gesture to give you room.

In spite of all this, I felt safe with Max at my side. Max was a full-blood Aborigine, born and bred in the Outback. He knew the *billibongs*, the watering holes in the bush, from the ceremonial songs his mother taught him and his siblings when they were very young. He knew where and when it was going to rain by the subtle changes in the direction of the wind. He knew how to track for rabbits simply by putting his ear to the ground. He knew how to hunt lizards and dig for witchetty grub. And he knew which flowers teemed with nectar you could drink and which would kill you within hours. With Max, we had no worries. On the other hand, it was comforting to know that the trunk of our car was loaded with supplies of water and familiar food. Before we left Sydney, Chris, my twelve-year-old son, and I filled a duffle bag with peanut butter, raisins, Robert Tims coffee bags, Cadbury chocolate bars, instant oatmeal, chocolate chip cookies, little wedges of pasteurized cheese, anything we could find to stave off hunger, just in case the wild tucker that Max had been trumpeting did not agree with us.

We had started from Sydney that morning, a six-hour train ride with local stops in every bush town dating back to the gold rush days of the last century. When we arrived in Dubbo, a rather sizable Outback town four hundred kilometers northwest of Sydney, a man from the car rental agency picked us up. One of the forms I had to sign stated in bold print that if I hit a kangaroo, I was responsible for the first thousand dollars in damage. "How often does that happen?" I asked.

"Poor Canadian bloke hit one yesta'dy," he said, flashing a token trace of emotion.

"What'd he do with the dead kangaroo?" my son asked.

The man was too busy checking my passport, visa, and Connecticut driver's license to answer.

Chris wouldn't leave it alone. He gave his best Aussie accent: "Did he throw it on the barbie?"

The agent took a lung-searing drag off a hand-rolled cigarette and said, " 'Oo's this joker?"

"The young fulla's me mate," Max spoke up. "I'm takin' him and his mum up to Enngonia where my people are. We've never had whites stayin' with us before."

"Yeah?" the agent said, adjusting his bush hat, studying the three of us. I gathered we were not a common sight here.

While Max and Chris went outside to begin loading the car,

the agent completed the paperwork. "So yer Aborigine mate's taken yuz on a walkabout," he said, as he handed me the rental agreement.

"Something like that," I responded. I slipped the yellow copy into my passport and followed him out to a red Holden that was parked between a car with a bashed-in front and a Jeep with a "roo bar"—a steel bracket mounted across the front grill for protection from kangaroos. The Jeep was twice the price of the Holden.

"Rough as guts out 'ere in the bush," he said, eyeballing the bashed-in car, giving me one last chance to spring for the pricey four-wheel Jeep. "Be glad you got a full-blood with yuz." He nodded respectfully toward Max. Max smiled and nodded back.

While Max examined the tires, the agent checked the speedometer and jotted down the mileage on the palm of his hand. "How far ya goin', mum?"

Max piped up, "Back o'Bourke."

"Awwwgh, Back o'Bourke." The agent sucked in air as if there was no way he'd be caught dead going there.

There's a common saying all through Australia that when somebody lives very far away, they live Back o'Bourke. There's a good reason for that. Bourke is the point of no return. Venture farther and you're into the land Back o'Bourke—the back of beyond. Back of the black stump. But for Max it wasn't the back of beyond. It was the land he grew up on the land where he fished, hunted, and learned about the Dreamtime, when ancestral spirits traveled the land creating people, animals, rivers, oceans, sky, mountains, and sacred sites. Those sacred sites abounded in the Outback. They were the stopping-off places where the Great Spirits paused on their journey. For many of us Westerners, the Dreamtime is poetic, lyrical, but for the Aborigines, it is the core of their being. They are linked, each of them, to an ancestral being.

The soil is the very source of life, and the Aborigines' identity and position within their tribe is based on the place where they were born. The earth owns and controls them, not the other way around. So they must live in harmony and balance. Max had his own way of putting it. "We are the caretakers of our land. We take only what we need. Not a witchetty grub more. When ya meet my people, ya'll understan' the way the Aborigine live an' think."

I was just hoping that when Chris and I met Max's people, we didn't do or say anything that would offend them. I told this to Max, but he was much more concerned with the breakfast menu. His sister would be preparing her specialty. "Ya haven't tasted anything till ya 'ave Katie's johnnycakes," Max said, whetting his own appetite.

"What time's breakfast?" Chris asked.

"Whenever ya tummy tells ya," Max replied. "Aborigine don't eat on white people time."

"Cool," Chris said.

"Chris," I interjected, "I think we're going to be learning a lot of cool new ways." That much I knew for sure. But what I didn't know that early fall evening when I pulled into Max's bone-dry village was why on earth I was there. I didn't know why I had taken my son out of his sixth grade class in the middle of the school year, and why I was using every dime I had saved that should have gone into his college fund on this trip. But there was one thing I did know for sure. Max was different from any person I had ever met. It was not because of his black, black skin and cornflower-blue eyes, or because he was born and bred in the Outback and I was raised in the white suburbs of Cleveland Heights. It was much more basic than that. There was something beyond the gates of his eyes that beckoned to me. From our first hello, I couldn't shake the feeling that we had come together for a reason. And so within a few short weeks of my meeting Max, we had set off on a journey that would soon draw me into a world of power, mysticism, and deep spiritual commitment to the laws of the universe.

Two months earlier, on February 1, 1995, at JFK International Airport, Christopher and I had maneuvered our way down the narrow 767 aisle of American Airlines Flight 117 to seats 38 A and B. We were loaded down like L. L. Bean pack mules. I half expected one of the flight attendants to nab us for going over the two-bag carry-on allowance. We settled into our seats, and moments later the captain announced it was time for takeoff. The chimes rang, and the plane lumbered down the runway. Chris immediately started fumbling for the airsick bag. "We forgot the Dramamine," he blurted, then gagged into the plastic-lined sack. As the plane banked over the Statue of Liberty, I headed for the galley to get a wad of paper towels.

I was quickly hustled back to my seat and asked to wait until the seat belt sign was turned off. When that happened, two flight attendants came to our rescue with wet towels, Dramamine, and a ginger ale to settle Chris's stomach. They started to walk away when the male flight attendant stopped and did a double take. I thought he was going to reprimand me for something else I'd done.

He studied my face briefly, then asked a little coyly, "Could I have seen you in a play in New York a few months ago? *Me and Jezebel?*"

"Why, yes," I said, exhibiting enough false modesty to cause Chris to roll his eyes.

"Well, I'm Rob," the flight attendant said, extending his hand. "Your show was a riot! It's all really true, isn't it?"

"Every word." Before I could elaborate, Rob motioned for a fellow flight attendant to come over, and then he began to recap the entire show.

"This lady wrote this off-Broadway play about the night Bette Davis came to her house for dinner and then moved in. She played herself. And Randy Allen, this guy, played the part of Bette Davis." Rob turned to me and exclaimed, "You two were fabulous!"

"Thanks," I said, obviously pleased but not telling him that the "fabulous" play had closed. Not telling him that after our final performance I drove back home from the theater and sobbed like a baby.

"So this must be the Chris who's mentioned in the play?" Rob asked.

"Yep," Chris said, slipping a fresh airsick bag into the seat pocket in front of him. He was now as good as new.

"Can you remember what it was like to have Bette Davis in your house?"

"One morning she gave me Froot Loops and it was laced with cigarette ashes," Chris said impishly. "And she was always telling

5

my mother she should dump my father." He sipped his ginger ale and went on, already a master at knowing what material worked.

"Where's your dad now?" Rob chuckled.

"My dad died."

"I'm sorry," Rob said, looking genuinely sorry.

"That's okay," Chris said, glancing my way, making sure that I was okay with this. Four years after John died, we still checked on each other, now more out of ritual than pain.

Rob turned to me and said, "I am really sorry."

"It's fine," I said. "It's been some time now."

That was me. Stolid. A strong woman. I was Rose Kennedy. I was Mame. I was Mother Teresa. I was everybody but me.

"It's so great that you're taking your son off to Australia," Rob continued.

"Yeah," I said, "I want to open his eyes up to a world bigger than Connecticut."

Level with yourself, Liz. You're escaping to Australia because your show closed, and your dearest friend, your coactor in your so-called play, is back in Philadelphia dying of AIDS and you've had all you can take of death, illness, and disappointment.

"You're a lucky guy to have a mother like that," Rob said, in total admiration.

"My mom's really a little nutty," Chris said. "Two years ago she took me to go live with the Amish for six months."

Rob's eyebrows raised. "Is that true?"

"Yes," I said. "I've always wondered what it'd be like to live the way they do."

Again that was only part of the story. Two years after John's death, I was having a very difficult time adjusting to being both mother and father to Chris. To make matters worse, it was rough making ends meet even though I had turned part of our house into an apartment to help pay the mortgage. Then one day I was reading a travel piece in *The New York Times* about the Amish and how content they were on their bucolic farms, where the entire family pulled together in peace and hard work. I wanted that tranquil lifestyle for Chris and me more than ever. Three months later, with our house rented, Chris and I packed up the car and drove six hundred miles west to live the plain-and-simple life on a dairy farm in Winesburg, Ohio.

It was a real horse-and-buggy town with one main street. The only shopping was a store where you could get everything from shoes to Cheerios to horse feed. In the mornings I would write, and in the afternoons I'd walk over to the Winesburg Restaurant and have the pie of the day and a cup of coffee. It was during these leisurely visits that I began to make a rather startling discovery: The Amish are subject to the same frailties as the rest of us.

After the shock wore off, I began to open myself up to these people, and then, surprisingly, they began to open themselves to me. Eventually I became close friends with two women. Ann, a pert-faced brunette, was in her mid-twenties—a cashier at the store. Every afternoon at two o'clock, Ann took her sandwich lunch into the back room, turned on a black-and-white TV, and watched *The Young and the Restless*. TV for the Amish is verboten. My other friend, Mary, was in her early forties. She reminded me of Meryl Streep. One day I told her so, but she didn't know who Meryl Streep was. Along with all the farm chores, Mary looked after her aging parents and retarded brother, but at three o'clock every afternoon, she walked fifty feet from the family's white clapboard house to the barn, climbed into the black buggy, and treated herself to two Camels—no filter! After dinner, in the privacy of her pale green bedroom, she reached into the bottom drawer of her dresser and pulled out a bottle of Wild Turkey and an ashtray. She opened the window just a crack, sat in her grandfather's handmade rocker, and escaped with a Barbara Cartland romance novel—thanks to the penlight she bought at Whitmer's General. Electricity, along with reading anything but the Bible, is verboten. Both Ann and Mary dreamed of one day finding the right man and having children. Mary spent a lot of time worrying about her biological clock, and Ann worried about her future husband—whoever he was—being faithful.

Christopher attended the local school where he thrived academically. The school's philosophy was work and self-discipline. But they also believed that children needed to burn off energy and so three recesses were built into the school day. Often, I would walk over to the small country school and watch the kids on the playground. The boys would be clustered around the basketball hoop, and the girls would usually be pushing each other on the swings. Except for the bonnets and overalls, the scene was pretty typical of every school in the country.

"Well," our flight attendant Rob said, "I'd like to go for maybe *one* weekend."

He was about to leave when Chris asked, "Are there any good golf courses in Australia?"

"Some of the best in the world."

"Cool. I brought my golf clubs with us, and when my dad visits us next month we're going to golf."

"Dad?" Rob asked, confused.

"Oh, I have a new dad," Chris explained. "My old dad was a writer. My new dad's a pilot and a golfer."

Rob's face lighted up. "Chris, when you and your dad see the greens, you're going to be in golfer's heaven," he said. With that he walked back to the galley to begin the beverage service.

# TWO

*I* plugged in the airline headphones and lay back in the cramped seat thinking that if it hadn't been for my mother, I probably would have never met Reuel. It was six months after John died that my mother's favorite refrain became "When are you going to start to date?" She would always follow up with "Your father noticed that you're putting on weight. . . . You're not getting any younger. . . ."

"Mom, when I'm ready, I'll go out. Besides, I'm putting all my time and energy into writing my play."

"Ohhh, that's going to pay the bills?" she said, grounded in Cleveland Heights reality. "Wake up and realize that John's not coming back. That child needs a father. Get out there *now* while you still have a figure. You wait much longer, you'll end up like your Aunt Harriet. Poor thing. Her whole life she worked so hard?—for what—for nothing. . . ."

"I'm nothing like Aunt Harriet," I said defensively.

"Around the eyes," my mother replied, ending all discussion.

Just the suggestion of ending up like poor Aunt Harriet sent me out into the dating scene only to discover that a forty-year-old widow packing a few extra pounds had to be less than supremely choosy.

"Mom," I said over the phone one evening after a torturous date, "I'm not going out anymore."

"Don't say that. You're a young pretty woman. You'll meet a nice guy. You just have to keep looking."

"Nope, no more," I said. "I was married to the best. I'm not settling. Mom, John thought I was the most beautiful woman he had ever seen. I want him back." I began to cry.

"When your father and I first started dating, he used to show up with a white gardenia."

"That's really sweet," I said, pulling myself together. "He really did that?"

"Without fail."

My mother was a past master at distracting her children from painful issues.

"Mom," I said, "John was my sun, my moon, and my stars." I began to cry again.

"Your father's entire family told him not to marry me."

"I didn't know that."

"I was shanty Irish," she said.

"That's awful."

"That's how it was in those days."

"But I thought they were really crazy about you?"

"Oh, after we got married, it all changed. Your grandfather taught me how to cook Italian. He used to always say that I could make a better calzone than Mama."

"Papa was such a flirt," I said.

"They all are."

"Then why do I bother?" I asked.

"Some aren't as bad."


One year and several months after that conversation, I phoned my mother with some real big news. "Mom," I said, "remember how I once told you that John was my sun, moon, and stars."

"I remember," she said. "You read that somewhere."

I took a deep breath. "Well," I said, "I just got engaged to my anchor. My touchstone. My best friend!"

"Play hard to get."

"Mom, you're going to love him. I can't wait to bring him to Cleveland."

"Let me call your father to the phone." A moment later she returned. "What did you say his *first* name was?"

"Reuel," I said.

"What the hell kind of a name is that?"

The day before Chris and I were to fly off to Sydney, I called my parents to say good-bye.

"You're married one year and you're off on some cockamamie trip," my mother said. That was her idea of good-bye. "Do you know your father and I have been married fifty years and the only time I left was to have you kids?"

"Mom, that was your choice."

"I had no choice. And if I did, where would I have gone?"

"You tell me," I said.

"Timbuktu," she snapped. Ever since I was a kid, Timbuktu was her fabled point of escape.

"Seriously, Mom."

"How could I have left your father? He's never cooked a meal in his life. Do you know the other day he asked me to smell the curdled milk in his coffee to see if it was sour. And I'm going to leave him for one week?"

How do I tell my mother that a big part of the reason I was off was her? From the time I was a little girl, I remember my mother always asking my father for permission to do everything—to buy a new pair of shoes, to have her hair done, to drive over to the west side of Cleveland to pick up my grandmother. Absolutely everything. She was a bright, funny lady who never came into her own.

"Mom," I told her, "when Reuel and I got married, we agreed on one thing: Neither of us would try to control each other's life. We both lost our spouses and I think that made us more aware of the preciousness of life. You know, this isn't dress rehearsal. . . ."

"Your show closed and you're running away," she said.

"What?" Mom was also good at slicing through hours of dialogue.

"You heard me," she said. "It's the same as when you flunked out of Ohio State and two weeks later you became a stewardess."

It took twenty years for those two words, "flunk out," to stop stinging and become mildly amusing. "Mom," I said, "if I hadn't become a *flight attendant*, I wouldn't have met John Fuller."

"So now you've got Reuel—another wonderful man—and you're leaving him."

"He admires my sense of adventure."

"You're just like your grandmother," she said.

I took that as a compliment, although it wasn't meant as one. "Old Ma never traveled."

"She would have if she could have," my mother said. "Your grandmother was a good woman, but she had very little common sense. Common sense skips a generation."

"That's what made Old Ma so irresistible," I said.

"Pfffffff."

"Mom, I'm going to send you something nice when I get there."

"Save your money."

"Put Dad on," I said.

"Your father can't come to the phone. Gout."

But my father got on anyway. "Do you have rocks in your head?" he asked. "I thought I had heard everything when you took my grandson to live with the goofy Amish."

How do you convince your Italian-American father, who worked his whole life so he could build the biggest brick house on the street and park a Cadillac in the driveway, that the Amish aren't *goofy*?

"Dad," I said, "I'm going to send you a bush hat from Australia. What size head do you have?"

"Seven and a half. Don't waste your money."


We landed at the Sydney airport shortly before eight in the morning. By the time we cleared Immigration, changed our American dollars into Australian dollars, and got our duffle bags piled onto one of those steel carts, we had been a full twenty-four hours en route. Zombielike, Chris pushed the overflowing cart toward the sliding glass door that said Ground Transportation. I followed on his heels, toting a schoolbag and a canvas bag that cushioned my notebook computer and portable printer. I was still counting luggage to make sure we hadn't forgotten anything when suddenly the electronic double doors opened and we were out in the middle of the Australian summer.

"Wow," Chris said, ripping off his sweatshirt, "I didn't think it was going to be this hot!" He took a hearty whiff of balmy air, as if to give himself a reality check. "This sure beats Winesburg, Ohio!"

I stood for a moment, soaking it all in. Eighty degrees. A faint breeze. No horns blowing. Bronze guys toting neon surfboards. No clouds. Aussie accents. English accents. Indian accents. Tanned girls in tank tops and thick-soled sneakers. Cars with roo bars and steering wheels on the wrong side. We were Down Under, orright. There wasn't going to be anybody around who was going to say, "Hey Liz, I'm really sorry your play closed. And, by the way, how's Randy doing?"

"Mum!" the taxi driver flagged us. "Ya goin' into Sydney?"

"No, we're going to Manly!" I called back.

"No worries," he said. He loaded our bags into the trunk of his Ford Falcon for the forty-five-minute trip to the North Shore. I had read in my guidebook that in Australia you don't automatically slide into the backseat of a taxi. To do so would imply a class distinction. And there was no class distinction in the country, not among the whites anyway. This fact was confirmed by the salty Australian I sat next to on the airplane. "In Oz," he said, "it's all about character. Social status is for foreigners. Beer an' barbie, havin' a good time's the name of the game."

Chris hopped into the front seat next to the cabbie. As the driver jockeyed his way through the Sydney streets and onto the expressway that led to the famous Sydney Harbor Bridge, he shared all sorts of useful information with Chris and some shocking facts as well.

Chris was disbelieving: "You mean you only have *five* major stations and *no* cable?" He was too unglued even to give a cursory glance to Sydney Opera House, which I had been looking forward to seeing since we left the airport. When I actually caught sight of the majestic white shells jutting out on the water's edge, I was filled with complete delight. I snapped half a roll of film.

" 'Ow many TV stations 'ave yuz in America, mate?" the driver asked, also immune to the hundred-million-dollar icon off on our right.

"We get, like, *sixty-two* channels," Chris bragged. "Next year we're going to get, like, *double* that."

My son may have been sitting in the front seat—noblesse oblige—but he wasn't going to be mistaken for Gandhi. It crossed my mind that I would make up for Chris's attitude with a tip, although Australian taxi drivers don't expect one. On second thought, maybe a tip would make us look like ugly Americans.

"Yer gonna find out that there's no place in the world like Oz," the driver said, bursting with pride.

"What's Oz?" Chris asked.

"Din't ya ever see *The Wizard of Oz*, mate?" the driver said.

"Yeah, I saw it," Chris said.

"Ya know how Dorothy and her strange mates go searchin' for some bloke in a land called Oz?"

"Yeah?"

"Well mate, that's where ya are now. In Oz. A land of wonder an' opportunity," he said throwing his arm out the window. Cigarette ashes blew across my face.

" 'Ere we are," the driver said, slowing to a stop and shutting down the meter. "Yer one of the houses right up 'ere."

I looked around in awe at all the old homes—a mixture of Victorian and vintage New Orleans. Fancy wrought-iron balconies festooned with ivy and flowers. An elderly lady, right near our cab, hosing down an already clean sidewalk.

"My husband told me that the water swirls down the drain in the opposite direction here," I said to the driver.

He gave me a look as if to say, I'll give the tour, thank you. He began, "Manly—seven miles from Sydney, but a thousand miles from care."

The house wasn't a modest Florida ranch as I had envisioned back in the U.S. It was an old Victorian perched on top of a hill that swept down to the harbor on one side and Manly Cove on the other.

"Mom," Chris said, "is that dump up there our house?"

"Don't be rude," I scolded.

"It sucks," he muttered.

14

"Oi reckon that'll be twenty-seven dollars, mum," the driver said, snickering to himself.

I fumbled inside my Kipling money belt and peeled off a fifty. When he gave me the change, he had an expression that seemed to say that he not only expected, but deserved, a financial reward for suffering the kid. I gave him five, and he cheerfully helped carry our bags past a gigantic Morton Bay fig and along a geranium-lined brick walkway, right up to a large front door with gingerbread paneling below and etched glass on the upper half. A regal-looking cockatoo with white feathers and quite a distinguished yellow plume swept down to greet us.

" 'Em bloody cockies," the driver said, shooing it away. "Ya go feedin' 'em, they'll never let ya alone."

I jiggled the house key into what looked like a double bolt lock. "It doesn't fit," I said.

"Oi don't think anybody's livin' here," the cabbie said, peering through the window.

"That's because we've just rented it," Chris piped up.

"Oi can't see any furniture."

"You've got to be kidding!" I screeched.

"Don't go gettin' yer pants in a bunch, Mum," he said. He left to have a look around. Chris followed at his heels.

A few minutes later Chris and the cabbie made the discovery that the house had been divided into two separate units und our unit was around back.

"Hey Mom," Chris called, "we have the whole backyard!"

I picked up whatever I could carry and followed the pathway along the side of the house and into a magnificent garden that more than compensated for a less than gracious entranceway. Inside, the house was light and airy. The living room was in earth tones, the furniture was wicker, and modern art posters were scattered about. From the dining room, we had a view of the harbor. I would soon discover that you could virtually keep time by the ferry boats and speedier Jet Cat that arrived from Sydney's Circular Quay on the half hour. Upstairs there were two very small bedrooms that had not been renovated. They had a sweet Victorian charm that might have bordered on seedy if you weren't into cozy and old. Each room had its original French doors that led onto a slightly precarious balcony overlooking a tropical garden complete with a Spanish-style pergola bejeweled with pink roses. Hogging the better half of my balcony was a giant flowering tree called a frangipani with scarlet blossoms of the kind used to make leis in Hawaii. Looking over the garden—a riot of reds and pinks—I thought what *torture* it was going to be to have the lush frangipani in full bloom brushing my arm with its fragrant blossoms as I sipped my morning coffee under the warm, indigo sky.

The best part about all of this was the price. Only weeks before we left the States, friends who lived north of Manly, in a small beachside village called Avalon, found the house by running ads in the local papers. It turned out that the owner was much more interested in having her house well cared for by an American woman who adored plants and had an unbelievably well-behaved son than in making a killing on the rent. We cemented the deal with several faxes and eight hundred dollars a month.

It was somewhere around two in the morning the first night that I was awakened by a thump coming from outside my bedroom door.

"Christopher!" I called out. "Is that you?"

There was no response. I called out again. Still nothing. I must have been dreaming. I turned over and went back to sleep. But moments later I heard the thump again. It was footsteps. Somebody was walking on the wide-planked hardwood floor only feet from my bedroom.

"Christopher," I spoke from my bed, "what are you doing?"

He didn't answer. He was playing a trick on me. Of course, that's exactly what he's doing. "You're not funny, Christopher."

He's disoriented. The time difference has him confused. Maybe he had gotten too much sun. We had spent the entire afternoon at the beach.

"Christopher, answer me!" I demanded.

In an instant something told me that it wasn't my son. There was somebody in the house. Who could it be? It was the middle of the night. The owner? She was somewhere in Europe. My friends who found the house for me? They were vacationing in England. Did I double-bolt the doors? Yes. I checked the front and back door before we went to bed. Was there another door I didn't know about? What about the windows? Big Victorian windows. Easy access. I didn't bother to see if they were all locked. The balconies? An open invitation to a cat burglar. Hoist up on the frangipani tree and right through the French doors. But the French doors were all locked. False security. Any amateur can crack a lock. The basement? I never checked the downstairs. I will lie here, still. Pretend to be sound asleep. Too late. Whoever it is already knows that I'm awake. I shouldn't have called out. Stupid move. I'll let him take whatever he wants. I'll wait it out. What if he tries to hurt Chris? God, please. Please don't let anything happen to us.

The phone. Damn. It wasn't hooked up yet. I had cash on me. I'll go to my dresser, get my wallet, and tell him to take it all. Just leave us alone. My ring. My diamond ring. Reuel would understand. I'd throw in the IBM computer. I'll run to the window, open it, and scream as loud as I can. But Chris? He may go for Chris.

Why was he pacing? And pacing? And pacing? Was he some sort of psychopath? Torturing us first? Was there crime in Australia? Not in the town we were in. It looked safe. Outdoor café tables. Yellow sand beach. Two ice cream parlors. No litter. Pubs, though. Quite a few of them. Could be a drunk. Harmless drunk. God, just don't let it be a druggie. Anything but a drug addict.

Now, ten minutes had passed since I first heard the footsteps. All was quiet. Whoever had broken in was gone. I reached down and picked up a pathetic rubber sandal beside my bed. Holding it like an ax, I headed to Chris's room. He was fast asleep, sprawled across a double bed, still wearing his bathing suit. The TV was off. His French doors were open wide, but the screen door was locked, just as we had left it. I walked onto the balcony. It had cooled down dramatically. The fragrant frangipani was fighting for attention over the sound of crickets. Maybe it was the crickets? The living room and kitchen were undisturbed. All of our stuff was exactly where we left it. Doors double-bolted. I looked out the dining room window. Everything was dark across the road. Off in the distance, I could see faint lights in the harbor. I went back to Chris's room and sat on the side of his bed, stroking his sunburnt forehead, listening, planning a quick escape route in case I heard noises again. I waited a little while longer, then lightly covered him with a sheet and went back to bed.

It was almost three. I couldn't get back to sleep. What on earth could that have been? Did somebody break in, walk back and forth for ten, fifteen minutes outside my bedroom door, and then leave? And take nothing? Could I have really heard footsteps? Had jet lag caused me to imagine it all? But I knew what I heard. We'd better move! I'd *never* get my deposit back! God, I missed Reuel so much. I could see his less than joyous expression as Chris and I walked through the jetway at Kennedy. What if he was secretly furious with me for leaving—or had an affair to get even? Why was I so hell-bent on coming to Australia in the first place? Was I really always running from unpleasant situations? My mom brought up the time I joined the airlines. I had forgotten all about that. She related it to my flunking out of Ohio State. She was wrong. It was because my grandmother—Old Ma, I always called her—was in the hospital dying and I couldn't stand seeing her like that. Old Ma was the closest person in the world to me. We were inseparable—until she got sick. After John died, in the last two years, Randy and I were inseparable—until he got sick.

I looked at the clock. Four A.M. I tried to sleep, as the scene played itself out before me. Randy and I had been rehearsing for months. Everything was as set as it was going to be. Then the unimaginable happened. The day before we were to open in New York, Randy collapsed on the set. It was heartbreaking. Randy Allen stumbling across the stage, his breathing labored, costume disheveled, unable to remember his lines. There was the seasoned producer, Elliot Martin, sitting in the front row during the technical rehearsal, his terribly cultured face twisted into a state of profound shock. Mark Graham, our director, pacing up and down the aisle, pleading, "Randy, we open tomorrow. Pull yourself together." Stage manager Katie Rader, up in the lighting booth, her voice echoing through the empty theater, "Randy, take your place, please." Randy incoherent. Still stumbling. Still forgetting lines. Still not in the correct spot. Katie's voice continuing to echo, "Randy, we're blocking. Take your place, please." Elliot Martin ordering Katie to run next door and bring Randy back tea and cookies to get his sugar level up. Randy, sipping tea, nibbling a cookie, looking at me with a desperate, delirious, wild-eyed look. He's clutching a *Playbill* that was just delivered to the theater, our photo on the cover. "Liz," he says in a breathy voice, "look. We finally made it. We're off-Broadway."

Over and over I ask Randy what the problem is. I don't give him a chance to tell me. I give him multiple choice. Always multiple choice. "Flu? Exhaustion? Nervousness?" Randy looks at me, no longer a thirty-six-year-old accomplished actor, but a vulnerable six-year-old boy on the verge of tears. "Liz," he begs, "help me through this rehearsal. We gotta open tomorrow."

I hear Elliot's dulcet Waspy voice in the third row. "We open in less than twenty-four hours. Will somebody *please* tell me what the hell's going on." Mark answers the Tony-winning producer, "I don't know. Randy had the flu when he arrived in Westport for the rehearsals. But we thought he got over it."

I look at Randy. He's thinner than when we performed off-off-Broadway in the summer. Cheeks are sunken. Bonier. Quieter. Moodier. Randy blames it on the bad bout of flu. I turn to Mark and Katie, and we all suddenly know. But none of us will say the word, not to each other and certainly not to Randy. AIDS. Even Elliot Martin, with dozens of Broadway shows under his belt and God knows how many of his actors dead of the same dread thing, is in denial. He continues to blame Randy's condition on low blood sugar and exhaustion. "He needs a $B_{12}$ shot," Elliot says. The house manager—a gay man—climbs the ladder to the lighting booth and asks Katie point-blank how long Randy has had AIDS. Katie shrugs her shoulders. He asks Mark. Mark throws his hands out and snaps, "What?" The house manager tracks me down backstage. I am in collusion with the straight world. I give the golly-gee,-I-don't-know-what-the-blazes-you're-talking-about shrug. Somebody tell me this

19

isn't true. He can't have AIDS. What about our show? Randy and I worked two solid years to get it where it is. If Randy has AIDS, there'll be no show. Oh God, how can I be so selfish?

And later we would all wonder why Randy had kept it from us. We were such close friends with him. We would remind ourselves of all the times that we'd go out for dinner with Randy and we'd kill a couple bottles of wine and regale each other with crazy anecdotes. Never once did he fess up, "Hey guys, guess what? I've got AIDS."

Katie calls, "The lighting and sound crew are standing by. Liz, take your place." I ask Randy if he's sure he can get through the blocking. His eyes are glazed. He nods weakly and totters off in high heels to his dressing room to freshen up his makeup and to put on the first act costume. I enter stage-left. Randy, confused, enters behind me. Katie yells, "Randy, wait for your cue." Finally Randy enters, unsteady and undramatic through the French doors. His makeup, normally meticulous, is smeared all over his teeth and chin. One fake boob drops out of his dress. He remembers only half of his lines. I whisper them to him. I begin to overact. Elliot turns to Mark. "What the hell's she doing? This is the worst acting I've ever seen in my life." Mark defends me. "Liz is compensating for Randy." Elliot begins to pace. This is not what he had bargained for. He had moved our little two-person play from the Ballroom off-off-Broadway into the Actors' Playhouse on Seventh Avenue in the Village. It was going to be a piece of cake after all his multimillion-dollar musicals. No pressure off-Broadway. No huge overhead. One set. Katie calls, "Randy, move stage-right." Randy trips over the coffee table. Elliot stops the rehearsal. Randy wobbles toward his dressing room. As he leaves the set, he collapses.

One month later we opened with Louise DuArt, a terrific actress, but the audiences and the reviewers wanted Randy, and so after three weeks and with no hope of Randy returning, the show closed. Randy was out of the hospital and back at his home in Philadelphia, weak but holding his own. We spoke nearly every day. His spirits fluctuated with his T-cell count. He had finally stopped apologizing for not telling us he had AIDS. I had finally stopped apologizing for not having allowed him to. Our relationship was no longer based on lines and laughs. We had become real friends. Randy talked openly about his illness. I listened openly. But I didn't talk openly. I've always been pitiful when it comes to baring raw emotions. One time I wrote him a two-page letter telling him that the thought of his dying was eating me up. I never mailed it.

The doctor gave him six months. Randy wanted to die in Philadelphia. His mother wanted him to come back home to Indiana. He was the youngest, and the closest to his mom. They adored each other. From the time he was a young boy they had watched all the old movie classics together. That's how he first got hooked on Bette Davis, Judy Garland, and Marilyn Monroe. Randy was the only one of his siblings to go to college. He graduated from UCLA with a degree in directing, and then continued his theater studies in England. His first love was acting—something his father did not find very appealing. He wasn't close to his father, a garage mechanic, who was always on his case to "butch it up." His mother finally told his father about Randy having AIDS. His father sobbed, "Not my little boy! Please, God! Not my boy!"

On Randy's good days, he spoke optimistically about his future. "As soon as my T-cell count goes up," he told me, forcing air into his ravaged lungs, "I'll be given a combination of new drugs . . . I'm going to work again. . . . Liz, we have an offer to do the show in San Francisco next October." I calculated that to be nine months away. During one phone conversation Randy began making loose plans for moving to Australia. He had been there a year earlier, performing in a club during the gay Mardi Gras, one of the biggest events to hit Sydney each year. Maybe he'd come visit me in Australia, he said weakly, adding, "Honey, I'm glad you're going. You gotta do everything right now. No regrets—you got that, Liz? And when you get there, I want a handful of that yellow sand."

When I phoned Randy the day before I left, he told me that he'd decided to go home to Indiana for some of his mother's home cooking. Her meatballs, he said, were unbelievable. He'd be gone only ten days. I had to be sure to try the peaches in Australia. "They'll melt in your mouth," he said. "Have one for me."

I hung up and thought about the distinct possibility that I would never see Randy again. I couldn't bear it. Damn him. First Old Ma. Then John. Now Randy. I should learn to keep relationships on the surface. No loss. No pain. Who was going to phone and leave crazy messages from dead divas on my answering machine? I hated that I had begun to count on him as much as he counted on me. How was I ever going to see or eat a peach again without thinking of him?

# THREE

There was nothing more soothing to frayed senses than waking up after a restless first night Down Under with the sun streaming in through French doors and a snow-white cockatoo perched on a branch of red blossoms, hanging out under 70-degree sun. The *Sydney Herald* reported that it was 5 degrees Celsius with snow in New York. Such a shame, I thought, as I sank my teeth into a juicy peach and thought of Randy. All the while I was being watched by the cockatoo. I wasn't sure, but it looked like the same bird that the taxi driver had shooed away when we first arrived. In case it was, I tossed him a chunk of bread to make up for the uncivil way he had been treated. My largess was not appreciated. The foot-and-a-half-tall bird glanced down at the bread, and then over at me, probably thinking, Don't do me any favors, sister. I watched to see if he was going to make a dive for it. "Ya want some bread?" I asked, in a condescending Polly-want-a-cracker? tone. The bird fixed his eyes on me, unflinching, totally disgusted. "Okay, I'm sorry if I insulted you," I said. "You are much too distinguished with that handsome yellow plume to be talked down to."

"Mom," Chris called out from the kitchen, "who are you talking to?"

"Come and find out."

"Cool bird," Chris said, appearing at the door with his math book tucked under his arm.

"Don't startle him," I cautioned. "He's been sitting on that branch staring at me for fifteen minutes now."

"Why?"

"How do I know?"

"Can I feed him?" Chris asked.

"I threw him some bread, but he didn't take it," I said. "It's over there on the balcony."

Chris picked the bread up and walked slowly to the bird. "Have some bread, little buddy."

The bird turned his haughty head. *Little buddy?*

"Chris, isn't he royal looking?"

"Yeah, he looks like Prince Charles."

"A little around the beak," I laughed. "Now finish your math."

"Prince Charles," Chris said in clipped, curt British, "your-breakfast-is-being-served."

With that, Prince Charles flew away. But he would return. In fact, Prince Charles was soon to become a permanent fixture around the royal household. I only wished he wouldn't drop by during Chris's schoolwork hours.

The following evening was a repeat of the first, but with a bonus. Eerie-sounding music emanating from the basement stairs. This time I resolved not to keep it to myself. When morning came, I sent Chris to pick up croissants and orange juice at our corner grocery store and I went next door to see our neighbor, Mrs. Simpson. Actually, we had spoken briefly the day we arrived. I had been setting up a couple of lounge chairs in our garden when she called over the fence, "When ya get settled in, drop by an' say hello."

"You can call me Gladys," the spry octogenarian said, opening the door and stepping out of her well-kept Victorian. Visibly delighted that I had taken her up on the offer to come by, she showed me to a rose arbor in the back garden where we sat on white wrought-iron chairs still damp from the morning dew. She wasted no time telling me that she liked Yanks. We were allies in the war. We were much more open than the Brits, who were otherwise referred to as Pommies, a name that went back a couple hundred years to when the king of England loaded his convicts on slow boats to Australia. When the criminals disembarked, their clothing was stamped with POHMIE—Prisoners of His Majesty in Exile. The Aussies are adamant, of course, that calling a Brit a Pommie is in no way an insult.

Gladys loved the "telly" show *The Nanny*, but she didn't get a lot of what the girl said, New York accents being tough to make out. My faded Cleveland twang was no problem, though, which I was glad for because I didn't want her to miss a word of what I was about to say. I was desperate to share the goings-on of the last two nights. But first, I had to give her a little bit of background on me to show her that I wasn't entirely wacky.

I began by telling her that my husband would be joining us in a month. He wasn't able to come sooner because he was a colonel in the Air National Guard—a reserve contingent of the Air Force. I punched up *colonel* and *Air Force*. She nodded, getting the point, and I went on, "He flies C-5's." Flew during the Gulf War? "Yeah. When he's not flying," I said, leaning over to smell one of the Queen Anne roses, "he's a financial consultant."

"Harold was an artilleryman in the Aussie Army," she said, finding common ground. "So oi heard that you're a writer, are ya?"

"Yes," I said.

"Whaddya write?"

"Well, I write plays. Just had one last winter."

"Yeah? What was it about?"

"Bette Davis—the movie star."

"Aww, oi like her."

I offered no more information. There was no delicate way to tell an eighty-year-old lady with her hair in a bun and a print housedress on that I performed on stage with a man dressed in women's clothing and then follow it up with the strange happenings in the house and expect her to think I wasn't a wild woman, a flake.

"If ya like plays, then you an' your son will have to go into Sydney and see Shakespeare in the Botanical Garden. Oi think *Midsummer Night's Dream* is on now."

"We'll do that."

She looked at me as if she were sizing up my financial situation. "They don't give those tickets away."

"Just like in New York," I said. We chitchatted a little longer and then when I felt as if there was some bonding going on, I dropped the bombshell.

"I think there's a ghost in my house," I said. I proceeded to tell her about the first night with the footsteps and how I thought some-one had broken in but didn't take anything. I told her how yesterday I bought a pepper spray at the pharmacy, in case something like that ever happened again. I told her how before I went to bed last night, I pushed heavy furniture against the front and back door and checked every window twice. But all that wasn't enough. At two in the morn-ing, I was once again awakened by the sound of footsteps outside my bedroom door. This time I didn't lie idle. I grabbed the pepper spray under my pillow and silently slipped out of bed. I was preparing a full-scale attack when suddenly the footsteps surrounded me. I was like the pickle in the middle. But nobody was there. No matter what direction I walked, the footsteps followed. And when I got near the stairs that led to the basement, I heard that weird, unearthly music. I didn't dare go down there. Instead, I went into Chris's room and sat at the side of his bed. I was still clutching the pepper spray, but the footsteps were gone. For a while longer the music droned on, and then it, too, disappeared. I sat there for a half hour, and then I moved the chair I'd propped against the front door and went outside and lay on the lounge chair in the garden. And that's where I stayed until the sun came up.

As I spoke, Mrs. Simpson raised her white eyebrows, practically to the hairline. Her eyes locked onto mine like heat-seeking missiles. When I was finished with my unlikely tale, she bent down, plucked off a few wilted geranium buds, and said, "The secret to keepin' geraniums healthy is to let 'em thoroughly dry out. Then ya give 'em a good soakin'. Ya pinch off the dead bud right 'ere." She demon-strated her technique.

Okay, so she had me pegged as a nutcase. Before I told her all this, she seemed on the verge of inviting me in for "bikkies" and tea, but now she was backing me down the walkway, safely away from her door.

"I know how it must sound, Mrs. Simpson," I said, making a quick decision not to call her Gladys. That might scare her. A crazy lady being a little too friendly. "But all I can tell you is what happened to me. Do you know *anything* about the house?"

"It's an old one, orright," Gladys said. She spied a prickly weed springing up between two small boulders. "Ya never wanna just go liftin' rocks. Not with the bloody snakes around 'ere."

"I guess it was one of the first houses built in Manly," I said, nudging her back on track.

"Reckon it was," Gladys sighed. She spotted another weed.

"I think if it were my house," I said, "I would have left it looking Victorian on the inside."

"Awwwgh, something's always goin' on over there." Gladys rested her plump wrists on Mother Goose hips. "This past winter, they put in some rooms down in the basement. For weeks, dirt an' dust was flyin' everywhere. Made a bloody mess of me garden." Then she softened. "The owner's a fine lady. She's with her daughter in Paris, France, now. Goes there every summer. Aww, when Pat's out in her garden an' I'm in mine, we bat the breeze. I never even brought up the mess."

"But she never mentioned anything *odd* going on over there?"

"Can't say she did." There was a long pause and then she dropped her voice to a whisper. "I heard a story."

"Story?"

"Nothin' about the house," she confided, "but I heard somethin' strange happened in that tree over there." She pointed to the large tree on the curb in front of my house.

"In that tree?"

"Yeah, the Morton Bay fig," Gladys said. "The bloke who works at the used bookstore, over on the Corso, saw somethin' one mornin' while he was walkin' to work."

"He saw something?"

"It's been a while now." She returned to nipping her buds. "Maybe you'd better go ask him. He'll be there. Ask for Norman. Tell 'im Gladys sent ya."

"Okay," I said. "So I'll ask Norman what strange thing he saw in that Morton Bay?"

"Right-o," Gladys answered, cutting me off. But as I turned to leave, she got talkative. "For a long time, he stopped walkin' this way after it happened. Scared the britches off him. Right up there in those higher branches." She took a few moments to recall the exact location and then went on, "Norman claims to have seen naked little Aborigine children playin'."

"I don't understand."

"One minute they were playin'. The next they were gone. Disappeared."

"Like ghosts?"

"If ya wanna hear the story, go ask Norman. Tell 'im Gladys sent ya."

I intended to rush right down to the used bookstore and meet Norman. But then I went back home to eat breakfast with Chris and began to tidy up the house and everything seemed so peaceful that I decided to forget about anything to do with ghosts. Why spook myself all over again?

That turned out to be a wise decision because for the following three weeks, I slept like a baby. If there were footsteps and music, I didn't hear them and they didn't disturb my sleep. Of course, just when I had myself convinced that my imagination had played one gigantic trick on me, the footsteps and music started up again. But things were different this time. Rather than alarm me, in some bizarre, unaccountable way, the footsteps and droning music were actually comforting, soothing—if that makes any sense. Whatever it was, or whoever it was, was not out to harm us.

Hearing unearthly noises and not being alarmed would have seemed pretty far-fetched, had I not once been involved in extensive research for my late husband John Fuller's book, *The Ghost of Flight 401*. Back in 1976, John and I spent ten months interviewing scores of pilots and flight attendants who actually claimed to have had a firsthand encounter with a dead flight engineer. Surprisingly, the crew members were not frightened by the unlikely encounter; they felt reassured. In fact, when the dead flight engineer did reappear, it was usually to warn of impending danger. One such incident occurred on an Eastern Airlines flight into Mexico City back in 1973, and it had first been reported in *The Flight Safety Foundation* newsletter. A flight attendant was in the lower galley of the L1011. During the meal service, she happened to glance into the window of an oven, and there, looking out at her, was the face of the flight engineer who had lost his life in an Everglades crash several months earlier. He had been below, checking the position of the nose gear, when the big trijet slammed into the swamp. Immediately the flight attendant summoned another flight attendant, and both women saw the apparition in the window of the oven. They picked up the galley phone and called their flight engineer to come below. He, too, saw the apparition, and he also talked to the ghost, who said, "Watch out for fire on this airplane." Shortly thereafter a fire developed in one of the engines. Fortunately the crew made a safe landing in Mexico City.

It was three years after this incident that John and I were finally able to locate and interview the crew members who had been involved in this report. But before they agreed to talk, we first had to give them our word that they would never be identified by their real names. They were fearful of losing their jobs. And for good reason. When they told their supervisors what had happened, they were sent to the company shrink.

Recalling all of this brought up another point. Should I mention anything about the footsteps and music to Reuel when he arrived in less than a week? Although Reuel didn't exactly clap for Tinkerbell, he was not closed-minded either. We had actually met fifteen years earlier, after Reuel's wife, Cindy, phoned John and me shortly after *Ghost of 401* came out. She said that we were neighbors and would we consider coming to dinner with several of their airline pilot friends, who like them were fascinated with the book. Music to an author's ear. We went to their home, but I have only a vague recollection of the evening. Reuel's memory is much better than mine. On our first date, Reuel not only recalled the evening from cover to cover, but also brought along the autographed copy of the book. He said that it had been a favorite of Cindy's, and that after she died, he had found it inside her night table. He had completely forgotten John's inscription: "Reuel, I admire your benevolent skepticism. I also admire your authoritative martinis."

Yes, Reuel was a benevolent skeptic. I would tell him *everything* that had been going on. I just wouldn't hit him on the head with it the minute he walked through the door. I'd first give him an authoritative martini.

Reuel arrived at the Sydney Airport in a torrential downpour. It had been raining six days, nonstop. All my plants and flowers were waterlogged, wilted, and doubled over, as if they had been punched in the stomach. Every last blossom had been washed off the frangipani, and the Morton Bay fig had made a brown, slippery mess on the brick walkway. It was a sad-looking garden. The weather, I was told, was highly unusual. The locals blamed it on strange weather patterns and left it at that. Good thing I had Gladys to commiserate with.

"My geraniums can't take all this bloody rain," she complained when she was over for tea the afternoon before Reuel was to arrive.

"It's supposed to clear tomorrow," I said. "Then more rain for the weekend." I poured us each a cup, bemoaning the fact that the romantic garden dinner I had planned for Reuel and me would now have to be moved into the dining room. What a shame. From the moment I first glimpsed the Spanish pergola in the garden with its delicate pink roses climbing up four white trellis columns toward a canopy of grape leaves, I envisioned Reuel and me underneath it, sipping chardonnay and eating mango and papaya. My carefully chosen dinner of Tasmanian shrimp with angel-hair pasta, set off with pink candles, cried out for the pergola—to say nothing of my new slinky, black frock, which I had picked up at a funky boutique down at the wharf. The salesgirl, who cultivated the Madonna look to near perfection, promised that if I wore the dress to greet my husband, I could forget about the dinner. "You are one shit-hot blond tart," she said, clinching the sale. After I turned forty, being referred to as a tart became a compliment of titanic proportions. When I slapped my Visa card down on the counter, the younger tart between us suggested that the money I'd be saving on the fattening dinner could be wisely put toward black platform sandals.

"We're gonna get bit bad by the mozzies when this weather pattern moves out to sea," Gladys said, snapping me back to the present moment. She adjusted the cloth belt on her floral housedress, took a swig of the Twinings, and went on. "I heard from my rellie outside of Perth yesterdie. She hasn't seen rain in seven years. For Christmas she sent me a prezzie of beautiful kangaroo paws. Awwwgh, they can't survive in this weather. When Harold was alive, he could grow anything. I'm just sorry you weren't here last summer. Poor Chris, I see him pop his head out the door all mornin'. Just waitin' for the sun to show."

"Yeah, we're really getting on each other's nerves locked up in here."

"Why don'tcha take him over to Ocean World? It's just down the road."

"We went twice," I said. "The second time we brought our camera. We have great photos of a diver in the tank feeding the sharks."

"I've got a friend up in the Northern Territory," Gladys said. "Years ago her brother was on a surfboard—a handsome bloke—his whole lower body was ripped clear orf."

"Ripped off?"

"Like a robber's dog."

"A shark?"

"Great white," Gladys said, sinking her teeth into a lemon meringue tart. "Awwwgh, it was in all the papers. The poor bloke never even knew what hit him. But I'll tell ya somethin' even worse. My cousin's son, George—for years, George was a camel trainer out near Alice Springs. One die, while he was saddlin' up the ugly beast, he was kicked roight between the eyes. Sorry bloke's been on the dole ever since."

Sometimes I wondered if Gladys really knew the people all these horrible things happened to, but it didn't much matter. She held my attention and it sure killed time on rainy days.

"So ya never went down to meet Norman at the used bookstore?" Gladys suddenly asked.

I was caught off guard. I never expected her to bring up anything to do with ghosts after her rather cool reaction to my ghostly saga. But okay, if she was going to open the otherworldly door, I was going to walk right in.

"Gladys," I said, "remember I told you that I heard some weird, droning noise coming up from the basement?"

"Oh, yeah." She nodded. "I remember that."

"Well, as of last week, I now know what I heard."

Gladys helped herself to a second cup of tea and a creme biscuit. "Whaddya hear?"

"A didgeridoo."

"The Aborigine wind instrument?"

"That's right. And I'll tell you how I know that's what it is. Last week," I began, "I was walking along the beach. The surf beach. Before the rains started. Well, I was just about at the pavilion when I heard something that got my attention. I looked around to see where the sound was coming from. It almost seemed like it was coming from *nowhere*. I stood still for a minute, listening. Then it all connected. It was that *exact* same unearthly sound that I've been hearing. You know, right over there," I said, pointing to the basement steps—steps I hadn't ventured down since I first heard the creepy sound.

"Yeah," Gladys said. She followed my finger.

"So I walked on past the pavilion. In the direction of the music. And there, sitting crossed-legged in the sand, was an Aborigine man. Probably about twenty-five. He was blowing into a long, hollowed-out tube that was elaborately carved and painted."

"I think I've seen the bloke," Gladys said. "Sometimes he sits in front of Hungry Jack's."

"I didn't want to just stand and stare. I walked on down the beach toward that little Mexican restaurant. Then I thought, What the heck, I'll go back and sit near him. I waited until he put the instrument down. Then I struck up a conversation."

"Women aren't allowed to play the didgeridoo," Gladys interjected.

"Yeah, that's what he told me. "It's supposed to bring bad luck, especially if you're pregnant. Anyway, he said that it's a sacred instrument and that it's used during Aborigine rituals. I thought about telling him how I heard the same sound coming from my basement. Then I thought, maybe he would be offended. So I said nothing."

Gladys nodded.

"But the very next day," I went on, "I opened the *Sydney Morning Herald*. And there's this big headline: SCHOOL'S PACT WITH ABORIGINES WILL KEEP THE DREAMTIME INTACT. The article said that a public elementary school somewhere outside Sydney had been built on top of sacred Aboriginal grounds. And at *night*, people claimed to hear the drone of the didgeridoo. The Aborigines explained this by saying that it was an echo, like a reminder, of the four tribes who used to meet there and bury artifacts there something like five thousand to seven thousand years ago."

Hearing that, Gladys downed the rest of her tea. "Well, I'm not gonna take up any more of yer time," she said, getting up quickly. "Ya gotta get ready for your husband."

At first, I couldn't tell if I had suddenly bored her, or if she just wasn't comfortable with the eerie talk. I assumed it was the latter. I followed her into the hallway to get her rain gear. As she walked past the stairs that led to the basement, she lingered for a moment, as if trying to hear something. Then she said, "When they put in those new rooms down there, I thought they were diggin' to Antarctica. Rocks an' dirt flyin' everywhere. Made a jolly mess of me garden. But as I told ya, I never once complained to Pat."

Gladys slipped on yellow rubber boots and called to my son, who was in his room watching TV. "Come on, Chris. I'm gonna make ya some fairy bread. 'At'll cheer ya up."

"What's fairy bread?" Chris called back.

"Aww, that's just sliced white bread with lotsa sprinkles," Gladys said loudly. "When my grandchildren come up from Melbourne, they can't get enough of it. They'd rather have fairy bread than lollies."

There was no response from Chris's room.

"I'll send Chris over," I said.

"Right-o." Gladys turned to leave, but then she stopped dead in her tracks. She had spotted a copy of *Playbill* on the dining room table with the photo of Randy and me on the cover. "What 'ave we got here?" she said, picking it up.

Oh Jesus, I thought, that's the last thing she needs to see. "Remember I told you how I had a play off-Broadway this past winter?"

Gladys studied the photo. "I didn't know you were an actress."

"I'm not. I just played me."

She continued to study the photo. "Is this supposed to be Bette Davis?"

"Yes," I said. I steeled myself.

"She's a very good resemblance. She's got her eyes, orright."

I breathed a sigh of relief. "Yep," I said. "Looks just like her."

"If I didn't know she was dead, I would 'ave thought it was Bette Davis." Gladys smiled, shaking her head, adding, "I always liked those Bette Davis movies." Then, typically, she switched gears. "Say, have ya been down to the old Quarantine Station—over on the other side of town?"

"No," I said. "I read something about it, though."

"Some strange things are goin' on down there."

"Like what?"

Gladys looked around, making sure that we were alone. She dropped her voice. "It's haunted. I know that as sure as I'm standin' here."

"*You* saw something?"

"Ya might say that."

With those words, she did an about-face, opened the gate, and plodded her way home through the rain.

Chris was stretched out on his bed, glued to the TV. "Mom, *you* can have your little tea and crumpets, but *I'm* not going to sit around with Gladys and eat *fairy* bread! Golf's on in five minutes."

"Chris," I begged, "just this one time. Talk to her about Australia. She's really very interesting."

"Fairy bread with Gladys? No way. I can't wait for Dad to get here. We're gonna golf every day, and you and Gladys can spook each other with your ghosts."

Each time I phoned United Airlines, there was a new arrival time. Finally at midnight, after almost being diverted to Brisbane, the plane was allowed to land when the ceiling lifted. I was at the window when the taxi pulled up. I could barely see Reuel. It was miserable and foggy out there. Inside, however, the stage was set. The candles were lit, the wine was open, the flowers were perfectly arranged, and the hostess looked fabulous. Even Chris noticed. "Hey, Mom," he said, singing the pop lyrics, "I'm-too-sexy-for-my-clothes. . . ."

"You think Dad will like this?" I asked.

"Mom, maybe you should cover those things up a little more."

"Chris, you sound more like your Italian grandfather every day. Now go to bed. It's after ten. You'll see Dad in the morning."

I stood at the door in my new black platform sandals, peering down the walkway. I was as giddy as a seventeen-year-old on prom night. "Darling," I called through the pea-soup fog, "I can't believe you're finally here."

"Lizzy, is that you?"

"Well, who the hell else would it be!" I hollered.

Reuel called to the taxi driver, "Yeah, this is the right house!"

When I saw Reuel standing in the doorway, drenched, I remembered what it was that first made me fall for him. It was the deep smile lines, slicing into a sturdy jaw on a very boyish face. The fact that his brown eyes slanted downward toward great shoulders was an added bonus. And when he was in his Air Force flight suit, forget it.

"You are gorgeous," he said, wrapping his soaking arms around my very bare back.

"I missed you so much," I purred. "I got crazy thinking that maybe you were secretly angry at me for deserting you. And to get even, you were going to have an affair."

"Only one affair?" he said. "Lizzy, I had them stacked up in Connecticut like planes over Sydney. Never take your eyes off me again." He placed my hand over his stomach. "I've been working out on the Nordic."

"You were almost perfect before," I said, "but had I known the shape you were going to be in, I would never have left."

"Don't you know a woman's place is at home? In the kitchen," he whispered, kissing me, "and in the bedroom."

"What about dinner? I've been cooking all day. Or if you're not hungry, we could have just mango and papaya." He was the sexiest-looking man I had ever seen.

"Darling," he said, "after United Airlines's fruit cup, it would be all downhill."

It was his humor that captured my heart.

We woke the following morning still wrapped in each other's arms. Thanks to the crazy birds outside our bedroom window, we didn't miss the best part of being Down Under—Australian mornings.

"What the heck's going on out there?" Reuel asked.

"Kookaburras."

"It sounds like a mental ward," he said.

"Every morning they wake you up with their goofy laughs. Gladys told me that."

"You think Chris is still sleeping?" Reuel asked, moving even closer.

"Dad!" Chris yelled, "I don't see your golf clubs."

"I guess it's time to get up."

Reuel and Chris didn't always hit it off. For the first three months after our marriage, I thought I was living with an eleven-year-old Trappist monk who had taken a vow of silence whenever Reuel entered the room. And although Reuel tried to pretend that we were one big happy family, his actions said that he, too, resented sharing me. I felt like the woman in the magic act who gets sliced in half. Time, however, and low expectations started us on the precarious journey of becoming a family.

"So, Chris," Reuel said, "tell me about those nutty kookaburras."

"Gladys told me that they munch on little birds," Chris said, paging through the latest *Golf Digest* Reuel had brought with him.

"Who's Gladys?" Reuel asked, helping himself to another slice of mango.

"She's Mom's best friend. They both see ghosts."

"Ghosts?" Reuel chuckled.

"You're not going to tell Dad?" Chris said, never passing up an opportunity to let Reuel know that we had secrets that he was not privy to.

"I plan on telling Dad tonight," I said. "It's all too complicated to just blurt out at the breakfast table."

As it turned out, I didn't tell Reuel that night. And I didn't tell him the second night either. In fact, I might have never told him, had it not been for the next thing to happen—which was exactly six days later.

We had just returned from the beach. Chris was in his room, changing out of his bathing suit. Reuel was in our bedroom doing the same. They were getting ready to hit a bucket of balls at a driving range about twenty minutes away. I was not at all unhappy to get rid of them for the rest of the afternoon. I needed desperately to catch up on my writing, which I had neglected ever since Reuel's arrival. My goal had been to return home with a finished play. And thinking of that reminded me of Randy. Earlier in the week, I had received a note from him. His handwriting might have been a little shaky, but his spirits weren't.

"Liz," he wrote, "great news for both of us. We've both been nominated for MAC awards. *Manhattan Association of Cabarets & Clubs!* You for best writing, and me for best impersonator. Can you believe it? Ron's taking me to dinner tonight to celebrate." At the bottom of the note, he scribbled, "Honey, are you okay? I woke up last night with a strange feeling that something's wrong there. Please write! Much love, Randy."

There was a P.S. for my son, too, whom he'd been teaching how to play cards. "Chris, if you get a good hand when you're playing poker, remember: Don't make any funny faces—look like you're really bored. That's called a poker face."

I had just jotted Randy a quick note back when I heard a rush of water. My first thought was that either Chris or Reuel had decided to have a shower. It took a few minutes to register that nobody was in the bathroom.

"Who turned the water on!" I yelled. Reuel had no idea what I was yelling about.

"That's odd," he said, manipulating the shower head and faucets. "Nothing's loose here."

"Chris," I said, "did you turn the shower on and forget?"

"Look at me," he answered, throwing his arms out, "I'm all dressed for golf. Why would I turn on the shower?"

"When we get back," Reuel said, slinging his golf clubs over his shoulder, "I'll check the pipes in the basement."

On their way out the door, Chris gave me a look that said, Don't make anything more of it, Mom.

I calculated that it had been a full week since the last time I heard the footsteps and music. Now this. Why? Everything had been going along perfectly. Even the weather was cooperating. For the last three days, nothing but 85 degrees and scorching sun. Twice, Reuel and I had a late-night dinner under the pergola. Now that the sun was back in full force, new, more interesting flowers and greenery were shooting up everywhere. Gladys was so busy pruning, pulling, and spraying that she barely had time to say more than a quick hello from across the wrought-iron fence. Twice she passed plum jelly over the fence.

By the time the guys returned from the driving range, it was practically dark. Chris burst through the front door with a Big Mac, fries, and Coke. "Mom," he said, "Dad's taking you out for dinner tonight!"

I naturally assumed it was to celebrate my MAC nomination.

"I think he feels guilty."

"Guilty? Why would he feel guilty?"

Chris clammed up.

"Tell me why he would feel guilty," I said, commandeering the remote from his hand.

"I don't know," he shrugged.

"No television till you fess up." I could put my foot down when I needed to.

"Well, maybe because we sorta laughed all the way to the golf course about the spooooooooky shower."

"So you guys got a big chuckle outta that one?"

"Sort of," Chris said, preparing his feast in front of the blank TV screen. "Mom, I hope you don't mind, but—well—I told Dad about the footsteps."

"What'd he say?"

"Oh, nothing," he replied, guilty, but not that guilty.

"Chris," I said, dangling the remote control, "tell me what Dad said."

He hesitated. Then he sang like Joe Bananas: "That we should just, like, humor you."

"*Humor* me?"

Chris shoved a handful of fries into his mouth. "Now, can I *please* have the remote?"

That night, Reuel and I had dinner at one of the outdoor cafés that lined the Corso. It was called Crystals, and it was touted to have the best seafood. Over a bottle of Australian chardonnay, I told Reuel my version of the story from beginning to end, every ghostly detail. The entire time I spoke, he had a half smile on his boyish face.

"Liz, I've been here one week," Reuel said, opening the oversize menu. "I haven't heard any footsteps or weird music. Except that stuff Chris blasts."

"What about the shower?"

"Probably sudden pressure."

"So you think I'm crazy?"

"No, I think that there's a logical explanation for it. Honey," Reuel said, clutching my hand, "you're in an old house. And old houses make creaky noises."

"I know what I heard," I said. I slid my hand out from under his patronizing grasp and topped off my wineglass. "You just don't believe me."

"Liz, I'm an Air Force pilot. I have spent my entire life dealing in hard, cold facts. Casper doesn't make it for me. Shall we order?"

"So that's it?" I said.

He broke out into a big grin. There was no way I could be angry. But I wasn't silent, either. So for the first time since we met, I began to explain to Reuel some of my past experiences in the paranormal. After all, twenty years earlier, I had been tested for psychic ability at the University of London by Dr. John Barnowski, head of the physics department. At the end of the three-month testing period, Dr. Barnowski concluded that my psychic sense was "highly developed."

"Oh yeah?" Reuel said. Although he still had that half smile, he seemed genuinely impressed.

"But the doctor also mentioned that I shouldn't get too cocky, because the average person on the street is not far behind. We all have this ability to a greater or lesser degree."

"I definitely believe women are more intuitive than men," Reuel said, offering the olive branch.

"So you're not just 'humoring' me?"

"Of course not. Women *definitely* have a sixth sense. I honestly believe that."

Okay, I said to myself, I got him to admit that much. Now, drop it. I just want to enjoy the next four weeks that we have together. And that's exactly what we did. After dinner we walked along the beach, holding hands and kissing. And then the goddess of Australian yellow sand led us to a very secluded spot, and taunted us, until we could no longer resist the temptation. I was wearing the black frock.

Three days after our dinner at Crystals, the resident white cockatoo flew in through the opened front door, circled our dining table a few times, and did something that got Reuel's attention. And the best part about it was that *Reuel* saw it happen. He had been sitting in a chair directly opposite the dining room table, reading the *Sydney Morning Herald*. I was in the basement doing the laundry.

"Lizzy," he called down, "that bird—the one Chris is always talking to—just flew into the house and took off."

"You mean Prince Charles?"

"I guess," Reuel said, suddenly appearing in the laundry room. "The damn bird dropped this clamshell right on your computer keyboard. Looks as if it's petrified."

"That's strange," I said, examining it.

"We'd better keep that front door closed," Reuel warned. "That's all we need—bird shit around the house."

"You know," I said, "the other night I promised myself that I wouldn't bring up anything weird again. But I'm about to break that promise."

"Here we go," he said, steeling himself.

I put the detergent in the machine, turned the knob to permanent press, and said my piece: "That bird just brought us a message."

"Oh, Lizzy, Chris has been feeding that bird, and this is nothing more than that bird taking advantage of a good thing."

"Wrong," I said. "The shell alone is no big deal. But combined with the footsteps and the music, it's too much to ignore." I scooped the clothes out of the dryer. "Somehow, I get the feeling we're standing on Aborigine soil."

"Darling, right now, you are standing on my golf shirt."

I spent the rest of the evening using every convincing argument I could think of to get Reuel to see that these things *can* and *do* exist. I told him how some very respectable people have believed in the paranormal. "You know what Albert Schweitzer said about all of this?" I didn't wait for a reply. "He said that the only road to a greater grasp of reality is the exploration of supernormal perception."

"Yeah?" Reuel mumbled, head buried in *Golf Digest*.

"And you wanna know what *skeptical* Sigmund Freud had to say?"

"Ummm."

"He said, 'If I had my life to live over again, I should devote myself to psychical research rather than psychoanalysis.' And you wanna know what . . ."

"You wanna know what Reuel Dorman says?" he asked.

"Not really," I answered.

"He says it's a crock of shit."

"Okay, forget it," I said, resigned to his tunnel vision.

When he realized that I was no longer going to pursue the subject, he came around. "Liz," he said, following me into the kitchen, "what do you want me to do?"

And I told him. "Tonight, after Chris goes to sleep, I want you to come downstairs to the basement with me and try out my new homemade Ouija board."

"Huh?" Reuel said, truly baffled.

"What's the matter? They didn't teach you about Ouija boards at the Wharton Business School?"

"I don't think so," he laughed.

I told Reuel how John and I had started off thinking the Ouija board was just a silly game too, and that we pooh-poohed the whole idea. But as we dug deeper into the theory of the paranormal, we discovered that it could actually produce verifiable messages. One evening, on the suggestion of two senior Eastern Airlines pilots who had actually encountered the ghost, we gave it a whirl, dubiously. After a string of garbled words, we suddenly began to receive coherent messages—presumably coming from the dead flight engineer! Eventually these messages were confirmed by his widow, whose first reaction was one of shock and disbelief. Later, however, she confided that *nobody* but herself could have ever known the information we had received.

"Okay," Reuel said, "enough of the sales job. What do I have to do?"

"I'll show you tonight," I said.

# FOUR

"Boy, you can really smell the earth down here," I said, as I placed the candle on a small oak table beside the bed.

"I don't know about earth. Smells like fresh paint to me," Reuel replied, ever the hard-facts guy.

"Gladys did say these rooms were built only a few months ago."

Reuel poked around and looked out a window that was about eye level. "This is a pretty deep basement," he observed. "They really had to do some excavation to get all this headroom."

I tried one of the twin beds and suggested that Reuel pull up a wicker chair and sit facing me. Once we were settled comfortably, I placed the Ouija board between us, resting it on our knees.

"What'd you make this crazy thing out of?" Reuel snickered.

"A TV tray," I said. I had covered it with cardboard, then written the letters of the alphabet with one of Chris's Magic Markers. "Clever, huh?"

"A regular Marconi," Reuel said. No way would he allow himself total cooperation—another reason why I was crazy about him. He picked up a clear piece of plastic from off the board and examined it. "What the hell's this little device?"

"It's what we're going to rest our fingers on. See," I said, demonstrating. "It slides around the board to the various letters of the alphabet. When it stops over a letter, we simply look through the clear plastic and call the letter into the tape recorder."

"No, I mean—what is it?"

"What difference does it make," I snapped.

"I'm just curious. What is it?"

43

"It's a compact lid for face powder," I said, annoyed. "I got it at the pharmacy today. Now stop stalling and let's get on with it."

"This is ridiculous," Reuel said. He got up.

"Sit!" I commanded the colonel. "You promised that we'd give it a try."

He sat back down. "So explain what we're supposed to do."

"First, I'm going to lead us into an altered state of consciousness through a deep breathing process."

"Oh, brother, if any of my flying buddies ever—"

"*Please*, suspend your disbelief," I begged. "Just for the next half *hour*."

After the deep breathing process, I told Reuel to imagine himself encircled in a spiritual white light. That pushed him over the brink.

"I'm outta here!"

For fear of losing my Ouija partner, I immediately ended the meditation and cut to the chase. I instructed him to place his fingers gently on the plastic indicator. I did the same.

After a minute or so, it began to move. At first weakly.

"Liz, you're moving it."

"I'm not!"

The indicator proceeded in slow, irregular circles.

"If you're not moving it, and I'm not moving it, then who the hell's moving it?"

"I told you the theory," I answered, trying to keep calm. "It could be your own subconscious mind, or it could possibly be spirits."

"How silly of me," he said. "I totally forgot."

I closed my eyes and imagined myself encircled in a protective white light, just in case there were evil spirits around. "Is there anybody here?"

The plastic indicator began to pick up speed and made its way up to the corner where the word YES was written.

"Your subconscious is moving this thing?" Reuel asked, sarcasm showing through.

"Do you have a message for us?" I asked the board, ignoring him.

Our fingers moved swiftly toward the letters of the alphabet.

Now it was my turn to accuse Reuel. "*You're* moving it! You want to get this thing over with and *you* are moving it."

"I swear, I'm not! Look—my fingers are barely touching it."

A cold shiver came over me.

The letters were now being run off, one after the other. But they made no sense whatsoever.

B-A-G-E-E-Y-N

"Is that a word?" I called out.

The indicator was moving in wild circles. It was frightening. It was as if somebody were standing directly over us, guiding our fingers. I didn't recall being this spooked during the Flight 401 research.

"Are we on Aborigine soil?" I asked.

YES

"Liz, it went to 'yes,' because you think we're on Aborigine ground," Reuel, reclaiming his voice of reason, spoke up.

"Well, maybe," I said, secretly welcoming a rational explanation. "Let's ask something else."

"Ask about the shower."

"Whoever's here, did you have anything to do with the shower?"

N-G-I-T-Y-A-L-I

"What is this crap?" Reuel asked the board.

Our fingers slowed to a stop.

"Have you been doing things around the house to get our attention?" I asked.

The indicator began to circle wildly again, dragging our fingers across the board from letter to letter with an energy I had never experienced before.

K-I-R-A-W-E-E

"What's *kirawee*?" I asked.

M-E-S-S-A-G-E

"It was a message?" I asked.

YES

The chill I felt had now gotten worse. "It's *freezing* down here," I said to Reuel.

"It *is* a little damp," he said, a tad conciliatory. "Let's call it a day."

"Wait. Is *kirawee* an Aborigine word?" I asked the board.

YES

I looked up at Reuel. "Do you have anything you want to ask?"

"Yeah," Reuel said. "Can we see the spirit?"

"That's ridiculous!"

"Why?" Reuel argued. "Didn't pilots and flight attendants in John's *Ghost of Flight 401* see the ghost?"

"But they didn't *ask* to see him."

"Liz," Reuel said, "tell whoever it is that we want to see him."

"Fine." I threw my head heavenward. "My skeptic husband doesn't really believe in any of this. Could you please do something physical to prove to him that you're really here?"

W-A-I-T

I felt a sudden icy cold wind blow past me. "You will do something to prove that you're really here?"

YES

"Liz," Reuel said, "ask how long we have to wait."

M-A-N-O-N H-O-R-S-E

"We're going to see a man on a horse?" I said to the ceiling.

YES

Reuel again: "Ask *where* we're supposed to see this 'man on horse.'"

T-R-G-I-L-A-C-K-I

Reuel's response: "Nothing but more nonsense."

"Wait a minute," I asked the board. "Could we get clearer messages if I tried an altered state of consciousness?"

T-E-S-T

"What's an altered state of consciousness?" Reuel wanted to know.

"I'll just lie down and go through a meditation. And then I'll ask for the messages to come directly through me."

Suddenly I got the whiff of smoke. I worried that I'd left the stove on.

"Do you smell something?" I asked Reuel.

"Somebody's having a 'barbie' in their backyard," he replied with his skeptical half smile.

"Smells more like burning leaves."

"It's a barbecue, Liz."

"I think I'll try that altered state."

"Now?"

"Yeah," I said. "Aren't you curious to learn more?"

"Lizzy, I think I've had enough of the *Twilight Zone* for tonight." Reuel wasted not a moment removing the Ouija board from our laps. "Let's go to bed," he said, sliding next to me on the twin bed.

"Here, on this little cot?"

Reuel slipped off his shirt. "You weren't very shy about the sand."

"But we had the whole beach to ourselves."

"And now we have the entire haunted basement to ourselves. We'll just stay here and wait for the man on the horse. Spoooooooky . . ."

"Let's go upstairs," I said. But I soon gave in and melted into his arms.

We woke the following morning to the kookaburra alarm, or as Gladys would say, the ha-ha pigeons telling us that it was time for breakie.

"You can hear those damn birds guffawing all the way down here," Reuel said, kissing my ear and at the same time easing on top of me with all the expertise and refined strength of a guy who could land a plane and a woman in one smooth move. In that instant a silly, nervous sense in me went off.

"Hey, you better never screw around on me," I said, not totally joking.

"You are the most beautiful woman I've ever known," Reuel answered, moving to the other ear. "I-am-mad-crazy-in-love-with-you."

"That's the way I like it," I said.

"And you're a little nutty. You and your Ouija boards and your flaky friends."

"Go on."

"And because we were married in the Vatican, I'm stuck with you forever."

I was ready for it to be forever, too. Reuel and I really had, a year and a half earlier, repeated our vows in the Chapel of the Choirs at St. Peter's Basilica. It was so wonderful, so romantic. Just Reuel and me, vowing our never-ending devotion amid the incense, gilded cherubs, and marble statues of saints sculpted hundreds of years before. If ever I thought that I wasn't really a Catholic, the notion was dispelled the second Reuel slipped his great-grandmother's wedding band onto my finger and Father John J. Foley intoned in a thick Irish brogue: "By the rites of the Catholic Church, I pronounce you man and wife."

Often when Reuel and I made love, I thought about the sanctity of our vows, and the intensity of the moment would grow. I loved the fact that we were married. That we couldn't leave each other. We'd grow old together. What a sense of security.

"Hey," I asked as we soared thiry-five thousand feet above the cot and still hadn't reached cruising altitude, "will you still love me if someday I have to see a periodontist and have serious root work?"

"Ohhhh, yes, yes, yes," he whispered into the top of my head. "My cousin's a periodontist."

"He's an ophthalmologist," I said, flying straight to paradise.

"Ohhhhhhh, so that's what he is," Reuel cooed.

Back on the cot where the oxygen was plentiful, I suddenly recalled the dream that I'd had that night. Slowly it began to emerge in full detail. It was a humdinger.

"Time for coffee," Reuel said, planting the old lovemaking wrap-up kiss on my forehead. He jumped up and slipped on his Timberland moccasins.

"I dreamed I met an Aborigine spirit doctor," I blurted out.

"Oh yeah?" Reuel smiled.

"God, it was sooo real."

"Lizzy," Reuel said, standing over me, bright-eyed and bushy-tailed, "what'd you do with that new white golf shirt?"

"It's in the dryer," I said, amazed at his capacity to switch from one passion to another without missing a beat.

"I hope it didn't shrink."

"Hey, wait a minute. You gotta hear this dream."

"Shoot," Reuel said, accommodating me. He sat beside me on the bed. "So you saw an Aborigine in your dream?"

"Yeah. He was standing at the top of the stairs. By the kitchen sink. His skin was pitch-black. As black as my T-shirt here," I said, reaching for it on the floor. "His chest and face were painted with white powder or something. All around him there was a pungent odor of burning leaves."

"That's because before we went to sleep last night, you thought you smelled burning leaves. Remember, Liz, that was one of the last things on your mind."

"True. Anyway this Aboriginal whatever had on some sort of headdress. With feathers and shells."

"Like an African witch doctor?"

"Pretty much. But the strangest part about all of this—I wasn't scared."

"It was only a dream," Reuel reassured me. Now it was with the kind of smile a parent gives a hysterical child awakened by monsters under his bed.

"Yeah. But it really seemed real," I said, as more details came back to me. "He told me that he was a healer. That his tribe once occupied the site where this house stands."

"Now *that* was on your mind, too," Reuel said. "Remember when we asked that crazy Ouija board if we were on Aborigine soil?"

"You're right," I admitted.

"So go on," Reuel said, anxious to interpret and bring reason to the conversation.

"He said that he was going to give me a healing."

"A healing? What's wrong with you?"

"I didn't think anything was wrong with me. In fact, I asked him if he could give Randy a healing."

"And?"

"He said that *I* was to be given the healing. And that I was going to be led to someone who'd give me knowledge that would help Randy."

"Who's the person you're going to be led to?"

49

"He showed me a black man sitting on a horse."

"Another thing we got off that Ouija board," Reuel said. "See, Liz, dreams are nothing but what's on your mind during the day." He chuckled. "Continue."

"He told me that I was here for a specific reason."

"What reason?"

"He said that I'd find out soon. I remember telling this spirit doctor that I wanted to wake up my husband . . ."

"Where was *I* supposed to be?"

"You were sleeping next to me."

"But you never woke me up?"

"That's right. Before I got the chance, he took some sort of painted stick and began to whirl it over my head while he chanted in a high-pitched voice. Then he took paperbark—you know, that soft bark you see . . ."

"Oh yeah, the bark that just peels off the trunks of trees around here."

"Right. He crushed it and sprinkled it beside my feet. As if he was performing some sort of ritual. I began to cry. And then laugh. I wasn't afraid, though. His face was so serene. And so filled with compassion."

Reuel checked his watch. "Sounds like quite a dream." Then he stood up and gave his golf swing one last test. "How 'bout if I run down to that little store and pick up the *Morning Herald* and some croissants?"

"Great," I said, getting out of bed, pleased that he'd at least heard my dream through. I, too, was anxious to start the day. I was going to spend the morning writing. Then I had a lunch date on the Corso with Gladys. "When you come back, let's have breakfast out in the garden," I called to Reuel. He was in the laundry room, examining his golf shirt for shrinkage.

"Terrific!" he said.

From the tone of his voice, the shirt had not shrunk. As I headed to the bathroom, I once again called to Reuel, who was halfway up the stairs. "Honey, could you start the coffee?"

I turned to step into the shower, and that's when I heard Reuel shout, "Liz! Liz!"

I grabbed a towel and ran upstairs. Reuel was standing at the kitchen sink. He was holding the coffee grinder in one hand and the bag of coffee beans in the other. All the color had drained from his face. Outside, I could see Prince Charles perched on a bare frangipani branch, looking in through the opened window.

"What's wrong?" I asked.

"Look," he said, motioning with his foot to the floor in front of him.

"What's all that?"

"Paperbark."

"Huh?"

"*Crushed* paperbark. Your dream, Liz. Remember your dream?"

It was midafternoon when I returned from lunch with Gladys, during which I told her about the dream, the paperbark incident, and about the clamshell that was dropped onto my computer. That's when she reported that during the excavation for our basement, clamshells were flying all over the place. A lot of them had landed in her garden. They were old shells, petrified, she said. Hearing that, I speculated, perhaps wildly, that the cockatoo was a messenger sent by the spirit doctor. Gladys's response was in keeping: "Orrighty, we'd might as well get the tab for the fish an' chippie an be orf."

I was just about to do a little work around the garden—to burn off some of the fish an' chippie—when the phone rang. It was Victoria Williamson. She and her husband, Peter, who had found the house for us while we were still in the U.S., were back from visiting her family in England. How was I surviving Manly? Was I satisfied with the house? She was dying to hear every little detail, and could I possibly drive up to Avalon the next day and have lunch? It was only forty-five minutes north of Manly. The drive was spectacularly breathtaking. I must be careful, though. The coastal road was narrow and twisting and in many places carved smack into the mountain, leaving a sheer drop down to the ocean. Whoa! When I heard "sheer drop," I thought, The only way I'm getting to Avalon is riding shotgun in Reuel's rental. I had yet to get behind the wheel when everything was on the wrong side of the road. I certainly wasn't going to start my Aussie driver training on a linguine-narrow coastal road. Reuel, on the other hand, loved nothing more than death-defying curves in foreign countries. It brought out his Grand Prix complex.

So Reuel and Chris dropped me off in front of the Avalon Café at noon. They were headed fifteen minutes south to Long Reef, a golf course that overlooked the ocean. Their only concern was that I would have nothing to do after lunch while they finished their eighteen holes. They had no intention of cutting their game short—not with the greens fees. I reassured them gently—I loved nothing more than to wander around expensive villages, fingering the finery. As they pulled away, Chris called out, "Mom, if you get bored, look for some cool T-shirt shops."

I laughed. One glance up and down the village of Avalon told me that there was going to be no scrubby T-shirt shops. The town had the ambience of a Palm Springs or Sarasota. Liberally dotted along the main drag were palm trees, flower shops, European boutiques, outdoor cafés serving hummus and bean sprouts on pita, bistros with French menus, shoe stores selling Ferragamo and Gucci sandals, Italian designer kids' clothing shops waiting for a Princess Fergie, and a plethora of women who looked like Olivia Newton-John hopping in and out of earth-toned four-by-fours with strollers and Boogie Boards.

I went into a flower shop where I found the most perfect card for Randy—a hand-painted watercolor of a peach tree with a white cockatoo sitting on top. I sat on a bench outside the shop and jotted off a note congratulating him (and me) on the MAC award nomination. Then I walked over to the café where I ordered a freshly pressed lemonade and savored the fall sun beating down on the awning above my head. What's that saying? Women can't be too thin or too rich. In my case, I can't be too hot or too underdressed. But I was not inappropriate—khaki shorts, tank top, rubber thongs, and John Lennon shades.

I calculated that I hadn't seen Victoria in over five years. We had first met fifteen years before in an art class in Westport. It was our differences that initially attracted us to each other. She was precise and liked realism, delicate flowers that took weeks to complete. I was sloppy, preferred abstract—it was quick and easy—and everything I painted had a somber, tragic tone. I remembered Victoria studying one of my rather threatening canvases and saying in her terribly British accent, "Elizabeth darling, have you given any thought to pastel seascapes?"

I was smiling about this to myself when I saw Victoria standing at a traffic light across the road. There was no mistaking her—fifty-something and striking with shiny, shoulder-length dark hair, tailored white trousers, long-sleeved cuffed shirt, and loafers that smacked of old money. It had often crossed my mind that she was some sort of deposed British royalty. As she neared, I wasn't surprised to see her porcelain complexion totally covered in sunscreen. She was worried about the ozone hole, and so rumor around Westport was that Victoria had to have moved to Australia to please her Aussie husband, Peter.

There was no small talk. In that respect, Victoria was not typically British.

She removed her Sophia Loren sunglasses and gave me the Continental two-cheeked kiss. Once we were seated in the restaurant, she got to the point. "Darling," she said, "Peter and I were *shocked* to hear you married a businessman. We thought you'd end up with another writer. Is it working?"

"Better than I imagined," I said

"Really?"

"Yes. We're as different as night and day. I adored John. But, Victoria, it's not always easy to live with another writer."

Victoria took a rubber band from her Chanel shoulder bag and pulled her hair into a ponytail at the nape of her neck, a protest against the heathen heat of the Southern Hemisphere. "Elizabeth, I know exactly what you mean. Sometimes I wish Peter were *anything* but a writer."

"I don't believe you for a second," I said to Victoria's unconvincing grin. Victoria thrived on the literary scene and it wasn't to wolf down the wine and cheese. She and Peter spent all their free time at plays, concerts, and museums. I wasn't quite sure what *our* friendship was based on. A typical conversation with Victoria would be her discussing, maybe, Puccini's final opera, with me sitting there with a hoity-toity puss, not knowing what the hell she was talking about, and thinking that the last thing I saw was *Dumb and Dumber*.

"Darling, Peter and I were over-the-moon to read the review your play received in the *London Times*."

"Oh, that was because Randy Allen was so terrific as Bette Davis when we did it off-off-Broadway," I said.

"It must have been quite a shout playing opposite a man in drag?"

"I'll tell you what was quite a shout," I began. "The day Reuel came home from a flying trip and walked into the living room where Randy and I were rehearsing. As long as I live, I'll never forget the scene. Reuel in his Air Force flight suit and Randy in his high heels and fur hat. They stood looking at each other as if each was from another planet. After several uncomfortable moments, they tentatively shook hands. There was no chitchat. Reuel grabbed his flight bag, went into the kitchen, and poured himself a double martini. He told me to count him out for dinner if Randy arrived at the dinner table in the high heels and the fluff ball on his head."

"Elizabeth, what a position you were in!"

"Of course I couldn't tell Randy to take off the heels. He was breaking them in."

Victoria laughed. "What on earth did you do?"

"I didn't do anything."

"And?"

"When it was time for dinner, I ordered some Chinese takeout. And when it arrived, I called Reuel."

"Was Randy still in the heels and hat?"

"Just the heels."

"Did your husband come down?"

"Yep. He came down. I was a total wreck. I didn't know what to expect. But Reuel just walked over to the refrigerator and said to Randy, 'Hey buddy, how 'bout a beer?' "

"Did Randy take it?" Victoria asked, hanging on my every word.

"No. He asked for a Sprite. And Reuel rolled his eyes. Randy picked up on that and then *he* rolled his eyes. And from that moment on, they more or less tolerated each other."

Victoria laughed some more. "Darling, how does one spell your husband's name?"

This wasn't the first time I'd been asked this. "R-E-U-E-L," I said.

"But it's pronounced like 'rule'? Not 'Raoul'?"

"You got it. Rule."

"Rule," she repeated with uppity flair.

We each ordered an arugula salad with sweet red peppers and gorgonzola dressing. No bacon cheeseburgers in Avalon.

"The house is suitable?" Victoria asked, flinging open Pandora's box.

"Well, we're getting a lot for our money. And I mean a *lot* for our money."

Victoria adjusted a dull gold monogrammed cuff link on her linen shirt and chuckled, "How do you mean, darling?"

I gave her the uncondensed version, which took from the salad to caffè latte and finally on back to iced tea and lemonade. Unlike Gladys, when I got to the end of the saga Victoria had all sorts of thoughts about how and why this was happening to us.

"Darling," she whispered, "one must take this very, very seriously. I know things like this can happen. I had my own experiences back in London." Then she asked, "What is Reuel's reaction?"

"After he found the crushed paperbark, I naturally assumed that we'd talk about it. But he swept it up. And that was that."

"He never mentioned anything afterward?" Victoria asked, stunned.

"He said that he thought Chris had played a joke on us."

"Elizabeth, could that be possible?"

"No. Chris was sound asleep when we first went down to the basement. And he was still sleeping when he discovered the paperbark."

"Have you pointed that out to Reuel?"

"Of course."

"And?"

"He said that it was the bird."

"Prince Charles?" Victoria asked.

"That's right. He said that Prince Charles flew in through the open window and created the mess."

"Poor man," Victoria said. "He's in denial."

"You can take that one to the bank."

Victoria sampled the carrot cake we were sharing. "Your next move?"

"To get to the bottom of this whole thing," I said, tasting the dessert. "Ummm. Great lemon frosting."

"It's prepared with sour cream," Victoria informed me. "One of the house specialties." She slid the moist, nutty cake closer to me. "How does one go about such a mission?"

"I want to go back into the basement and try that altered state I told you about."

Victoria's large green eyes darted around the room. "The Australians are very funny when it comes to the idea of the spirit world." She was whispering again. "They simply don't understand it. One must keep that in mind."

I immediately thought about Gladys.

"Another thing, darling, there is a great deal of guilt over how the white man has treated the Aborigine. Our Aborigines have been dislocated in much the same manner as your American Indians. Most have been shuffled off their land onto reservations in the Outback. Oh yes, there is guilt."

"But if there's so much guilt, how come I read in the paper every day that the government is still building roads and drilling for oil on sacred grounds?"

"Because the white Australian simply doesn't understand the Aborigines' relationship to the land. For some reason they cannot comprehend that there is a deep spiritual link between an Aborigine and the specific site of his birth." Victoria went on. "Humans, spirits, those who have died, those yet to be born, all hold the land in trust. In fact, darling, it's even deeper than that. In the spiritual sense, they are the land. It cannot be removed from the Aborigine. Not even by death. Land is considered to be eternal."

"You seem to know a lot about Aborigines."

"I've read a bit," Victoria said, modestly. "I've taken a few courses, as well. But darling, there is much to learn. Their culture is so rich. So beautiful. It is highly undervalued by the white man. Such a pity. One could study for a lifetime and not even scratch the surface." She sipped her caffè latte. "A great deal of the religion is secretive. Unless one is an Aborigine, one will not be privileged to know many of their sacred laws, and—"

"Victoria," I interrupted, "to be totally honest, I'm scared by all of this."

"Darling, you must not be. Perhaps you have been selected for a specific purpose."

"That's what the spirit doctor said in my dream."

"Elizabeth, had you ever had a dream like that before?"

"Never."

"How was it different?" Victoria asked.

"You know how most dreams eventually fade in your memory. Oh, you think about it when you first wake up, then by the end of the day it's all hazy in your mind. But not this one. If anything, it's become clearer and stronger in my mind. It's become part of me. I wish I could explain it better. I'm just so confused by everything that's been happening. I keep saying, Why me? And now even Reuel is treating me like I'm a little weird."

Victoria nodded. "I see what you mean."

We sat silent for several moments. Victoria looked as if she was in deep concentration. "Elizabeth," she started, "you never explained why you came here in such a rush. When you rang up from the States, you were quite frantic for a place to live. Frankly, Peter and I worried that the marriage wasn't working out."

"I don't know about frantic," I said, "but I was hell-bent on getting here. And that's what has me so confused. It was as if there was some sort of transcontinental bungee cord strapped to my ankle that was pulling me from Weston, Connecticut, to Manly, Australia."

"Elizabeth, you haven't changed a bit," Victoria laughed.

"Seriously, Victoria, part of me feels like packing it up and going back home."

"Darling, we've been friends for fifteen years. I know you. You will pursue this to the finish."

"And that's what scares me. I'm afraid that this time, I'm in over my head. Reuel leaves in two weeks. Right now, I'm tempted to go with him."

"Elizabeth," Victoria said, placing her hand over mine, "I feel so responsible."

"Why on earth would *you* feel responsible?"

"It was Peter and I who found the house for you."

"That's nonsense," I said. "You went out of your way to help me. I'm really very grateful."

Victoria sat back, pensive. "What seems quite odd was that your house in Manly was the *only* house available, after we had run all those ads in the local paper. . . . Darling, as unreal as it may sound, that house rather had your name on it."

Suddenly I had this thought: If what Victoria said could possibly be true, then I was under some sort of spiritual obligation to follow this through. I should have learned in my Flight 401 research that when a spirit wants to get a message through, the spirit will not rest until the message is conveyed to the person intended. How ridiculous to think that I could run away. "Victoria," I said soberly, "do you know any Aborigines?"

"For you to meet?" she asked, surprised.

"Yes."

"No, darling. I really don't. Most of the Aborigines are in the Outback. Oh, wait a minute, come to think of it, there is a rather large community of Aborigines in Sydney. I'm sure Peter will have a better idea of exactly where. I'll ask him when I go home. But you must remember that they are very private people. They don't readily open up to the white man."

"I think I'll start with library research in Manly."

"Yes, and the Mitchell Library in Sydney is an excellent source. They have a large and important Aborigine collection," Victoria said. Then she leaned forward and mused, "Perhaps there is a whole world inside that house just waiting to be explored."

"What's that Eastern saying?" I said. "To regard the world as ultimately real is a delusion."

"Precisely!" Victoria motioned for the waiter to bring the check. "If one is privileged to experience other worlds, one would be better suited to see this world as it really is. Not what it simply appears to be."

Our waiter had arrived just in time to catch the tail end of our philosophical discussion. I gathered from his Birkenstocks, ponytail, and crystal pendant that he felt comfortable with our energy. On our way out, he confided that the lapis crystal was for harmony.

"Avalon attracts a fair share of New Agers," Victoria said, hugging me good-bye.

"I'll have Peter call you tonight."

It turned out that Peter knew of a Catholic priest in the Redfern district of Sydney who worked very closely with the local Aborigines. "Redfern," he said, "is where many Aborigines live, and they don't live very well." Peter equated the area of Redfern to Harlem in New York City. He had never actually met the Irish priest in charge there, but he had read about him more than once in the *Sydney Morning Herald*. He was Mother Teresa-like in his devotion to the Aborigine people. Father Ted Kennedy—a name not easy to forget—was known to have opened up his church doors to house the homeless, to have fed them, become their friend, and asked absolutely nothing in return. Father Kennedy had a deep respect for the Aborigine religion and had no interest in making converts—a controversial issue with the Catholic Church.

At nine o'clock the following Sunday morning, Reuel and I set out for Redfern with our car doors locked and windows rolled up, expecting Harlem. It wasn't even close. In fact, many of the old houses were in excellent condition. A number of the houses and buildings had been freshly renovated, restored to a Victorian charm. The streets and sidewalks were litter-free. If there were "bad" streets, Reuel and I had somehow managed to avoid them. Directly across the street from Father Kennedy's parish, St. Vincent's, was an upscale cappuccino bar where a few yuppie-looking sorts (white) were having a leisurely Sunday breakfast waiting for the ten o'clock mass. The only Aborigines I spotted in the area were the ones in front of St. Vincent's—lying on the ground, drunk, passed out. About six or eight men. Occasionally an Aborigine woman came by and yelled an obscenity at one of them. We figured it was a disgruntled wife or girlfriend. We were twenty minutes early so we sat in our parked car directly across the street from the church and watched the drama unfold. I was glad Chris had decided to stay home and finish his math homework, although this might have been more of an education.

We had only been waiting for a few minutes when a car pulled alongside the curb directly in front of the church door. A white couple, the woman driving. I assumed they were husband and wife, but the moment the car stopped, all the guys who had been lying el stinko on the ground, jumped to their unsteady feet. They all but saluted the gray-haired man, who was wearing dark slacks and a white short-sleeved shirt. There were instant and profuse greetings: "Wossgowinon Father Ted. Sister Dorothy. . . " One older Aborigine man wrapped an arm around the priest, almost knocking him over. Out of nowhere a gang of small Aborigine kids, barely dressed, ran up and draped themselves around the priest's knees and the sister's skirt. One of the kids fell. Crying, he pointed out his scraped knee. While Sister Dorothy inspected it, Father Ted took a handful of lollies from his pocket and passed them out to the children. It was a scene out of a Bing Crosby movie.

After the hellos, I expected everyone to follow Father Ted and Sister Dorothy into church, but as soon as the priest and nun disappeared through the large wooden door, the soused fell back to the ground and the kids scampered off down the road. About five minutes to ten, a few white people in jeans, khakis, and lightweight dresses and skirts started up the pathway, nonchalantly stepping around the bodies as they made their way into the church. One young man matter-of-factly picked up his two small daughters and carried them over the human obstacle course. On that note, we locked up the car and followed them in.

Inside, the church was bare. No stained glass. No statues. No plaques depicting the stations of the cross. There was just a simple crucifix on the wall behind a tidy makeshift altar. Reuel and I slipped into the second-to-last pew behind the young man and his two little girls. Off to my right was a middle-aged woman whom I immediately pegged as a nun. Silver cross and simple dress. We nodded hello. She had a gentle smile. I was sure she recognized us as first-timers.

If there had been any doubt that we were truly in God's house, there wasn't the moment Father Ted appeared at the altar in a plain white cassock over his street clothes and began to say mass. His voice was as kind as his face. His sermon was pure and from the heart. Ornate gilding, cherubs on ceilings, and marble statues would suddenly have seemed like an unnecessary and extravagant backdrop for the unadorned message delivered that late-summer morning. "For us whites," Father Ted began, "reconciliation starts not with guilt, but with the acknowledgment of truth. Guilt cannot be passed down, for Christ has taken guilt away. Guilt is unproductive, indeed harmful. When Aborigines notice that we non-Aborigines are beginning to see that our own liberation is bound up with theirs, the healing power of truth will begin to set each of us free."

As I sat on the worn and shaky bench, listening to what Father Ted was saying about the necessity for overcoming destructive feelings of guilt and fear, I thought about my latest decision. I wondered if it had been based on fear. In the last few days, I had decided that when Reuel left for the States in less than two weeks, Chris and I would be with him. I hated to admit it, but my mother was right. Married only one year and I'm off on some cockamamie trip. Reuel needed me with him. Although he would never say that. Then there was Randy. He needed me, too. We had spoken earlier in the week. He was unable to gain weight, to get rid of a cough. He didn't sound good, but it was good to hear his voice. He was eager to see me. We'd dine at Café des Artistes in the City. With any luck he'd win the MAC award and give his career a boost. His mother and brother were driving up from Indiana to stay until he got back on his feet. Had I tried the peaches? I hurt.

I would thank Victoria profusely for going to all the trouble of finding us the house, but that darn transcontinental bungee cord that had pulled me from Weston, Connecticut, to Manly, Australia, was now pulling me back to Weston. Sorry. Time to go. The fat lady had sung.

The bench was hard. I really wished that Father Ted would stop talking on and on about how fear is a major stumbling block that stands in the way of our achieving inner peace. Why was he looking at me? Or maybe he wasn't. Was *I* suddenly looking at *me*? Did I know at that moment, as I sat in St. Vincent's Catholic Church in Redfern on an uncomfortable, unsteady pew, that my fears were holding me captive? Did the ringing of the communion bell trigger a full-blown awareness that I was scared to death to stay in that house—a sitting duck for God knows what kind of spirit?

I watched Father Ted move around the altar as he completed preparation for communion. Damn, I'd thought I had fear beat when I picked up my life again after John died. The communion wafer was simple. A soup cracker. When I accepted it into the palm of my cupped hand and looked into Father Ted's soulful blue eyes—eyes full of pain, sorrow, and love—I silently asked for guidance. "Please God, what do I do? Do I stay here or go home? Do I communicate with the spirit? Is there really a spirit? Am I crazy? Lead me wherever I'm supposed to go. Who is that black man in the row behind me?"

At the point during the mass just before communion, when we turn to greet those around us, the man with the two daughters turned to me, shook my hand, and said, "Peace be with you." "Peace be with you," I said back. The entire church was alive with the feeling of Oneness. While Reuel turned to his left and extended a hand to a teenager and her mom, I turned to my right and shook hands with the woman I took to be a nun. Then I turned around to the pew behind me. For a second I stood still, literally mesmerized by the black, black skin and blue, blue eyes. At once, I tried to hide my astonishment. I threw out my hand and gave a no-nonsense handshake. "Peace be with you," I said. "Peace be with ya," the Aborigine man said, returning a no-nonsense handshake.

———

"I'm Max Eulo," the man with the black skin and blue eyes said after mass.

"I'm Liz Fuller," I said, reaching out to shake his hand for the second time. "My husband's over there pouring himself a cup of coffee."

He straightened a very tattered bush hat and gave a smile that revealed a few missing teeth. "Ya first time here?"

"As a matter of fact, it is."

"Where ya from?"

"United States."

"Got lotta cowboys 'ere?" he asked.

"That's in the West. We live in the East."

"No horses where ya are?"

"Oh sure, but the cowboys are out West."

"I was a stockman—Aborigine cowboy," he said, throwing his rather broad shoulders back. He was wearing a western-syle shirt and a red bandana tied around a good-sized neck.

"I can see that."

"Ya can?" he said, and broke out into a grin that turned his leathery, square face perfectly round.

"The way you dress," I said. "And your bush hat. It's decorated with all those horse pins." I spotted Reuel approaching. "Honey," I said, "meet Max Eulo."

Reuel handed me a cup of coffee and then extended his hand to Max. "Pleasure to meet you, Max."

"Good ya come to our church." Max clutched Reuel's hand with both of his.

"It was a beautiful mass," I said. "The sermon was very moving."

"Fatha Ted's a good fulla. Have ya met him an' Sister Dorothy?"

"No," I said, "not yet."

"Ya wanna follow me?" Max said. He led us over to where they were chatting with a group of others. "Fatha Ted, Sister Dorothy, I'd like ya to meet a fulla an' his missus. They come all the way from America."

Father Ted and Sister Dorothy couldn't do enough to make us

feel at home. They immediately ushered us to a long table loaded down with freshly baked breads and cakes. As Father Ted asked us all sorts of questions about ourselves, he helped himself to a large hunk of coffee cake. This did not go over well with Sister Dorothy, who Max quickly explained was a nun, as well as Father Ted's biological sister. Father Ted wasn't supposed to be eating sweets because of his health; he mumbled that he'd skip lunch. Max burst out laughing.

When Max was certain that Reuel and I were comfortable, he walked off to say hello to a few other people. "I'll be right back with ya," he said. "Pour ya-selves another cuppa."

Father Ted and Sister Dorothy went on about how they wouldn't know what to do without Max, who was more or less the "mayor" of Redfern. "He tries so hard to keep his brothers on the straight and narrow. They depend on him. We all depend on him," Sister Dorothy said.

"As you probably noticed," Father Ted said, "there's a major drinking problem here. Not Max," he quickly added. "He doesn't touch the grog."

"Max was the only Aborigine I noticed in the church," I said.

"They rarely come into the church during mass," Sister Dorothy replied, "but Max is different. He's here almost every Sunday."

"Then he doesn't practice his own religion?"

"Oh yes," Father Ted said, "he most definitely does. It's part of him. The fact that he comes to mass does not alter in any way the importance of his own religion in his life. He's here because we're very close friends."

Just then the other woman whom I had pegged as the nun walked up to us. She was introduced as Sister Pat. "I see you've met Max," she said, smiling.

"Yes, he seems like such a terrific man."

"The best," Sister Pat said. She turned to Father Ted and Sister Dorothy and asked, "Did you tell Liz and Ra-ool what happened when the pope arrived last month?"

"Awww," Sister Dorothy said, delightfully throwing her hands up in the air. "What a time we had. Max was supposed to have led the pope's parade. He was to be riding a white horse as the representative of the entire Aboriginal people."

"Holding a smoking torch," Sister Pat added.

"Yes," Sister Dorothy nodded. "But then, at the last minute, things went awry and Max didn't get to do it. What a magnificent sight it would have been to see our Max on a horse leading the pope."

"But he did lead the parade of his people on foot," Sister Pat added.

"He was very disappointed, though," Father Ted said. "He wanted to be on that horse."

A few minutes later Max came back and joined the conversation. Sister Dorothy, Sister Pat, and Max began to tell us how we were not to miss the Easter Show when it came to town the next month. Quickly, however, the conversation switched from prize sheep to the unfortunate fate of a young Aborigine man who had just arrived in Redfern from the Outback. From what I could gather, the man fled his village to escape a bone that had been pointed at him to avenge some misdeed he had committed. The double whammy had been put on him. Sister Dorothy suggested that Max bring him around for a cup of tea later in the day and they would arrange a place for him to live.

It was just about noon when Max walked us back down the church pathway toward our car. "Ho!" Max belted out on seeing his sloshed brothers spread on the sidewalk. The crooked crew popped up as quickly and as wobbly as jack-in-the-boxes. Max did not look happy. "Gowon an' get ya-self a feed!" he ordered. He watched the six men stagger single file through the large church door. When the last one disappeared, he turned his attention back to us. I detected a distinct look of embarrassment. "I'll look fa ya next Sunday," Max said, forcing cheer.

"Well, Lizzy," Reuel said, as we got into the car, "I guess you just met your man on the horse."

# FIVE

That night Reuel and I went back down to the basement, and for the first time since experimenting with my homemade Ouija board, we attempted to contact the spirit world. After we met Max, Reuel's whole attitude took a dramatic turn. He finally admitted that something mighty odd was going on. And more than that, Reuel was the one who suggested that I attempt that altered state of consciousness that only days earlier he had affectionately referred to as a "crock of shit."

"So is this going to be spooky?" Reuel asked as we headed down the steep stairway to the basement.

"Not at all," I said, stretching out on the twin bed. "I'm just going to do some deep breathing exercises, the same as with meditation." I went on about how breathing helped separate the stresses of the physical world from consciousness and helped one enter into the spiritual realm so that contact could be made with higher energy forces.

Reuel sat beside me holding the tape recorder, staring at me as if I were going to float above the bed or something.

"Honey, stop staring," I said.

"What should I do?"

"Just close your eyes."

"I might fall asleep."

"Then breathe along with me. Take a deep relaxing breath through your nose."

"Do I keep my mouth shut?"

"Please do," I said. "Now as you inhale, picture that you are pulling strength into your body. With each breath, imagine yourself lifting above your physical body."

"Hold it, Lizzy," Reuel said. "I'll just be your secretary."

"Fine," I said. I continued to deep-breathe. Gradually I began to lose sense of time and space. My body became feather light. Slowly everything around me started to fade out of existence. Later, Reuel told me that I remained in this state, motionless and expressionless, for almost a half hour. Then, without warning, I began to make high-pitched birdlike noises that startled him out of his skin.

The following is an unedited transcript of the taped session:

REUEL: What the hell's happening!

LIZ: Dwango here.

REUEL: Liz, you okay?

LIZ: Yes.

REUEL: Who's Dwango?

LIZ: Spirit doctor. One of his nicknames was Birdman. He was very light and graceful. As a youngster he would fly through the air.

REUEL: Is he speaking English now?

LIZ: I just know what he's saying.

REUEL: Is it mental telepathy, Liz?

LIZ: Yes. He's showing me that he's playing the didgeridoo. During healing sessions, he sings. He says that singing and healing are interconnected.

REUEL: Then the music you sometimes hear in the basement is Dwango playing the didgeridoo?

LIZ: Yes.

REUEL: What about the bird? Prince Charles?

LIZ: It's Dwango. He's able to manifest himself as a bird. He's saying that if you are a spirit doctor you have powers that don't go away with the physical death.

REUEL: Are we on sacred ground?

LIZ: Yes.

*[At this point on the tape there is more singing
and birdlike noises.]*

REUEL: Why's he coming through you? What's his message?

LIZ: He says that the path of life for the Aborigine are the lines
in the earth that they follow. When they go on their walk-
abouts, they are following a path. A path that nourishes them
physically and spiritually. It is the unknown path that leads
you to knowledge. [*A chantinglike sound is on the tape.*] The
road you take fulfills your inner knowledge. It feeds you. He's
saying that each person was put on this earth to take a different road. Our very own road. We must follow our own
path that will twist and turn and go up and down, and sometimes appear that it's going nowhere. It is out of nowhere
that you will find your peace. He says that I'll soon be led
along the path, and the answers will be revealed.

REUEL: I don't understand.

LIZ: When we transcend the world of sense, then we will begin
to know.

REUEL: What will you learn along this path?

LIZ: How the mind and the soul work together for spiritual en-
lightenment.

REUEL: Go on.

LIZ: I must start along the path to learn more. He's showing me
the man on the horse.

REUEL: Is it Max?

LIZ: Yes. He will lead me.

REUEL: How?

LIZ: When the lizard appears, I will know I'm on the right path.

REUEL: Can you ask him to explain that?

LIZ: Stay close to the ground and follow the source. Open yourself up to the earth, and look to the sky.

REUEL: Anything else?

LIZ: [*Pause*] Yes. [*Pause*] Something about . . . something about
an . . . emu?

REUEL: [*Chuckling*] What the hell's an emu?

LIZ: A bird. [*Pause*] A very large bird. Do you think I'm crazy?

REUEL: Maybe. [*More chuckling*] Let's finish off that Danish ice cream.

*End of taped session*

One week later we went back to St. Vincent's and met Max as planned. In fact, he greeted us as we entered. His hat was off and his hair was freshly combed and slicked to one side. He reminded me of Chris on school picture day. He was wearing a brown Western-style shirt and pressed brown trousers that had a bell-bottom look. Tying the outfit together was a blue bandana that drew attention to his blue eyes. He was the most unusual-looking person I had ever seen.

"I almost didn't make it 'ere this mornin'," Max said, giving a warm, welcoming handshake. "I had to take my niece food shoppin'. The bus was late."

"Well, we almost didn't make it here today, too," I said. "Our son had a fever last night. I was a little concerned about leaving him. But he's starting to feel better now."

"What's ya young fulla's name?" Max asked.

"Christopher," I said. "I'd love you to meet him sometime."

"That'd be good."

"Max, do you ever have any time for lunch?"

Max thought for a moment. "Tuesday," he said. "I gotta take one of my bruddas to the doctor in the mornin'. After that I'll be 'round."

"Great, where should we meet? Anywhere's fine with us."

"Ya wanna come on down an' have lunch at our Aborigine coffee shop 'ere in Redfern?"

"Terrific," I said, instantly committing Reuel and Chris. "What time?"

"Whenever ya can make it."

"One o'clock," Reuel said, cheerfully resigned to the outing.

I had read that Aborigines were very casual about keeping appointments, but Sister Dorothy later told me that Max was different. If he set a time, he'd be there. And he was.

Reuel and I arrived at the Redfern train station just before one. Christopher was not with us. He said that he'd rather eat a loaf of Gladys's fairy bread than sit around an Aborigine coffee shop. Just as well. I'd never be able to talk to Max about what was going on if Christopher was there rolling his eyes and making wisecracks. We gave Christopher his daily schoolwork assignments and then money to have lunch at McDonald's on the Corso. We also gave him strict instructions to stay away from the beach and off his skateboard.

"Hey!" Max hollered as we stepped off the train platform.

We had originally intended to drive, but then Max phoned us late Monday evening and suggested that it would be easier and a bit safer if we took the train. He said that his coffee shop was close to the station. "Jus' wait right there till ya see me," Max instructed. "I don't want ya wanderin' aroun' Redfern."

"Where's ya young fulla?" Max asked, briskly leading us through the spic-and-span railway station.

What's that saying? Often kindness is more honest than truth. "He's still not feeling too good," I said.

"Awwghh," Max said. He led us out into a drizzling rain. "Ya hungry?"

"Starved," Reuel said. He squeezed my hand and muttered, "Steel yourself for Aussie roadkill."

Following at Max's heels, I gave myself a quick reality check. Yes, I was about to have lunch with an Aborigine whom I met because of a spirit doctor who spoke through me. Yes, my husband—a hard-ass colonel—witnessed the whole thing. And no, I probably wasn't crazy. I just hoped that when I told Max about all the strange things that had led up to our actual meeting that morning in church, he didn't become offended by a presumptuous white lady. This was going to be tricky. Over the years, John Fuller and I had had the opportunity to meet and interview some pretty exotic people—from Tibetan monks to Pygmies to British royalty. But the anticipation of this rendezvous had really gotten the adrenaline pumping.

As Reuel and I followed Max across the road to a shabby storefront in a rough part of the city, I thought about how John had taught me everything I knew about interviewing—even if this wasn't exactly an interview. Let them do all the talking, John would say. Nobody wants to hear about your life. If you feel you need to talk, ask *them* questions about *them*. Then listen, listen, listen. Often in stressful times, I'd feel John's presence. Sometimes I'd close my eyes and feel him so strongly that I'd open my eyes and expect to see him standing before me in khaki slacks and fishing hat, taking a long, thoughtful drag on his pipe. He was with me opening night off-Broadway. That's how I really had the nerve to face twenty-two New York critics. "Liz, our doubts are traitors," I heard John say. I heard him so crystal clear that I walked out of my dressing room and onto the stage confident and cocky, oblivious to the fact that a few acting lessons could have helped. The next day when I read the New York papers, I blamed my mentor for the pathetic reviews: "Will somebody please tell Elizabeth Fuller the hard, cold facts: SHE CAN'T ACT." Another favorite of mine: "I know I've seen worse actresses than Fuller. I just can't remember where or when." I think that one was compliments of Clive Barnes, *New York Post*. "Fuller," I said to John, tears dripping onto the papers, "what the hell was that advice of yours all about?" Again, I heard him say clearly: "Liz, you did it!"

Now, a few years later, I know what he meant. It's about the journey. It's all about what you do along the way. It's about following the path Dwango spoke of: the path that twists and turns and seems as if it's going nowhere and then suddenly—*bam*—you know what it's all about. You're trusting your inner nature. Your awareness becomes more alive than it's ever been before. You're seeing and hearing on a higher level. And soon you're walking by sight and knowledge. You're no longer ruled by emotion. Fear, anger, anxiety, are gone. You have stopped becoming overwhelmed by the demands of everyday life. Because nothing can overwhelm you when you're guided by a higher consciousness. No longer are you a hostage to the "shoulds" and the "should nots." What others think of you is irrelevant. You have the guts and the wisdom to know you're on the right path—the path you were born to follow. You're living *you*.

And when that happens, you've lifted not only yourself but all those around you to a spiritual level where deep and powerful knowledge resides.

Of course, I didn't have this awareness the afternoon we followed Max into the coffee shop, which reminded me of a fifties-style place in a working-class neighborhood. The second I walked in, I thought of Mildred D's—a corner luncheonette on the west side of Cleveland that my grandmother and I used to go to for burgers and malteds. I was relieved to see recognizable food on the menu. I was also grateful to see a cappuccino machine. A shot of caffeine never failed to help me think more clearly.

"The ham sandwiches are real tasty," Max said, guiding us to a table next to the sandwich counter. I could feel all eyes on us as we sat down. Nobody looked too friendly. When we placed our order at the counter, the short-order cook nodded hello to Max. He, too, looked rather unapproachable. Maybe that's what Max meant about not wanting us to walk around Redfern without him.

So over ham sandwiches and cappuccino, Max talked. He told us about his childhood, and how, when he was nine, his mother and father packed him and his eleven brothers and sisters up and took a horse and buggy from their home in Queensland into New South Wales to avoid having the children taken away by missionaries in an assimilation process. He told us that when his mother saw her first airplane, she thought it was a big bird. And he told us how a *koradji* in the Aborigine community could point a bone at someone and the next day the person would be dead.

"Bone pointing still happens, doesn't it?" I said, recalling the young man who Sister Dorothy and Max were trying to help with a place to live.

"Ya don't hear about it the way ya used to," Max said. "But it still goes on in the *mulga*."

"Mulga," I later learned, was an old Australian word for the Outback.

"Max," I said, breaking John Fuller's cardinal rule, "I need to tell you about something sort of unusual that's happened to me since I've been here. In your country."

Max took a sip of cappuccino. "Yeah?" he said.

I looked around to make sure nobody could hear. Frosty faces looked back. "Max," I said in almost a whisper, "do you believe in ghosts?"

"Goats?"

"Ghosts," I said, giving Reuel a little elbow nudge to stop smirking.

"Awwggh, ghosts," he said. "Whaddya, see somethin'?" His eyes suddenly darted around the dimly lit room.

"Oh, not here!" I said. "At our house in Manly." I made a quick decision not to play the part on the tape where Dwango says we were living on Aboriginal ground. And I would definitely steer clear of the part where Dwango says that Max will lead me along some unknown path. Mainly, I wanted to find out if the words that made absolutely no sense to Reuel and me made sense to Max.

"I've had some communication with a spirit—you know—like a ghost."

Max looked from me to Reuel and back to me.

"My husband and I are both totally baffled by what this spirit has told us."

"Liz," Reuel said, "you brought along the tape, didn't you?"

"Would you like to hear some of what came through?" I asked with great trepidation. "We recorded it."

"That'd be good," Max said.

I took the Sony out of my canvas shoulder bag. "It may be a little noisy here."

"Ya wanna move over in that corner," Max said. "Nobody's sittin' aroun' 'ere."

Once we got settled, Max said, "Go on. Play ya machine." His blue eyes were both inquisitive and questioning.

Before I started the tape, I told Max that one of the things he was going to hear was the spirit coming through me saying that we were going to meet a man on a horse.

Max folded his arms across his barrel chest—not receptive body language. "Ya sayin' that I'm the fulla on the horse?" he asked ingenuously.

"Max," Reuel said, coming to my rescue, "it's very strange. We were told by this spirit that we were going to meet you. I was right there. I heard it. You'll hear it."

Everything seemed so bizarre—my husband, an Air Force pilot, sitting in an Aborigine coffee shop trying to convince a full-blood Aborigine that a spirit had led us to him.

Max looked down at the tape recorder. "Start ya machine," he said. I couldn't seem to get a reading if we were treading on dangerous ground or not. I pressed the PLAY button and said silently, "Fuller, wherever you are right now, I need your help."

The tape had only been playing a matter of moments when Max asked, "Who's Dwango?"

"That's the spirit who came through," I said.

"He talked to ya?" Max looked directly into my eyes, and then downed the rest of the cappuccino.

"Yes," I said. "I was in sort of a trancelike state. And this spirit who called himself Dwango spoke through me."

"Awwwgh," Max said. He put his hand up to his chin and rubbed it. Talk about universal body language. "Who's makin' them bird sounds?"

"That's Liz," Reuel said. "The alleged spirit was making the noises through Liz."

"Awwwgh," Max said as if it was all beginning to make some sort of sense. "Who's singin'?"

"Dwango."

"Can ya play that singin' part again fa me?"

I rewound the tape, turned up the volume and played it again.

"That's Aborigine awright," Max said. "Them bird noises ya hear when a koradji doin' a ceremony. My grandfatha was a clever fulla."

"Max," I said, "what's a clever person?"

"Same as a koradji."

"Like a spirit doctor?" I said.

"Yeah," Max said, "like a spirit doctor."

I got shivers. In that instant I felt Fuller at my side.

"Do any of the words make sense?" Reuel asked.

"Hard fa me to make out the words," Max said. "We got hundreds a tribes. I'm from the Bujedi. About thirty, forty in my tribe. It's not our language. But the feelin' like Aborgine is there awright."

"Max," I said, "do you think that this person could really be a spirit doctor?"

"The clever fullas all died out," Max said.

"So there're no spirit doctors around?" Reuel asked.

"Ya right."

"But could it be that this 'dead' clever man spoke through Liz?"

Max's eyes shifted to mine. It was as if he were scanning behind my eyes for an answer. "Yeah," he said, "it can happen."

Numbness set in. I wasn't so sure that that was the answer I was looking for. "What should I do about all of this?" I asked.

"Maybe I should come out to ya house an' smoke the spirit."

"Huh?"

"Ya house," Max said. "Might 'ave to be smoked."

I looked over at Reuel and lightly kicked his foot under the table. He was totally without expression.

"What do you mean by smoke?" I asked.

"If ya got a bad spirit in ya house, I'll smoke 'em outta there."

"But what if it's a good spirit?"

"I'll know when I walk into ya house."

I turned to Reuel. "Should we do that?"

"Max," Reuel said, "what exactly does smoking a house entail?" He asked in the same tone he would ask a builder what it takes to redo a deck.

"I'll smoke branches an' talk to the spirit. Tell 'em to let ya alone."

"Do you perform the ceremony inside or out?" I asked, when I suddenly thought, What would Gladys think if she saw Max smoke a spirit in our garden?

"Liz," Reuel said, "you can't smoke a spirit in the house. You'll have smoke damage."

"Sometimes ya gotta smoke in the house," Max said, overriding Reuel.

"Max," the colonel said, "you'll have serious smoke damage if you do that in the house."

"Well, why don't we just have Max come to the house and then we'll see if we even need the house smoked," I said, calmly kicking Reuel under the table again.

"I got nothin' on Friday," Max said.

That was three days away. Reuel was scheduled to leave Thursday. By now I had decided to stay and play it out. I did not come to that decision lightly. Reuel and I spent many long hours discussing the pros and cons. At one point, I had even gone so far as to call the airline to find out how much I'd be penalized for changing the return date on our tickets. It was a chunk of change. Then there was the lease I had signed. If I broke it, I'd lose my deposit and then some. But the money was not the determining factor. The final decision to stay was the fact that I had met Max—a black man on a horse— just as Dwango said I would. And according to Dwango, this black man was going to lead me somewhere to help Randy. And, oh yes, something else weighed heavy on my mind. Victoria's words during our lunch: "Darling, as unreal as it may sound, that house rather had your name on it."

"Max," I said, "my husband is returning to America on Thursday. Do you have any time before that?"

Max started to think about how he could rearrange his schedule, but Reuel interceded, saying it really wasn't necessary for him to be there. Max grew hesitant, maybe thinking it wasn't proper for him to come by without Reuel, but Reuel reassured him that Friday was just fine. Once that was settled, we began to make our plans. Mid-morning, Max would take a bus to the Circular Quay at Sydney Harbor and then the ferry over to Manly. I'd be at the wharf to meet him. With any luck Gladys wouldn't be out in her garden. I certainly didn't need to explain to her what Max was all about.

As it turned out, the afternoon Max and I walked up the hill toward our house, Gladys was standing at our corner waiting for the local bus to take her into town. Naturally Max had his little brown leather satchel with him, and this did not look good. She knew Reuel had left the day before. "Keep an eye on my wife!" Reuel had hollered to her as he got into the taxi to go to the airport. "Right-o!" Gladys called back. "Have a safe journey."

When Max and I approached the bus stop, Gladys turned away.

She began to dig furiously into her pocketbook, pretending she had not seen me. To make matters worse, before Max and I were able to get close enough to set the record straight, the bus screeched to a halt and Gladys scooted up the steps as if she were being chased by unleashed hounds.

I didn't bother to explain Gladys to Max. We just continued on our path. Then at our sidewalk Max surveyed the garden. "Got ya-self a plant over 'ere that's real good fa burns," he said. He tore off a leaf, examined it, and then slipped it into his shirt pocket. "Poison berry plant over in that corner. Ya don't wanna go eatin' it."

Before we took another step, Chris came rolling up on his skate-board. "Mom, Mom!" He was with his friend Collin. They were quite a pair—Chris in his oversize Chicago Bulls shorts and ripped T-shirt and Collin in his Little Lord Fauntleroy school uniform, gray shorts, knee socks, white shirt, and a straw boater hat, which all public and private school kids wore to protect them from the scorching after-noon sun. The younger children even wore a khaki hat with a flap that came down around their necks—very Foreign Legion.

"Wow, hi!" Chris said on seeing Max.

"Good to meet ya," Max said, shaking hands with the two twelve-year-olds. "Ya got ya-self a real good board 'ere, fulla."

Chris's face lighted up. "Wanna try it?"

"Awwwgh, Aborigines like to feel the ground under their feet," Max said, chuckling. I glanced down at Max's polished but very worn brown shoes.

"Can you stay for dinner, Max?" Chris asked, instantly bonding. That was one of the things I cherished about him. From the time he was a small boy, Chris was so open and accepting of people different from himself. He was that way with the Amish and he was the same way with Randy. I remember after one show, Chris came into my dressing room and said, "You know, Mom, some of the kids at school make fun of you because you do this show with a drag queen." I asked Chris how he handled that. "I just tell them to mind their own business. And that Randy doesn't always wear pumps and a dress. He's a cool guy who teaches me how to play poker and do different voices."

"I'd really like to be stayin' fa dinner," Max said to Chris, "but I gotta get back to Redfern fa church service."

Collin took off his straw boater and tucked it under his arm as if out of respect. "Chris told me that you're a full-blood," he said.

"Ya never met a full-blood before?"

"Not in person," Collin said, "but we're learning about Aborigines now in school."

For a few moments, Max was quiet. But then with a bit of hesitation, he asked, "What are ya learnin' about us?"

Collin became very serious. "Today we learned about a bloke named Arabanoo. He was the first Aborigine captured. It happened right down there at Manly Cove." Collin pointed down the hill.

"Yeah," Max said, "the Gamaraigal tribe used to live all 'round 'ere."

"Mom," Chris squeezed in, "me and Collin are going inside to watch TV."

"No, you're not," I said, tugging him back. I certainly didn't need them hanging around the house. I slipped Chris a couple of dollars. "Why don't you guys go get an ice cream."

"Thanks, Mrs. Fuller," Collin said. He adjusted his schoolbag that was strapped on his back, put his boater back on, turned toward Max, and said, "It was nice to meet you, sir."

Chris hopped back on his skateboard, did a cocky show-off jump, and said, "See ya later, Max!"

In moments the boys had disappeared down the road. I opened the front door. Max walked in first.

"Ummmmm," he said, standing in the foyer, peering into the living room and dining room. I steeled myself for whatever. I thought of Madame Arcati, the eccentric psychic in Noël Coward's *Blithe Spirit*, and forced myself to keep a straight face.

"Would you like to put your bag down?" I asked.

"Yeah," he said. But he didn't put it down. As I led him into the living room, I saw something that looked like weeds sticking out of a torn corner of the satchel. He'd apparently brought along the tools that he'd need to smoke the house. Who would ever believe this?

"I'll give you the Cook's tour," I said.

"Cook's tour?"

"Oh, sorry. That's an American saying for 'I'll show you around.' "

Each room Max entered, he paused as if he were soaking in some sort of invisible energy. Occasionally he muttered, "Ummmmm."

When we got to Christopher's room, Max asked to go out onto the balcony.

"It's a little shaky," I said, unlocking the screen door.

"No worries," Max said, though he did look a bit worried when he stepped out. It was high off the ground, and Max had said how he liked to feel the ground underneath his feet. I was sure he meant that literally. Then again, he had been a stockman.

"We have a bird who visits us regularly," I said, scanning the backyard for Prince Charles. "He loves the frangipani."

"Awwwgh," he said, nodding and coming back inside.

When we got to my bedroom, Max stood outside the door and peered in as if to respect my privacy.

"I'll show you the kitchen," I said, leading him down a long, narrow hallway.

As Max passed the stairs that led to the basement, he stopped. "What's down 'ere?" he pointed.

"The basement. Would you like to see it?"

"Yeah, that'd be good."

I purposely hadn't told him that the basement had recently been renovated and that during the renovation, spirit bones may have been disturbed, which might be why Dwango had surfaced—so to speak. I worried Max might be offended.

Halfway down the steep steps, Max stopped cold. "I smell smoke."

I thought that I smelled smoke, too. I ran back upstairs to check. It was probably Chris burning the popcorn or leaving his French fries in the oven too long. But neither the microwave nor the oven had been used. I got back downstairs to find Max standing about a foot from the twin bed where I had communicated with Dwango.

"Ya on top of the clever fulla's land," Max announced with a solemn reverence that chilled my bones and warmed my face at the same time.

It had been one thing for me to *speculate* that we could possibly

79

be over an ancient Aboriginal site, but it was a whole other thing for me actually to hear it come from Max's lips. I stood flushed and motionless, feeling detached from the here and now.

"We're standin' where the clever fulla did his work," Max said. "Ya got a good spirit fulla 'ere."

I gave a sigh of relief. "So you don't need to smoke the house?"

"Naw, ya only smoke out a spirit if it's no good."

"Can you feel the spirit now?"

"Yeah, ya can feel it real strong," he said almost in a hushed whisper.

I was too numb to feel much of anything. "Max," I said, "why has this spirit been coming through me?"

Max shrugged. "Sometimes spirits talk to people who will listen."

"And he knows that I'll listen?"

"Yeah, he knows that ya'll listen."

I felt a breeze whip by me. The small window above our heads was closed.

"What's the message?" I asked.

"Don't know." He shrugged.

I still had not mentioned anything about Dwango's message that Max was supposed to lead me along a path. I tried to ease into it. "Max," I said, "would it be possible for *you* to speak to Dwango?"

Max thought for a moment. "If ya want, sometime I'll come back to ya house an' sleep down 'ere. See if the spirit fulla will 'ave a yarn with me."

"A yarn?"

"Talk to me while I'm sleepin'." Max folded his arms and dropped his eyelids. Could he be trying to imagine what the land must have been like hundreds and maybe thousands of years earlier when Dwango and his people were standing right where we were?

For a long while neither of us spoke. Finally I said, "So the spirit could speak to you while you sleep?"

"Ya right," Max said. He moved over to the small window above our heads and gazed out to the back garden.

"I think you should sleep over," I said suddenly.

"Awright," Max said, adding, "There's ya bird."

It was Prince Charles all right. He was sitting in the frangipani, showing off his royal profile.

Max opened the small window and made a bird sound. The cockatoo turned toward us.

"What'd you say?" I asked.

"I jus' said it's real nice to meet ya."

Dwango had said he was able to manifest himself as a bird, but I decided to keep quiet about it. See what developed. Instead I asked, "When can you come back?"

"The end of next week," Max said, still looking at Prince Charles in the tree.

"Perfect." That would give me a week to prepare. I wasn't sure, however, what I would be preparing for.

When I told Victoria and Peter that Max would be coming to spend the night, they thought I was out of my mind. To bring a man I hardly knew anything about into my house for the night was flirting with danger. It was irresponsible, and if I wasn't concerned for my own welfare, I should be for Christopher's. "Besides, where's he going to sleep?" Peter asked.

"In the basement," I said.

"And what's to keep him from coming to your bedroom in the middle of the night?" Peter snapped.

"He wouldn't do that," I snapped back.

"But darling," Victoria said on the extension, "you really know precious little about him."

"Liz," Peter said, "would you bring a man from Harlem that you just met into your house to spend the night with you and your son?"

I told Peter and Victoria all the wonderful things Father Ted, Sister Dorothy, and Sister Pat had said about Max. I was speaking to deaf ears. I hung up the phone a wreck. I went to bed convinced that I was putting our lives in peril. After tossing and turning half the night, I got up and phoned Reuel in Connecticut.

"You're worried about Max?" Reuel chuckled. "Lizzy, he's one hundred percent safe."

The instant Reuel gave his seal of approval, I felt ridiculous for having bought into Victoria and Peter's fears. I told this to Reuel.

"Liz," Reuel said, "you can't expect Peter and Victoria not to be concerned for your safety. They would have had to meet Max and spend time with him to know what a good guy he is."

"Of course," I said, "you're absolutely right. Once you meet Max, you know that he's a very special person."

"So when's the big night?"

"This coming Monday," I said. "Chris and I already have the entire day and evening planned. Chris is dying to take Max to the beach and teach him how to use his Boogie Board. We'll have a picnic lunch and then for dinner, I'm going to make pasta. Max said that he loved pasta. After that we'll just hang out until it's time for Max to retreat to the basement and see if the spirits speak through him."

"Just another humdrum day in the life of Lizzy Fuller," Reuel said. "Promise to call me Tuesday morning."

Before we hung up, Reuel gave me the good news. Randy had left a message on my machine—he had won the MAC award!

"He did!" I screamed. "He's gotta be ecstatic."

"Liz," Reuel said, "you might want to give him a call and congratulate him."

I knew instantly from Reuel's tone that things weren't at all good. "He's in the hospital, isn't he?"

Reuel didn't need to answer.

"In Philadelphia or Indiana?" I asked.

"Philadelphia," Reuel said. "He left the number."

One fear alleviated—a worse one to take its place. I steeled myself and dialed Philadelphia.

A nurse answered. I heard a coughing spasm, and a few moments later Randy got on. "Darrrrling," he said in his dead-on staccato Bette Davis voice, "where-are-you? And-when-the-hell-are-you-coming-home?"

"I'm still in Oz," I said. "Everything's up in the air."

There was more coughing. "I won the MAC, Liz!"

"That's why I'm calling. You're the best!"

"Ron and I went to the Awards."

"When was it?"

"Last week. At the Copacabana."

"Were there any other stars there?" I asked, feeding Randy a line from our show.

"Darling," he said, slipping back into vintage Bette Davis, "there-are-no-other-stars." Then he asked, as he always asked, "How's the voice?"

"Like I said—you're the best."

"I know," he replied, cocky as ever. Randy knew he was the best. The London Times called his peformance in our show "a little short of miraculous."

"Remember, Liz, we're doing San Francisco in October."

"I'm out of the acting business, Randy. We're going to have to find somebody to play me."

"No, it just wouldn't be the same." A moment later he said, "Who can we get?"

"So I'm that easily replaced?"

He gave a weak chuckle. "I liked you fine, Liz."

"Randy," I said, kicking into a serious gear, "how's everything going?"

"I'm getting out of this dump for the weekend," he said. "On Monday I'm back. My doctor's going to start me on a new combination of drugs."

I listened to Randy describe a new, very aggressive treatment of the virus, and was suddenly reminded that Dwango said that I was going to be led to someone who would give me knowledge that would help Randy. What kind of knowledge? Maybe that wasn't the message at all?

"Liz, I've been doing a lot of writing." There was more coughing. "I'm almost done with the children's book."

"I can't wait to read it," I said, still thinking about that message from Dwango. "Do you have a title?"

"Punky and the Enchanted Forest."

"That's so sweet," I said. "When will it be done?"

"I'm trying to come up with an ending."

"Beginnings," I said, "are hardest for me."

There was a long pause. "Endings," he said, "are hardest for me."

"Oh, I'm sure you'll come up with something terrific," I said, pretending I didn't understand.

He had another coughing spasm. "Honey, are you and Chris okay?"

"Everything's great."

"You sure?"

Do I tell him about Dwango? No, too complicated to explain over the phone, especially halfway around the world. "Randy," I said, "what makes you think that there's anything wrong?"

"It's just a feeling I have that something's keeping you there. That's all. There's no more."

Obviously there was. But for the moment, I was back to wrestling with what on earth I could say to Gladys about why Max was coming to spend the night. I shuddered each time I thought about the distinct possibility of Gladys spotting Max arriving at my door Monday afternoon and departing Tuesday morning—toting the brown satchel. I was grateful for this frivolous worry. I wouldn't dwell on Randy's worsening condition. I just wished he hadn't made that comment about endings.

# S I X

All my worrying about what to say to Gladys was wasted energy. The Friday before Max arrived, Gladys shouted over the fence that she was going to Melbourne to celebrate her granddaughter's twenty-first birthday. She would be gone a week. Would I mind taking in her mail and newspaper? And if it didn't rain in the next day or two, would I water the plants? Give the geraniums a good soakin' and then let them dry out thoroughly. Then she presented me with a jar of her plum jelly, which she was under the impression that we liked.

"I know how ya like my plum jelly," Gladys said. She presented it to me with her house keys.

"Yes, it's really yum," I said. I reached over the fence for the sickening sweet goop. This was the first time we had eyeball-to-eyeball contact since she had pretended not to see Max and me walk up the hill.

"I'll need to have the jar back so I can fill it up again for ya."

"You'll have it back sooner than you think," I said, hoping the purple goo wouldn't clog the kitchen sink drain.

"Have ya tried it on damper?"

"Damper?"

"Os-try-ya bread. When I come back, I'll make ya some."

So in spite of the fact that I brought a black man to my house the day after my husband left town, we were still mates.

"I've met a full-blood Aborigine," I said, getting it out into the open.

"Ya have?"

She was playing that game. "Yeah," I said. "He was here a few days ago. For lunch. His name is Max. Great guy."

"Aww, that's nice."

"Maybe next time he comes up—if he ever comes up again—you can meet?"

"Fine." She tucked strands of gray hair into her bun and said, "I hope I'm not puttin' ya out too much lookin' after my garden an' mail."

Her garden and mail? Doesn't she want to know where I met the Aborigine? She was great at not dealing with things in her face. "Oh, the garden and mail's no problem at all. I'm here all day anyway— working on my writing. Just Chris and me."

"Well, it might not be just you and your son," Gladys said, giving a sly smile.

"Huh?" Was that a snide comment? Did she think I was going to sneak Max into the house? What did she take me for?

"I was talkin' to Norman yesterday."

"The guy down at the used bookstore?"

"That's right. I was tellin' him that ya might be comin' around to see him sometime. To talk about the ghost children he saw in that tree."

Here goes Gladys again. Playing cat and mouse. She brings up ghosts, I bite, she drops it and runs.

"Oh, I'll get there," I said, cool, casual. "So are you taking the train down to Melbourne or flying?"

"The train." She yanked up a wild vine and then steered the conversation right back to the spook and kook. "Yeah, Norman was tellin' me that somebody else has seen the same thing."

I bit again. "You-are-kidding-me?"

"I guess it happened late at night. The bloke heard birds. Up there in the Morton Bay."

"But they weren't birds?" I said, feeling creepy all over again.

"Aborigine children one minute an' birds the next."

Somebody get Alfred Hitchcock. "I'll go see Norman now," I said.

"Right-o."

_____

I found Norman behind a stack of books in the tiny and cluttered used bookstore off the Corso. He was crouched down, rummaging through an old wooden trunk filled with dusty books, magazines, and little knickknacks.

"When I opened up the store this mornin', this bloody trunk was blockin' the front door," Norman said, standing up to greet me with a welcoming smile. "Apparently it's a gift from an anonymous donor. It was sittin' outside all night."

"It could have been stolen," I said.

Norman was a tall, slight man with little, round wire-rim glasses and a mustache. I figured him to be in his mid-seventies and to have spent his life surrounded by books. "They don't pinch books around here," he chuckled. "The dole bludgers are just keen on footy an' a frosty."

"Oh," I said. "Incidentally, I'm Liz Fuller. A friend of Gladys Simpson."

"Jeez," Norman said, brushing dust off the front of his tweedy jacket, "it's jolly good to finally meet ya. Gladys told me all about ya."

"She told me all about you, too," I said, equally enthusiastic.

"Aww, I'm not a writer like you. I'm just buggerin' about tryin' to keep some sort of order in this grotty place."

"It's got a lot of atmosphere," I said. The shop did not look like a dump, though the line was fine. "Looks sort of Dickens-esque."

"That's one way to put it," Norman laughed. "By the way, I have the hardcover copy of *The Ghost of Flight 401* here."

"You do?"

"Gladys didn't tell you?"

"No."

Norman looked surprised. "When I lent it to her, I told her to be *sure* to tell ya how much I enjoyed it."

"Gladys had the book?" What the heck was going on? Why wouldn't she have told me she was reading it? What's the big secret?

"She returned it just yesterday," Norman said. He went over to the cash register by the front door and held the book up. "She wanted to buy it. But I told her it's not for sale. Just for loan. Would ya mind autographin' it?"

"I'd love to," I said, pulling out my pen, totally bewildered by Gladys's selective secretiveness.

"Have yourself a look around," Norman offered, "but mind the books on the floor. Don't want ya to go trippin'."

In between browsing among the stacks, I learned the story of Norman's life. He had been a fighter pilot in the Royal Australian Air Force and had flown in North Africa and the Pacific. When he was only twenty, he married a "kiwi"—a girl from New Zealand. They were still married—over fifty years now. Last year they spent two weeks on Bali—a "prezzie" from their five children. He and his "bride" each knew what the other was going to say before they said it. After he "saw" the Aborigine children in the Morton Bay fig, the two of them began to read books on phenomena.

I had been leafing through an ancient-looking book on New Guinea wildflowers when I came across a pressed specimen between the pages. "Hey, look at this!" I called to him.

"By jingo!" Norman said, inspecting it. "Ya can still see the seeds."

"If I buy the book, do I get the flower?"

"No buts about it."

"Then I'll buy it and give it to Gladys."

"Old Gladys will be like a possum uppa gum tree," Norman said.

As I reached into my money belt for three dollars, I said offhand, "Gladys mentioned this morning that you weren't the only one to have seen the ghost children in the tree."

"Right-o," Norman said. "Must be a good month now since Gladys had her experience."

"Gladys had an experience?"

Norman brought his hand up to his chin. "If memory serves me correctly, I think it was during that bad heat wave at the end of the summer. Yep, that's right. Gladys came in complaining that she couldn't sleep. The bloody heat. I was complainin' that the blasted moist air brought the mozzies."

"Mozzies?"

"Insects," Norman translated.

"Oh yeah," I mumbled, recalling my new vocabulary.

"She said that she went for a midnight stroll. Cool herself down. And that's when it all happened."

"You mean to say—*Gladys* saw Aborigine children in the Morton Bay?"

"She didn't tell ya?"

"She told me that some *bloke* saw them."

"It was Gladys orright. Awwwgh, come to think of it, she asked me to not tell anyone. She's a funny old bird."

"Do you know why she wouldn't have told me?"

"Buggered if I know," Norman said. He thought for a moment and added, "Aww, a lot of older folks aren't keen on talkin' about things that scare them. That's why I gave her your husband's book to read. Very sane people—airline pilots—saw the unbelievable."

"Norman, did Gladys mention anything sort of out of the ordinary that's been happening to me since I arrived?"

He thought for a moment. "No," he said, "can't say she did. She just told me how much she liked you an' your family. Quite fond of Yanks. Ya don't seem to have much fear of strangers." He chuckled to himself, "You're a lot like the Ozzies in that ya don't censor what ya say."

Why disappoint him? "Norman," I said, "I believe I'm in touch with an Aborigine spirit doctor."

"By cripes!" he exclaimed, crossing his long arms and leaning against the front counter. "Gladys never peeped a word."

I proceeded to tell Norman about everything that had happened, and when I got to the end of the saga, I knew that I had made a lifelong friend.

"Liz," he said, "could ya bring in that Ouija board transcript. I've got quite a collection of books here with Aborigine words. I got a real funny feelin' that the words aren't all gibberish."

Later that afternoon, I dropped off the Ouija transcript and the altered state transcript, and early the next morning Norman phoned.

"Strike a light!" he said.

"Huh?"

There was a pause. I heard papers being rustled. "K-I-R-A-W-E-E means sulfur-crested cockatoo!" Norman sputtered as if he had just won the lottery.

"You're kidding!"

"It's a Gamaraigal word."

"A what word?" I got the feeling I'd heard it before, but I couldn't place it.

"Gam-a-rai-gal. That's an Aborigine tribe."

"How on earth did you find that?"

"I didn't get much sleep last evening," Norman laughed. "So I guess this ties your Prince Charles in with Dwango."

I checked my copy of the transcript. "You're absolutely right," I said, nervous but delighted. "Reuel and I asked the Ouija board, 'What does K-I-R-A-W-E-E mean?' And the answer was M-E-S-S-A-G-E. So that means that the bird was a message sent by Dwango."

I heard more papers being shuffled and then Norman said, "Liz, turn to the top of page six, third line down. Your husband asked, 'What about the bird, Prince Charles?' And you said, 'It's Dwango. He's able to manifest himself as a bird. He's saying that if you are a spirit doctor ya have powers that don't go away with physical death.'"

As Norman paused, I thought, Reuel is going to love this!

"I came across something else you might find interesting," Norman went on. "The Gamaraigal tribe had many members who were koradji. . . ."

"That's a spirit doctor," I said.

"Right-o. The Gamaraigal tribe occupied the land right down at Manly Cove. According to *The Aborigines of the Sydney District Before 1788*, the Gamaraigal koradji had a most important role in the spiritual and ritualistic side of life."

"Norman, it's not only possible, but probable, that where my house sits is where their ceremonies took place."

"Too right!"

"I wonder how long they'd been in the area?"

"According to some deposits in nearby rock shelters, there's a radiocarbon age of a mere twenty thousand years."

I was so eager to phone Reuel that I hung up before asking Norman if any of the other words made sense. But we must have been on the same wavelength because just as I was checking for how to dial the States, Norman rang back to say he hadn't been able to find any other words but that he'd keep looking.

I never got hold of Reuel that morning. He was out on a four-day flying mission. I left him a detailed message on the answering machine.

When Reuel rang back, it was early in the morning of the day Max was due to arrive, and he had his own bit of juicy news. "Lizzy," he said, "the school called this afternoon."

"What for?"

"Apparently Christopher wrote the class a very interesting letter." Reuel's amused tone told me to brace myself. "Your little Stephen King wrote that he was being held captive in a haunted house."

"What?"

"You heard me," Reuel said, chuckling. "Spirits were ripping the place to shreds. Spirit voices were coming through his mother's voice box. Something about his next door neighbor trying to poison him with 'fairy' bread."

"Oh brother!"

"There's more, Liz," Reuel continued with great delight. "There were spirit birds flying around the house, 'crapping' all over his schoolbooks."

"Why am I not laughing?"

"He ended the letter with a P.S. If he never returns, give the stuff in his locker to the poor."

"That kid is a real piece of work," I said.

"Maybe you'd better clear things up before he goes back to Weston Middle next year."

"You mean, you didn't say anything?"

"Oh, I reassured them that his mother was coaching him along in creative writing."

"Quick thinking," I said, then moved on. "So you got the message about Norman and the Ouija transcript?"

"Lizzy, I wasn't really surprised."

"You weren't?"

"Remember, I was there. It's just another piece of the puzzle that's fitting together."

"You really have come a long way."

"Yeah, I guess I have," Reuel said, chuckling some more. "But the guys I was flying with thought it was a crock."

"You told your pilot buddies?"

"What else do you do for eight hours crossing the Atlantic in a C-5?" Reuel said. Then he added quite casually, "When we got back, the squadron was asking for volunteer crews to fly supplies into Bosnia. I respectfully declined. Hope this isn't a sign of things to come."

That was an instant sinker. "What do you mean, you respectfully declined?"

"I don't plan on going, but it could be turned into something nasty and you know who gets called up first when that happens."

"But you can't go," I said.

Reuel jumped on that one. "What do you mean—I can't go? If we're called up, I go."

Exit loving, sexy husband. Enter stiff-assed colonel.

"So now we're even."

"What's that supposed to mean?"

"It means that you're pissed off that I left you to come to Australia and now it's payback time."

Twelve thousand miles of silence pressed against my suntanned ear.

"Just admit it," I said. "You're mad that I'm here."

I could hear him light up one of his foot-long cigars. "I hope you're not stinking up the bedroom," I said, irritating him into opening up. Something not taught in pilot school.

"You're right," he said. "I would have preferred you stayed."

"I knew it! I saw it in your eyes that day Chris and I walked through the jetway at Kennedy."

"You're an amazing psychic, Liz." The irony dripped.

"Very funny," I said. "I don't know why you couldn't have just leveled with me."

"Leveled with you! You were so goddamn determined to leave, if

I'd even suggested you stay, you would have smothered me to death with those stacks of lousy reviews."

"Now you're hitting below the belt."

"Get over it, Liz. You're not the first person to have a show close. Until you left, all I heard about was the show and Randy. You were more worried about leaving Randy than leaving me. I'm sorry for Randy. I'm sorry about the show. But I'm sorrier for me. Your goddamn show and friends were taking precedence over us. You're my wife. I want you here with me. I want to wake up in the morning with you next to me. I want to have coffee with you in the morning and make love to you at night. I'm horny. I'm fucking miserable. I'm pissed. I'm lonely. So there. Happy? I'm not the guy you thought I was. Feel better? If I told you anything different, I'd be a goddamn liar."

"I'm coming home," I said, alive and in love—and frustrated. Why did he have to wait until *now* to tell me how he really felt? I wanted nothing more than to fall onto our queen-size mattress and make insane love to that horny, miserable, pissed, lonely, unhappy guy. And then I wanted to get up and make us coffee. And after that I wanted to do the whole routine all over again. But I couldn't! That goddamn bully ocean was standing between us—cackling with laughter. "I'm calling the airline right now," I said.

"Oh no, you're not."

"What?"

Silence—a Waspy version of medieval torture.

"Explain what you mean!" I demanded.

"I mean that the other part of me has fallen in love with the crazy nut who takes off and does what she goddamn well pleases. The five-foot-four-inch blonde who gets kicked in the teeth by reviewers—who don't know from their asses about a great show—and gets back up again ready to fight. And ready to fight for the life of her best friend who just happens to be a drag queen. Oh, Christ—what I'm stuck with."

Two thoughts went through my mind at the same time. First, I'll spend the rest of my life trying to become the exciting woman he believes me to be. And second, I'd better get home before he finds out the truth. But all I said was, "I love you more than anything in the world."

"Yeah, well, you're goddamn lucky to have me, sister."

Just before noon, Chris darted down the hill toward the wharf in an Olympic attempt to beat the ferry in. I was trailing far behind, toting a plastic bag filled with sandwiches, chips, and lemon crush for our beach picnic. It was a perfect Aussie beach day. Mid-80s—a fall heat wave. The autumn flowers were in full bloom and there was a sweet fragrance in the ocean air that summer's humidity kept under wraps. From the top of a shaded path, I watched Max's ferry bull its way through the turquoise water as it entered Manly Harbor. And right at that moment, I thought, this is as good as it gets. There was something so magically alive about Oz—the captivating land down under that seemed to be an exotic and wonderful mixture of mystery and earthiness all wrapped as one. The fact that Chris and I were about to spend the day and evening with a full-blood Aborigine sent to us by a spirit doctor who lived hundreds—maybe thousands—of years ago seemed to be testimony to the magic of the land.

The afternoon was filled with surprises. For starters, Max didn't know how to swim. When Chris insisted he try out his Boogie Board, Max laid out the ground rules. He'd go into the cool salt water three kangaroo lengths—or up to his waist.

"Come on, Max," Chris pressed him. "You can't ride a wave twenty feet in."

"I told ya the day when ya was on ya board that we like to feel the ground under our feet," Max said.

"My mom has a book at home that shows Aborigines swimming," Chris taunted him. "You can swim—you're just chicken of the rips!"

"Yeah," Max said. He scooped up the skinny kid, ran out into the waves, and tossed him, arms and legs in all directions. Chris squealed with delight and Max did it again and again and again until Max, on the verge of total collapse, called to me, "I can't tire ya young fulla out!"

"It's time to eat!" I yelled, holding up the picnic bag for my drowned rat to see. Food was the only thing that would get Chris's attention.

Max and Chris wolfed down the sandwiches, each accusing the other of eating too much and too fast. After lunch, Max stretched out on the beach towel, rested his head on his brown satchel, and had a snooze. I got out one of the books Norman had lent me, and Chris headed back to the water where he rode the waves until the sun finally ducked behind the trees, chilling the afternoon air. At five o'clock we packed our things and headed back up the hill to our house.

By the time we sat down to the pasta dinner, it was after nine. We had had a full day.

"Noodles look real good," Max said, tucking the paper napkin underneath his neck, protecting a faded red plaid shirt.

I lifted my wineglass. "Cheers."

Max lifted his coffee cup. "Cheers."

Chris lifted his glass of milk. "Over the hot sands!"

"Over the hot sands?" Max questioned.

"That's what my first dad used to say when he clicked glasses."

"Ya 'ave a first dad?"

"My *first* dad died," Chris explained. "Reuel's my *second* dad."

"What did ya fatha die from?"

"Lung cancer," Chris said. "Smoker."

"Awwwgh"—Max shook his head—"it's no good to smoke. The grog's bad fa ya, too."

"Grog?" Chris asked.

"Alcohol," I told Chris.

"I'm off the grog now fa ten years."

"Were you an alcoholic?" Chris asked innocently.

"Christopher," I hissed.

"Yeah, I was a bad alcoholic," Max said without a second thought. "Ya saw all the scars on my chest an' back at the beach."

"You had your T-shirt on, Max," Chris said.

"I always keep my shirt on. It's no good to be lookin' at scars." Max cut the pasta into bite-size pieces and went on. "I got drunk one night an' rolled into an open fire pit. I come real close to dyin'.

When I got outta the hospital, I left the cattle station an' come down 'ere to Sydney an' got myself into the program."

"Alcoholics Anonymous?" I asked.

"Like that," Max said, taking a sip of black coffee.

"Then you never went back to being a stockman?" I asked.

"Ya right. There were other things fa me to do."

"Like taking care of your Aborigine brothers?" I persisted.

"I'm real busy takin' care of my bruddas," Max said. He sampled the salad. "What ya got here in the greens?"

"Just lettuce, tomatoes, and onions."

"Onions are real good fa ya."

"Onions make me want to puke!" Chris announced.

"Puke, brudda?"

"Get sick," Chris said, clutching his throat dramatically.

Max laughed. "Maybe ya'd like witchetty grub?"

"What's that?"

"Insect larvae. Good tastin' tucker."

"I don't think so," Chris said, excusing himself from the dinner table.

I poured myself another glass of wine. "Where do you find witchetty grub?"

"Out in the mulga. Ya can find 'em in the roots of the *kempeana* bush. Take ya-self a real sharp stick an' jab the ground till ya feel grubs."

"Do you eat them raw?"

"Ya can do that. Or ya cook 'em in hot ashes. The skin swell an' get hard."

"What does it taste like?"

Max thought for a moment. "Ya ever tasted a nut—an almond? Like that."

I think it was the second glass of wine that prompted me to change the conversation from culinary delights to spiritual happenings. "Max," I started in, "my neighbor lady saw ghost children in our Morton Bay fig."

Max looked up from his second helping. "I thought you said it was a fulla?"

"Oh, it was," I said. "But as of three days ago, I learned that Gladys saw the same thing."

"Yeah?" Max said. Just then the phone rang. It was Victoria. "Darling," she whispered, "is he there?"

"Yes," I said. I was not surprsied to hear from her.

"Just answer yes or no," Victoria said, conspiratorially. "Do you feel comfortable with him in the house?"

I looked over at Max, who was looking out the window toward the Morton Bay. "Yes," I said. "One hundred percent."

"Darling, listen closely—if anything should happen, Peter and I want you to call any hour of the night. We can be down there in twenty-five minutes. Do you understand? Just yes or no."

"Yes. Great. Fine."

"You positive? Yes or no."

"Positive."

"Elizabeth," Peter said on the extension, "lock your bedroom door."

"Will do," I said. "Thanks for calling. I'll give you a ring tomorrow." Click.

"Ya wanna go out an' have a look up ya tree?" Max asked as I hung up the phone.

"Sure," I said, wishing Victoria and Peter could have seen Max playing with Chris at the beach. That would have allayed all their fears. "Would you like dessert first? I bought napoleons with Devonshire cream and fresh strawberries."

Max tapped his belly. "I'm full up. I'll have me one fa breakfast."

After I put the last cup in the dishwasher, Max and I stepped out the front door. It was quiet. The only sound was the occasional barking of dogs from the houses below. The kookaburras would not begin their insane cackling until just before sunrise. In spite of my trepidation of the spirits visiting Max as he slept, there was a feeling of peace and calm.

As we approached the Morton Bay, Max said, "There ain't no ghosts up 'ere now. Jus' a lot of real tired-out birds."

"Max," I said. "Have you ever seen a ghost?"

"Back home my mudda comes fa a visit."

"You mean, when you go home to your village?"

"Yeah, when I go home to Enngonia. Sometimes blokes that die come back an follow ya aroun'."

"Whoa," I said, getting a massive case of the willies. "Doesn't it scare you?"

"Awwgh, the bad people can make ya sick. Sometime ya don't see 'em. But they can see ya. Ya gotta smoke 'em away," he said, yawning.

"You're tired," I said. If I was ever going to be able to sleep myself, I'd better cut the ghost tales. "I'm afraid Chris really wore you out."

"It'll be good to swagger down," Max said, following me up the brick walkway and toward the house.

Once inside, Max grabbed his brown satchel and headed toward the basement stairs. "I'll be up early mornin'. I gotta get back to Redfern. Take my niece food shoppin'."

"There's an alarm clock by the side of your bed."

"No worries. Aborigines have a clock right here," he said, pointing to his gut.

"Well, my alarm is the loony kookaburras."

"Yeah," Max chuckled. "They sure got mouths on 'em. See ya in the mornin'." He retreated down the steep basement stairs.

"Sleep tight," I called out. "Don't let the bedbugs bite."

"Ya got bugs?"

"Ohh, sorry," I said. "It's just a silly American saying."

The moment my head hit the pillow, I was out. The next thing I knew, the kookaburras were guffawing hysterically outside my bedroom window. I looked at my clock. It was only five-thirty. I could hear Max snoring fiercely in the basement. I lay in bed shifting from side to side, unable to fall back asleep. At six, I got up and started the coffee.

I was on my second cup of coffee when Max appeared at the top of the stairs. He looked squeaky clean in a fresh shirt and slacks and of course the bandana around his neck, assuring that Wild West look.

"Good shower down 'ere," Max said. "I put the wet towel on ya sink to dry itself out."

"Perfect," I said, breathlessly waiting to hear more.

"Yeah, I had me a real good soakin'."

"You slept well?"

"Real good sleepin' down 'ere," Max said, double-knotting the bandana.

"Terrific. So—uhh—let me get you some coffee."

He sat down. "Cuppa sounds real good."

"Black?"

"Ya got milk?"

"Yep. Sure do. How about a hard roll or a bowl of cereal?"

"Ya got one of 'em cream an' berries?"

For a split second I didn't have a clue what he was referring to. "Ohh, the napoleon!" I went to the fridge and then placed the choc-olate-covered dessert on the table.

"Just half fa me," Max said, slicing into the three-inch-high goody.

"I'll take the other half." I figured I'd skip lunch. "So the kooka-burras didn't wake you up?"

"No, ya spirit livin' down 'ere woke me up."

Thank God it was daylight. I could handle anything as long as the sun was streaming through the leaded windows. I took a hearty swig of coffee, snapping my endorphins to full attention. "The spirit woke you up?" I said, feigning calmness.

"Yeah," Max said, preoccupied with the napoleon.

"So Dwango came to you in your sleep?"

Unruffled, Max said, "Ya right."

"And?"

"An' ya spirit told me that I'm suppose to take ya to my village."

"What?"

"I'm suppose to take ya and ya young bloke to Enngonia an' meet my people."

Pinch me, I thought. "That's what the spirit told you?"

"Yeah," Max said, scraping every speck from his plate. "That's what ya spirit down 'ere said."

At that moment nothing seemed real, and yet at the same time everything seemed real. So natural. As Reuel would say, it was just another piece of the puzzle. "Max," I said, "are you going to take us to your village?"

Max poured himself another cuppa. "Ya wanna go?"

"Yes, of course," I said. I caught myself. "I mean, no. I mean, yes. Maybe. Can I let you know?"

"Yeah, ya can let me know. I jus' need to be settin' everythin' up with Fatha Ted an Sister Pat an' Sister Dorothy."

"Set what up?"

"Tell 'em I'll be leavin' fa a while."

"How long would we go for?" I asked. "That is, if we could really go?"

Max shrugged his shoulders. I knew that Aborigines are not on any clock. Then again Max did wear a watch. And, at that moment, he was checking the time. "Awwgh," he said, getting up from the kitchen table, "I gotta get me the eight-thirty ferry back to Redfern." On the way out the door, he said, "I'll ring ya tomorrow an' let ya know when I can be takin ya 'ere."

And so that's how our journey to Enngonia began.

# S E V E N

The dashboard clock of the Holden read ten-thirty. It had been six hours since we left Dubbo. It was a long haul to Max's village up on the Queensland border. It was made even longer by my insisting I keep the speed below sixty. There was a good reason for this caution. Two hours earlier, at dusk, I had been clipping along at close to eighty when out of nowhere, two Big Grays darted out of the tall scrub, bounded over the hood of my car, and disappeared into the setting sun, leaving behind a cloud of red dust and me screaming, "Oh my God! I killed a kangaroo!"

"Ya didn't kill nothin'!" Max hollered above my screech. "There they go. Into the mulga. Two Big Gray fullas. Reckon that one fulla weighs as much as me."

Shaking, I pulled off the road, chastising myself for daring to drive in the treacherous Outback. Back in Manly, I wouldn't even *park* Reuel's rental. If only he could see me now—mowing down roo. "You *sure we* didn't hit them?" I said.

"Ya hit one of them clippin' along the way we was, this buggy be nothin' but a tinny. Yeah," Max said, " 'eir tails polished up our hood real nice."

Chris poked his head between Max and me. "Mom, I bet you hit them."

I got out onto the lonely Mitchell Highway and inspected the front end. I wiped down the hood with my Gap denim jacket, seasoning it with the dry earth. Max was right. Not a scratch. There was just a thick layer of red clay and clumps of spiky weeds clinging to the car, transforming it into some sort of camouflage vehicle. Inside, the damage was minimal, spilt coffee on the console and lemon crush all over my khaki shorts and down my legs. "Max," I said, "I'm a wreck."

"You'll be right. We'll stop up the road an' boil us up a billy of tea."

"I hate tea," Chris said, adding, "Mom, I told you we should have gotten a Jeep with a roo bar! But nobody would listen to me."

"Don't be givin' ya mudda a hard time," Max scolded.

"How am I giving her a hard time?" Chris answered back. "She almost got us killed."

"Chris," I said, "you keep an eye out for more roo."

"This place sucks!" he said.

"Yeah," Max said, "dusk an' dawn's when they're jumpin' into the road lookin' fa a drink." With that, he slipped in a scratchy Elvis tape that he had brought along. He began to hum along with "Are You Lonesome Tonight."

"Boy, it sure is getting dark out here," I said, feeling as if we were driving in a dusty black hole in outer space.

"No moon tonight," Max said, breaking into "Do-ya-stand-at-ya doorstep-an'-picture-me-'ere . . ."

Who would ever believe this? I'm in the middle of sixty million parched hectares—whatever a hectare is—with my snotty kid and a full-blood Aborigine crooning like the King. "Is Elvis popular here in the Outback?" I asked Max.

"Yeah, he's popular awright. When I was a stockman, the local pub had a jukebox. Fa ten bob we could hear ten tunes."

"Did you ever sing Aborigine songs?"

"When I was a youn' fulla, my mudda was always singin' aroun' the fire." A few moments later he added, "Yeah, she'll be comin' 'round to see me probably tonight."

Comin' round to see him? Probably tonight? I thought Max said that his mother was dead? Maybe I had misunderstood? I was trying to recall exactly what Max *had* told me about his mother when he set the record straight: "Before my mudda passed away, I used to get home a lot more often."

So she *was* dead. That's right—Max had told me that the town was crawling with spirits. I turned to the backseat to see if Chris was awake and listening. He was. He rolled his eyes and gave a snide little smile. Fortunately he kept his thoughts to himself. A sign of maturity, I thought. I would have to compliment him on that later.

"Awwgh, my mudda was a real good, strong woman," Max said. "A hundred years old, she was still doin' all the cookin' fa us."

A hundred years old? What was her secret? I stopped myself from asking any questions about her. The white man is not supposed to speak about the dead in ordinary conversation. Sister Pat cautioned me about that when I telephoned her for some guidelines on how Chris and I should conduct ourselves as guests in Max's village. She was incredibly knowledgeable about Aboriginal culture and, in fact, was preparing to move to the Northern Territory to live with the Aborigines up near Darwin. She would be teaching as well as writing a paper for her doctorate in Aboriginal studies.

"You are so lucky," Sister Pat had said. "Very few people ever have the opportunity to really get to know the Aborigine people. Max comes from a very good family. Sister Dorothy and I met his sister Katie when she came down to Sydney last year. A fine lady. You and your son will have a wonderful experience." Sister Pat went on to say, "Unless you're invited by an Aborigine, you will not be allowed onto their reservation. Uninvited people must apply for a special permit from the government. And even then they are rarely granted one."

"Why's that?"

"The Aborigine people desperately want to maintain their dignity and privacy. Tour buses are no longer permitted to cruise up and down village roads. Be aware when you visit Max's people that they have many sacred sites that must be respected. But you may be fortunate enough to be invited to one of their ceremonies that take place at the sacred sites."

"What happens at the ceremonies?"

"Most often they'll sing and dance. Act out their old stories."

"Dreamtime stories?"

"Yes, but if you ask them about the Dreamtime, most won't know what you're talking about."

"I thought Dreamtime is what they're called," I said.

"Most Aborigines refer to the Dreamtime as simply their old stories."

"Then we should never ask to hear their old stories told at the sacred sites?"

"Absolutely taboo."

"What if Chris and I should accidentally stumble onto one of their sacred sites?"

"No worries," Sister Pat said. "Max will be with you. Just stick by him. You couldn't have a better guide." Then she said with a slight hesitation, "Max mentioned to Sister Dorothy and me that a spirit in your house spoke to him in his sleep. Said that he should take you to visit his tribe."

Oh boy, I wasn't at all sure how Sister Pat felt about that one. "Yes," I said tentatively, "as strange as it may sound, that's what happened."

"Awwgh, with Max things like that happen often," Sister Pat confided. "Last week, Sister Dorothy misplaced an important document. We looked high and low for it. Couldn't find it anywhere. We had mentioned this to Max when he came around for a cup of tea. And the following morning, bright and early, Max was knocking at our door. Straightaway he led us to the missing piece of paper."

"The spirits spoke through him?" I asked.

"Right-o," Sister Pat said. "You're in store for quite a treat traveling with Max. Just remember to let him take the lead."

"So what you're saying is that we should just look, listen, and keep our big American mouths shut?"

Sister Pat roared with laughter. "Awwgh, the Yankee frankness is so lovely."

Before we hung up, Sister Pat reviewed the most important things for us to remember. There were six of them. I wrote them down and later went over them with Chris.

1. Don't ask their names. You may tell them your name.
2. Don't mention anybody who has died. The dead are not spoken of in ordinary conversation.

3. You may ask them the name of their tribe and where they are originally from.
4. Don't ask them to tell you their Dreamtime stories. They are sacred.
5. Don't be uncomfortable with silence. The Aborigine people are serene and gentle.
6. Don't go into their homes unless you're invited.

I was mentally reviewing this list when suddenly I spotted head-lights off in the distance. "Here comes a road train," I said to Max. I immediately pulled off to the side of the road just as one guidebook suggested.

"Whaddya gettin' off the road fa?" Max asked, perplexed.

"Road train's up ahead. See their lights?"

"That ain't no road train," he said, sitting up. "Light's over 'ere in the scrub."

For a moment, I studied the road. "Doesn't the road turn that way?"

"This 'ere road is perfectly straight. Ain't no bends fa a long while."

"Huh? What on earth could it be then?"

Max didn't have a clue— nor did he seem interested, which helped to take the edge off my concern.

"Out here in the mulga ya see a lot of things ya don't see in the big city," Max said.

"Can we get a radio station?" I asked, fumbling with the buttons, trying for a connection to the outside world.

"Awwgh, that radio's no good out 'ere." He put in a Willie Nelson tape and dozed off, leaving me alone with an unleashed, insane imag-ination, kept in check only by "Georgia on My Mind." When I could stand it no longer, I woke him. "Max," I said, shaking his arm, "that light's still just ahead of us."

Max lazily looked out the window as if I had just pointed out a pastoral scene on a Sunday drive. "Yeah," he said, "it's there awright."

"What the heck is that thing? Looks like a headlight."

Max shook his head. "I jus' told ya, I don't know."

"What's so weird," I said, picking up my speed, "is that we can't catch up to it."

"No worries. Up ahead 'bout twenty miles is Sylvia's."

"Who's Sylvia?"

"Store an' milk bar. We'll get Chris an ice cream."

I turned to the backseat. Fortunately Chris was sound asleep. "Do we really want to wake him?"

Max chuckled. "Yeah, he sure can talk. I got a great-niece jus' like him."

"She can't be as bad as Chris," I joked back, suddenly feeling like the worst mother in the whole world. Among other things, how could I in good conscience have taken him out of school in the middle of the year? And would a responsible parent be dragging her son back of the black stump where dusty roads lead to nowhere, bushfires are as common as campfires, and a three-thousand-kilometer dingo fence was erected to keep out the wild dogs, boars, and worse.

Max interrupted my guilt. "Wait till ya be meetin' Margaret. *Yap—yap—yap—yap—*"

"How old's Margaret?"

"Awwgh, 'bout ten," Max thought. "Her little cousin Matthew's a wild one. An' Henry's—he's another handful."

The light stayed with us all the way to Sylvia's. Chris awoke for the last few miles and saw the light, too. When we finally arrived at the tiny outpost café, we told Sylvia and the two men inside—characters right out of the guidebook—what we had seen.

Hearing our story, the bush folks sauntered out. The light had disappeared.

"It was there when we walked in," Chris said, unhinged. "Tell 'em, Mom!" He turned to Max. "Max, you saw it, too!"

The locals were definitely more entertained by Chris than the thought of a mysterious light.

"Wotssy flappin' his gums about?" Rusty elbowed Ned, who was about a foot shorter than his sidekick and walked with a distinct limp—a limp that he said he got while wrestling "crocs" in the Northern Territory.

"Come on, Max," Chris begged. "Tell them you saw it, too."

Max was too smart to get sucked in.

"I think the mate is a tinny short of a six-pack," Ned said. "Whaddya think, Rusty?"

Rusty seemed to think that everything was funny, especially Chris and me in our new bush hats. "Yuz wearin' Cunnamulla cartwheels on yuz heads," he said.

Max started laughing.

"What's a Cunnamulla cartwheel on our heads?" I asked him.

"I know that there's opal fields in Cunnamulla," Max said, adding. "An' I know a lady who lives 'ere."

Rusty helped himself to our new hats and began to manipulate the brims so that they weren't so stiff and new looking. "Now ya look like yuz belong out 'ere," he said, returning the hats to our heads.

Back in the rough-hewn milk bar/country store, Sylvia turned on a scratchy ham radio. "So ya seen the min light, ya 'ave."

"We saw something," I said.

"It was min light orright," Sylvia said, putting on a Foster's lager apron. "Nobody knows anything about it."

Rusty sat down at the wooden table with us, rolled himself a cigarette, and said, "I think it was a yowie." He pulled Chris's hat down over his eyes. "What do you think, mate?"

Chris wasn't biting. "Who gives!" he said, annoyed that nobody believed him.

Sylvia moved behind the counter and scooped out some of the richest vanilla ice cream I had ever tasted.

"This is really good," Chris said, instantly forgetting his grudge. "Can I have more chocolate sprinkles?"

"Mate," she said, " 'ow come yuz not in school?"

"I got my schoolwork in the car," he said, going at it with the sprinkles. "Are there any kids around here?"

"Yuz on a sheep station, mate. Come back in the daylight an' old Rusty and Ned 'ere 'ill show ya 'round."

"If ya don't mind gettin' foot rot," Rusty said.

"Gotta watch out fer the Big Browns out 'ere, too," Ned added.

"That's why me mate's walkin' with one leg shorter," Rusty said. "Big Brown got him right out that front door."

Chris jumped on that one. "Hey, you said it was a croc!"

Ned popped open a Toohey's to go with his meat pie. "I was just yankin' yuz chain, mate," he said. "It was a poison snoike."

Rusty and Ned laughed. It was hard to separate them from every known cliché about the Outback.

Chris turned to me. "Mom, we need a snakebite kit."

"Yeah," Max agreed, "be a real good thing fa us to have." He wasn't smiling.

"Max," I said, "you really think we need one?"

"Be a real good idea," he said. He turned to Rusty and Ned. "Yeah, my white lady friend an' the youn' bloke don't know nothin' 'bout the livin' in the mulga."

My pioneering spirit was shrinking to the size of the sprinkles on my ice cream. "Sylvia," I said, "do you know where we can find a snakebite kit?"

She thought for a moment. "Nowhere's out 'ere. Probably coulda gotten one back in Dubbo."

"Yeah, that's right," Rusty said. "Over on Macquarie Street. Across from the old Dubbo jail."

"On yer way back," Ned said, "ya can take the young sprocker over an show 'em the gallows. You'll see lifesize statues of Wild West outlaws that make yer Billy the Kid look like a raving poof."

"Who gives!" Chris said. "We need a snakebite kit!"

"Not gonna find one now, mate," Sylvia said.

"What do we do if we get attacked by a Big Brown?" Chris asked, clearly perturbed.

Rusty flipped a Crocodile Dundee-size knife from his back pocket. "Ya cut this way," he said. "An' this way. An' then ya suck."

This made my son's day. It was Rusty's only intent, and Chris's eyes widened in devilish delight.

When we got up to continue on our journey, Sylvia, Rusty, and Ned seemed visibly disappointed that we were leaving. I joined Max at the turn-of-the-century cash register. He got out his wallet. I reached into my money belt. "Put ya money away," Max scolded me. "Ya treated back at Nyngan."

"So we'll see yuz on the way back," Sylvia said, as the three locals escorted us to the car.

"Yeah, on the way back." Max waved.

"Watch out for the yowie!" Ned called.

"We got Bigfoot in our country!" Chris hollered out the window to our new Outback friends.

Moments later, we were back on the Mitchell Highway, heading north toward Enngonia. The mysterious light was gone—for now.

It was midnight when we pulled into Bourke—the historic port along the Darling River, 780 kilometers northwest of Sydney. It was a bleak frontier town, famous at one time for its wool that was transported by camel train, then loaded onto barges, and sent down the river, eventually to end up on the backs of the English and the Italians and the Americans and everybody else who bought prime Australian wool. As I approached the main drag, Mitchell Street, I was reminded of an Arizona ghost town.

"Check out that old hotel, Mom!" Chris said. "Bet there were a lot of shoot-outs there."

"It looks like Tombstone," I said. "Tombstone, Arizona, a town too tough to die. Where the Earp brothers and the outlaws shot it out at the O.K. Corral."

Max nodded knowingly. "That's the Old Royal," he informed us. "Been there fa a long time."

"Dead Gulch would be a cool name for this place," Chris said. "Wow, look at that saloon! Can we get out and walk around?"

"No way," I said. "When we get to the end of this road, we're heading right back onto the Mitchell Highway."

But we ended up taking a little detour after all. When we got to the end of Mitchell Street, Max told me to hang a right.

"What for?" I asked.

"Mightswell see if my nephew an' niece is home," he said, as if it were two o'clock in the afternoon.

"But it's midnight," I said.

"No worries," Max said. He directed me around dark, dusty, winding roads where stray horses were roaming freely on the red clay and a bunch of beat-up cars were parked every which way.

"Is this a reservation?" Chris asked.

"Ya right," he said, pointing to a nondescript trailer-type house on the corner. "That's 'eir house. Pull in that driveway."

"The lights are all off," I said. "We might startle them dropping in at this hour."

"What if they think we're burglars and blow our heads off?" Chris said.

"You'll be right," Max said. He flung open the car door. "They got a new baby."

A new baby! This was even worse. Two scraggly dogs came to greet us. "Max," I said, "Chris and I aren't getting out with those dogs here."

"Ya can wait right here," Max called back. "I'll go see if anyone's around."

While Max disappeared around the corner, Chris jumped into the front seat and began to try to get a radio station. "Max is so bossy," Chris complained.

"That's because we're on his turf," I said.

"He won't let me have a turn in the front seat," Chris said, getting to the heart of the problem.

"Well, it's been a long day and we're all tired," I said, trying to reason with him. I spotted Max walking back. "Here he comes. Let's all just get along."

"Can't find nobody 'round," Max said. He opened the car door. "Jump in the back youn' fulla!"

"I want to stay in the front seat!"

"Only women an' kiddies ride in the back. Now go on, mate."

"I get carsick in the back," Chris whined. "I'll puke my brains out."

"Chris!" I snapped. "In the back."

"No!"

"Okay," I said, "when we get to Max's village, you're grounded!"

"You crack me up, Mom," he said, climbing into the backseat. "Grounded in the Outback. Like this whole trip doesn't suck enough. . . ."

"Christopher, I don't like that word!" I looked over at Max. "He's just tired." I pulled out of the driveway and onto the lonely road that led us deeper into the red plains. "When are we officially Back o'Bourke?"

"Right about now," he said. "Next good-size town ya come to is up Queensland way."

At the edge of town, we passed a large billboard that read: GATE-WAY TO THE REAL OUTBACK. I couldn't help but wonder who put it up and why.

"I guess that sign means we're not going to find a McDonald's around," Chris said with a tragic tone.

"Jus' cotton an' sheep," Max said.

"He's kidding, isn't he, Mom?"

I ignored him. "Where do they get water?"

"Darlin' River," Max said. "When she's not dried all up. It's real bad this year."

I drove on, hypnotized by the nothingness. "It's hard to see the road," I said, yawning.

"Open ya window," Max said. "Get ya-self some fresh air."

Fall in the Outback was downright chilly at night. I slipped on a sweatshirt and rolled the window part way down. "They know we're coming?"

"I sent 'em a message four days ago."

"They get mail all the way up here?"

"Once a week," Max said, "but I sent 'em the message by bird."

"Bird?" I said, not quite sure I heard correctly.

"That's right. I sent 'em a bird."

I instantly stopped myself from intellectualizing. After all, a bird carrying a message from Redfern to Enngonia wasn't any less plausible than a dead spirit doctor leading me to Max.

"Max," I said, "how did you communicate with the bird?"

Max tapped his forehead. "Ya open ya-self up to the world an' talk to the bird. Tell 'em what ya need. He can fly 'ere easier than I can," he said, adding, "Nobody in my family got a telephone."

We drove on in silence. There was a peaceful eerieness about the Outback. In an inexplicable way, it was calming to the senses. I was as far away from home as I could get and yet, as I drove farther and farther Back o'Bourke, I began to feel some sort of connection to something bigger than my own world.

It was about an hour out of Bourke when Max called out, "Ho! We're here!"

I looked at the car clock. 1:15 A.M. "Do I stay on this road?" I asked, my heart literally pounding with nervous anticipation.

"There ain't no other road," Max said, amused. "Go on past the Oasis Hotel/Pub." He pointed to a low concrete structure with cactus and palm trees painted on the front. So the guidebook was right: "A small settlement with a pub and a petrol pump." If the writer had embellished, he would have been a clear liar.

"Nothing's here!" Chris grumbled.

"Got all my nieces an' nephews here," Max said.

"This is like one major joke," Chris whispered in my ear.

I turned to the back and hissed, "Enough!" Then I turned to Max, "I hope we don't wake anybody."

"Yeah, they'll all be waitin' fa us," Max said, unbuckling his seat belt and unbuckling my imagination. "Yuz our first white guests."

Max was totally unaware of the pressure he had just laid on me. I was glad that I had stocked up on chocolate bars back at Dubbo.

I followed the paved road for less than a quarter of a mile, past a small grocery store/milk bar, a newly built elementary school, and a police post that housed one white policeman. I wound around a bend and in seconds pulled up in front of Katie's house, which was sandwiched between other identical homes on about an eighth of an acre. The house looked just like Max's nephew's—a one-floor no-frills ranch. Tin roof. Wood front porch. Simple but tidy. The street—an Aborigine version of Levittown—was nothing like how I had envisioned an Aborigine reservation to be.

Before I even shut off the ignition, folks began to saunter toward our car. They seemed to be coming from all directions. It was evident that they had been waiting for us. Max got out of the car first. Everybody certainly looked happy to see him. I felt no warm smiles directed our way. Same as when we were in that Aborigine restaurant in Redfern. I poked around the glove compartment, giving Max a chance to explain us.

"Mom," Chris said, nervous, "everybody's just staring at us."

"They're curious," I said. I couldn't make out anything Max was saying to his relatives, but the lack of cheer told me that we had better be on our best behavior.

"Remember," I said to Chris, "don't go into their homes unless you're first invited."

"I'm not going anywhere near their homes."

"Don't be that way."

"Well, they don't look friendly," he said. "Look at that spooky old lady over there with no teeth. Just shoot me now."

"I'm sure they're very sweet," I said, though I secretly agreed with him. I took a deep, relaxing breath and forced myself out of the car. "Hi," I said to the aloof faces surrounding Max. "I'm Liz Fuller." I pointed inside the car. "That's my son, Christopher."

They blankly looked from me to Chris and back to me. I took another deep breath and gave a nervous, goofy sounding laugh, filling in the deadening quiet. I reminded myself that Aborigines were comfortable with silence. The worst thing I could do was start to gush neurotically. The next worst thing I could do was to start passing out chocolate bars.

After what seemed like hours, but was probably only fifteen, twenty seconds, Katie, the matriarch of the clan, spoke. "Ya ready to swagger down," she said in a flat monotone made even flatter by icy blue eyes and deep frown lines.

I didn't know if I should say yes or no. I figured that if I said yes, she might think that we were unsocial. If I said no, she might feel obligated to invite us in for tea or something. I split the difference. "We're sort of tired," I chuckled self-consciously. "Been on the road now over twelve hours. Isn't that right, Max?"

"Ya right," he said. I couldn't tell if he was embarrassed by his family's cool reception or not.

A little girl about ten years old began to giggle. I wondered if she was Margaret.

"Yeah, we're all tired," Max said. I was sure he was sensing what I was feeling.

With those words, the crowd dispersed. The little girl, however, was prepared to hang around, but one of the adults shooed her along. "Get ya-self home."

Max gave us a choice of accommodations. We could sleep next door to Katie in an abandoned house that had been taken over by a large sheep, numerous stray cats and dogs, and a sick relative, or Max would build a campfire and we'd sleep outdoors.

"Let's sleep around the campfire!" Chris and I said at the same time.

While Max went in search of firewood, Chris and I retrieved our duffle bags from the trunk and placed them around a fire that had burned down to a few glowing embers.

"Do I have to brush my teeth?" Chris asked.

"Not tonight," I said.

"I gotta pee," he said, hopping up and down.

"Go near that tall grass over there." Suddenly remembering that poisonous snakes were no joke, I added, "But don't step into it."

When Chris came back, I did the same. Big Browns were less of a threat than venturing into a dark, abandoned house.

And so that first night we camped under the vast Outback sky. The stars were hanging down like globes on threads. I had never before seen them look that way. They gave off a perceptible starshine that coated the barren landscape. It was magnificent. I might have loved being here except all I could think was that we were hours from the nearest hospital, no one had a telephone, and no one had shown us even a shred of warmth. In the faint glow, some ten feet away, I could make out the bare outline of Max. "Yeah, everybody was real tired tonight," Max said, making lame excuses for his rude family. "We'll have us a good yarn with them in the mornin'."

"I can't wait," Chris whispered. He was lying beside me, his small shoulder pressed next to mine, snuggled down into his new sleeping bag. "Mom, we gotta get out of this dump."

"Shhh," I said. "Go to sleep."

"I can't."

But a few minutes later he was out. I didn't have any such luck. The Outback was resonating with unfamiliar sounds. "Is that an animal howling?" I asked Max.

"Dingo," he said.

"Dingo!" I exclaimed, remembering a horrible story about the dingo stealing a baby somewhere out near Ayers Rock—or did I read that it was the mother who killed the baby? Maybe the Outback does bizarre things to people. "Don't they sometimes go after babies?"

"Chickens," Max said. "Small roo. Emu . . ." His voice drifted off. Moments later he was snoring. I was too tired to sleep. I lay on the hard red ground, shifting from side to side trying to get comfortable, trying to figure out why we received such an inhospitable reception. Katie sure didn't mention anything about cooking us up johnnycakes in the morning. Even the Amish had been friendlier when Chris and I first arrived. Then, again, they were prepared for us. And they were white, like us. I fell asleep certain that the Eulo clan would be much happier if we'd just leave.

Less than an hour later, I was startled awake by Max's rather loud voice. He was speaking to someone. "I'm okay, Mum. I'm just 'ere restin' with my white lady friend an' her youngin. She's a good woman. He's a good little fulla. . . ."

It was three thirty in the morning, and Max was talking to his dead mother.

" 'Ey come all the way from America. Lotsa horses 'ere. . . . Yeah, I'll be bringin' 'em aroun' tomorrah to meet ya. . . ."

Tomorrow? We were going to be on our way home tomorrow.

". . . I'm real busy with my bruddas in Redfern. . . ."

Chris's steady breathing beside me was comforting. That was about the only normal thing around. While Max went on chatting with his mother, I came up with a terrific excuse why we needed to go home: I had forgotten my allergy medication. If I didn't take it every day, I would risk a serious allergic attack. I dozed off confident that by ten o'clock in the morning, we'd be on the Mitchell Highway headed back to Dubbo for the train to Sydney. I only wished that one of Max's relatives had a phone so that we could change our train reservations. Perhaps, I thought, I could make a phone call at the Oasis Pub?

"Mom," Chris said, jolting me into semiconsciousness, "it's eight o'clock. Time to get up."

"Come on, fulla," I heard Max say, "let ya mudda sleep."

I burrowed down into my sleeping bag and drifted off again, only half aware of where I was. The next thing I knew, a stray dog was sniffing around inches from my face. "Get out!" Max said, chasing it away.

I pulled myself to a sitting position, waving at both the mutt and the flies. Slowly, my eyes adjusted to the ruthless morning sun. The scenery was less than captivating: prefab houses evenly spaced on the barren red clay, sparse shrubs, and a handful of unfortunate trees begging for a downpour. I recalled a quote from one of my guidebooks: "Anyone who'd venture into the Outback would go to hell for a pastime."

"Coffee ready fa ya," Max said, jiggling the Robert Tims coffee bag around in the steaming water.

"Terrific," I said, reaching for the tin mug. But there was already a metallic taste in my mouth. During the night I must have rolled over onto the ground, caking my lips with red clay, and I imagined I could taste the iron. "What time is it?"

"Nine," Chris groaned. He was twenty feet away, propped against our duffle bags, eating a bowl of instant oatmeal, giving me the evil eye. He was cooly ignoring a group of kids hiding behind a tree, spying on him. As I sipped the coffee, I tried to talk myself into staying just one full day.

"*Boogalie*'s runnin' down at the river this mornin'," Max said, enticing me into exploring.

"What's boogalie?" I asked.

"Crayfish," Max said. "Real sweet tasty meat. We'll get 'em fa lunch."

After my second cup of coffee and a trip into the abandoned house to use the toilet, I made up my mind. It was time to go. I reached into my knapsack and let out a screech. "Oh shit!"

"Whatsa matter?" Max said.

"My medication," I said, panicky. "I left it in Manly."

"What's it fa?"

"I have *very* bad allergies," I said, sniffling.

Max's reaction was better than hoped for. "Ya gotta 'ave it?" he said, alarmed.

I took a deep worried breath. "Twice a day," I said.

Chris looked bewildered. He wasn't sure if I had really forgotten the nonexistent medication, but he hopped right on the bandwagon. "Crap! We gotta get Mom back home."

I looked at Max's face. He looked confused. "Ya need to be gettin' back home then?" he said.

"Max, I have no choice. Ohhh, I am so disappointed. I can't believe this is happening. I am devastated."

"We both are," Chris said.

Nobody looked more disappointed than Max. He solemnly rolled up his two blankets that he had slept on and left to wash up.

"Mom, you are too cool!" Chris said, slapping me a high five. "Those kids are not at all friendly. Look at them over there now just hiding in that tall grass watching my every move."

"Okay, load the car. When Max gets back, we'll go over to Katie's and politely say good-bye."

"Yes!" Chris said, throwing his clenched fist up into the air. "We are outta here!"

My little deception would have worked just about anywhere in the world, except the Outback. Because Max had a cousin down the road who was quite knowledgeable about bush medicine. Twenty minutes later found Max and me sitting around a kitchen table where I was describing my symptoms to Medicine Tom and his stone-faced wife.

"I mainly have sniffles and coughing," I said to the white-haired man. His skin was pitch-black, his eyes a milky bluish-green that gave him a prophetic appearance and seemed to demand respect. Every instinct in my body told me to fess up. But I was already in it this deep. "Sometimes the wheezing can be very bad," I went on.

"Wheezing?" Tom turned to Max.

Max turned to me. "Can ya describe what wheezin' is?"

I let out a death gurgle that loosened up his wife's set jaw. "Awwgh." She clutched her chest.

"Mmmmm," Tom said. "Wheezin'." He looked over at his wife and rattled off something in Aborigine. She pinched her nose at the bridge and said something in return. "Yeah, yeah, yeah," he said, bringing his fingers up to his eyelids and stroking the inner corners while he consulted with his wife once again.

"A lot of water comin' outta ya eyes?" Tom asked.

There was no turning back now. "Sometimes so bad that I can't see," I said, at that moment feeling like I was back in elementary school on a phony visit to the school nurse, waiting breathlessly for her to finally say, "You may call your mother to pick you up now."

"Do ya eyes itch ya?" Tom asked.

"Oh yes, badly."

"Burn ya?"

The longer I looked at Tom, the softer his face became. The same went for his wife. I wasn't positive, but they actually seemed concerned about me. How could I keep this charade up?

"Ya eyes burn?" Tom asked once again.

I had to come clean. I hesitated.

Max interpreted this as my not understanding what Tom asked and so he repeated it slow and clear: "Do ya eyes sting ya?"

What the hell. "Yeah, they sting," I said. In spite of the cool morning, I was beginning to get very warm. I slipped off my jean jacket. The Gap label caught my eye. What I wouldn't give to be browsing around the Gap in Westport. Sipping cappuccino at Starbucks. Gossiping with friends about who is doing what to whom. Curled up with Reuel watching *Seinfeld*. I had to get out of Tom's kitchen. I had to get out of Enngonia. I turned to Max. "Max, could you *please* explain to Tom that I really appreciate his concern, and of course, his wife's concern, but I'm on a very specific medication. I need to take only that particular one. Would you pass that along?"

"Yeah." Max nodded. "I'll tell 'em that."

"And be *sure* to tell them how much I appreciate their concern," I added, in a pathetic attempt to lighten my guilt.

I couldn't pick up everything being said, but I did pick up a few key words: Manly, medicine, train, Dubbo, young bloke. After about five minutes of talking back and forth, Max rose from the kitchen table and announced, "Tom's gonna take ya into the bush fa some medicine now."

"What?"

"Tom's gonna fix ya up."

Holy shit! This was not happening. "Max, I'm on a prescription drug," I said, breaking out into a cold sweat. "I can't just switch medication."

"You'll be right."

"What about Chris?" I cried. "He's waiting for me back at the campsite."

"I'll go back now an' take the youn' fulla aroun' to be meetin' me great-nephews," he said, stepping out the door.

"Tell him I'll be back very soon," I said. I looked to Tom for confirmation.

Tom, however, was preoccupied filling up several bottles of water from the kitchen sink. "Radiator's not workin' fa a while now."

As we bounced along the dirt road in Medicine Tom's 1967 Toyota truck, which was minus a windshield, I tried to rationalize how I hadn't really lied. After all, I did have hay fever, even if I didn't take medication for it. Every spring and summer I got all the classic symptoms—runny nose, and burning, watery eyes. I was just too lazy to do anything about it. Perhaps Tom *could* fix me up—with a natural remedy. I looked over at him. His strong Aborigine face, framed with Einstein hair, inspired confidence.

"Where are we going?" I asked.

"Up 'ere," he said. He swung off onto a rocky pathlike road that followed a river. We had been driving for only a few minutes when

I saw something big and dead and half submerged in the muddy water.

"What is that?" I yelped.

"Roo," Tom said. "Be glad ya got allergies an' ya can't smell it."

Just then I got a whiff. "Phewwwww," I said.

"Awwgh, ya *can* smell it."

The bumpy ride, the putrid, decomposing carcass, and my lack of sleep combined to make me want to vomit. "I feel sick."

"Pinch ya nose," Tom said, flooring the accelerator.

I did as he instructed.

"You'll be right now," Tom said, heading down a barely negotiable dirt path lined with pine trees that scented the air. Instantly my nausea was gone.

From the way Tom maneuvered his truck, I had no doubt that he knew exactly where he was headed. But I didn't have a lot of faith that we'd get there. Broken Foster's bottles littered our path, and it was only a matter of time before I expected to hear the hiss of a tire going flat.

Fifteen minutes after we started out, the tires were still holding up. Tom rolled to a stop beside a big cactus flowering in a shade of red so vibrant that it tinged the surrounding shrubs a rose color.

"We're 'ere," he said, slamming on the shaky brake.

I gingerly climbed out of the truck, exaggerating my aches from sleeping on the rock-hard earth. But my bones weren't the problem. It was my feet. With every step, prickles, called goat heads, poked up through the rubber soles of my worn flip-flops.

"You'll be right?" Tom said, holding my elbow while I plucked the goat heads from my feet.

"I guess I have to toughen up," I chuckled, not wanting to appear even more of an ungracious wimp. We wound our way through a grove of tall pines and more flowering cactus until Tom found what he wanted. He pulled a pocketknife from his pants pocket and began to collect samples from a cactus in full bloom with large purple fruit. Medicine Tom's technique: cut, pinch, sniff, drop in plastic bag. I watched, fascinated. After he had taken about a dozen or so specimens from various parts of the cactus, it was time to head back. We got halfway to the truck when Tom remembered that he needed one other thing.

"Wait right 'ere," he said, handing me the plastic bag.

In no time at all he returned holding a single leaf. "When we're comin' up near that dead roo," Tom said, "put this up to ya nose."

I took the greenish-brown leaf, and sniffed. "Smells sort of like anise."

"Anise?"

"Licorice," I said.

"Ya like it?"

"I really do!"

Tom beamed. "If ya close ya eyes, yer not even gonna know when we pass it."

"Okay," I said, climbing back into the truck. I shut my eyes tightly and pressed the leaf to my nose.

"Awright," Tom said, starting up the truck. And then he suddenly shut off the ignition. "Awwgh, I gotta get some water in the radiator before we go anywhere."

A few minutes later we were bouncing back down the rocky dirt path.

"Got ya eyes closed?" Tom checked.

"Can't see a thing," I said, remembering how as kids my brother Gary used to blindfold me and lead me through the neighborhood and I'd have to guess whose yard we were in. That same playful spirit of adventure was now in the air. "Don't give me any hints," I said.

"Nawwww, I'm not tellin' ya nothin'."

A few minutes went by and Tom said, "Smell somethin'?"

"Hey, you promised to not tell me!"

"I din't say nothin'," Tom said, his voice crackling with amusement.

After about five more minutes, Tom said, "Ya can open ya eyes now. We're back on the main road."

"Unbelievable! This leaf *really* works! You know, Tom, I should package this plant and take it back home."

When I said those words, "back home," it suddenly occurred to me that ever since Tom and I started off on our little journey, I hadn't thought about leaving Enngonia. I hadn't thought of returning to Connecticut. I hadn't thought about Chris or what he and Max were up to.

Which was good, because there was absolutely nothing to worry about. Max had taken Chris and Margaret over to the Aborigine milk bar for a soda and bag of chips, and as we were driving by, Tom spotted them coming out of the store.

"Ho!" Tom called out as he came to a loud, screechy halt behind an eighteen-wheel tractor-trailer parked in front of the store. It was loaded down with sheared sheep and wrapped in flies.

Max slid in beside me. Margaret jumped into the back of the open pickup.

"Christopher, get ya-self in 'ere!" Margaret ordered, as bossy as Charlie Brown's Lucy. She even looked a bit like Lucy.

"Mom," Chris said, self-righteous, "it's against the law. There aren't any seat belts back there."

"You'll be right," Max said. "We're not goin' far."

Like a thousand-year-old man, Chris climbed into the open back and sat as far away from Margaret as he could get.

"So ya got ya medicine?" Max said.

"It's right here," I said, holding up the plastic bag. I turned to Tom. "What are you going to do with this now?"

"Fix it up fa ya," Tom said, downshifting for a skinny dog that was crossing the road. "It'll be ready by evenin'."

As promised, Tom showed up at dusk with a cloth sack filled with a concoction that had been pounded, soaked, boiled, and set out in the blistering sun to dry. I was instructed to inhale the pungent mixture immediately upon rising and just before going to sleep at night. In three days, he'd be back to check on me. He couldn't come any sooner because of an emergency in Lightning Ridge where a few nephews worked, mining for the precious black opal. If I had any problems, I was to go see his wife. The medicine would have to do its job, and I resigned myself to the fact that I wasn't going anywhere until Tom returned.

The following is a letter I wrote to Reuel on our third day in the Outback:

Dear Reuel,

I feel as if I'm on the face of the moon with alien creatures all around. We do a lot of staring at each other and very little talking. Max, however, is going out of his way to try and show us a good time. Today he taught Chris how to track for rabbits. He didn't get any—thank God—but it was such fun just watching Chris with his ear to the ground as he learned how to listen for the subtle sounds in the earth. It was the quietest and most concentrated I had ever seen him.

Max's sister, Katie, regards everything I do and say with deep suspicion. This morning I brought her over a cup of coffee with one of my coffee bags and she told me to just set it on her kitchen table and later when I went back to get my cup, she hadn't even taken one sip. I asked her if anything was wrong with the coffee and she said, "I drink tea." And then she continued to sweep down her front porch as if I wasn't there. She's much less hostile to Chris. In fact, she actually burst out laughing when Chris asked her if she was spooked living so close to the graveyard. Meanwhile, I'm walking on eggshells trying to not offend anybody.

Be glad you're not here. I haven't had a shower now in three days. This afternoon, Max is taking Chris and me to some watering hole for a dip. The water is supposed to be crystal clear and clean enough to drink. I'll believe that when I see it.

Today is the first day that the kids are all playing together. A guy by the name of Squeaky is jury-rigging a basketball hoop. Chris brought along his basketball. There's a little girl here named Margaret who is never more than ten feet from Chris. Romance is in the air. She's really very cute.

Darling, I'm going to sign off for now. I don't want them to think I'm writing about them. They watch my every move. Before we left, I arranged for Gladys to send my mail up here once a week, but that won't be necessary now since we'll be leaving the minute Tom returns from a place called Lightning Ridge. He's supposed to be back anytime. I just hope his old junker truck holds out. You're on my mind every second. I see those sexy smile lines and hear your gutsy laugh everywhere and I get a warm, tingling rush just like a teenager with a first love. How was I so lucky to meet you? In some strange, weird way, being here has made me more aware of my love for you. I can't wait to get back to Manly and make plane reservations for home. With any luck, by this time next week, we'll be together. I hope you don't have to fly to Bosnia. But I understand. I think a lot about our last conversation. I love the fact that you didn't want me to leave. This is my last trip away from you. I want my mother's life—spaghetti and chicken every Sunday. That's a promise. If I get too boring for you, I'll take an acting class. Hey—why didn't I think about that before. . . .

> I love you,
> Liz

P.S. Darling, would you call Randy and tell him what we're up to. I pray he's not back in the hospital.


Later that same day, Max took me down to the watering hole. I wanted Chris to come along, but he said that he was going to stay and help Squeaky make a sturdier basketball hoop. Chris suggested that we invite Margaret along. Hearing that, Margaret scrunched her turned-up nose, folded her arms, and said that she needed to make sure that the hoop was going to be big enough for the ball to pass through. "Fullas can't do nothin' right," she said, prompting my agreement. "You're absolutely right, Margaret," I said.

And so in the heat of the afternoon, Max and I headed down a path of struggling trees toward the promised freshwater spring that Max called by the Aborigine name, Winhthi. We must have walked for a good twenty minutes before we arrived at a pile of rocks in all sizes and shapes. I watched Max place a rock that he had picked up along the way on top of the pile, and I assumed the formation had a spiritual significance. Once the rock was in place, Max led me down a sandy incline festooned with anthills and scratchy scrub, and there, at the bottom of the hill, sat a pool of water shimmering in the bright sunlight like a precious sapphire.

For a moment, I stood dazed. Then I knelt down on the edge of the bank and scooped up a handful of the pure, cool water. "I feel just like Alice in Wonderland," I said, watching the water run between my fingers like liquid silver.

"We used to come here for initiations," Max said. He lowered his leathery cupped hand for a drink. "My grandfatha was a koradji."

"You mentioned that," I said, also having a drink. The water was as sweet as it was clear.

"Yeah, he made people better. And sometimes he made 'em worse."

"How did he make them worse?"

"Pointin' the bone," Max said. "Years ago a fulla from up near Tinnenburra stole a Eulo woman. My grandfatha called everybody to meet at this 'ere hole. Durin' the ceremony, he pointed the bone in the direction of the bloke that stole the Eulo woman away. Once the bone was pointed, the fulla's blood moved into the bone. Pieces of the bone went into the fulla making 'em real sick. After the ceremony, the bone was wrapped in emu feathers an' buried over there," Max said, pointing about ten feet away. "From time to time my grandfatha dug up the bone an' warmed it up, makin' the fulla more sick until the time he finally died."

I knew things like this could happen in the Outback. Sister Pat had told me that the Aborigine power of belief is so strong that if a victim becomes aware that he or she is a target of bone pointing, the results are certain death. I asked Max if there were any more magic men in his village. But he didn't answer. Maybe it was a tribal secret. I changed the subject. "Boy, I've never before seen such a beautiful watering hole."

"Ya wanna have ya-self a coolin' off now?"

"Ohhh, yes!" I said, unlacing my sneakers. "I can't wait."

"I'm gonna go off fa a little walk while ya have a swim," Max said, a perfect gentleman.

"You don't have to. I have my bathing suit on under these shorts."

"I'm gonna head on down the path a bit an' have a snooze under a tree I used to go to when I was a youn' fulla," Max said. "Call fa me after ya get out."

"Is this watering hole deep enough to dive in?"

"Deep as the sky is high," Max said, walking away.

With Max out of sight, I took off all my clothes and dove in, feeling at once the cool warmth of the embracing spring. There was a buoyancy bubbling from below that lifted not only my body but my mind to a place gentle and forgiving. I don't know how long I luxuriated in this transcendent state, but I do know that when I heard Max calling from down the path, everything seemed just slightly different. At the time, I thought that it was because I was refreshed. But it was much more than that.

"Max," I said, "did you bring me here for a special reason?"

"Ya said ya wanted to get cleaned up."

"But something happened to me in that water."

His face was quiet and serene. "I wanna take ya somewhere," he said. "Follow me."

I laced up my sneakers and began to follow him up the bank. I had only walked a few feet when something bright and flashing caused me to look back toward the watering hole. It was a ball of light. It was gracefully bobbling in the water, almost playful, in an uncanny way, almost human. As I studied the dancing light, I felt the strong presence of another, accompanied by a vibration that lifted me above the spring to where I seemed to become one with the light that now was everywhere. Joined with the warm rays, I looked down into the deep, blue spring, and there I saw Dwango's crystal clear reflection on the surface of the water. "The spiritual gateway has been lifted for you to enter," the spirit doctor communicated.

# EIGHT

We took a different path back. Max wanted to show me the tree that he had a snooze under while I swam, and I followed along, as free and happy as when I was a kid running through the sprinkler on our front lawn in August. When we got to the very ordinary gray-green tree, Max said that he hadn't really slept after all. He had just sat there and thought about a woman he had known many years earlier. Her name was Thaalangay. It meant fresh. He called her Gay. She was strong, with small hands, deep brown skin, and eyes bluer, clearer, and deeper than the spring. They had met at the end of the dry season and spent every day together. In the early morning, when the dew was still on the tussocky grass, they swam in the watering hole, and in the late evenings they lay under the tree and sang, danced, yarned, and fell in love. They wanted to marry, but as an infant Gay was promised to her mother's mother's brother's son. When word got out that Gay and Max were more than friends, Gay's father sent her brothers to take her to her betrothed's camp where she married the older man—a man already with a wife and five children. For days afterward, Max didn't eat or sleep. He sat beneath the tree, remembering when his heart was not caged and he knew peace.

He believed the tree to have special powers. It was the only tree in the area to have survived every major bush fire in the past forty years. It had never been struck by lightning and never suffered from lack of water. "The roots," Max said, "have snaked down the path an' joined up at the waterin' hole where they look out fa each other."

"But Max," I said, "if this tree and that spring have special powers, why didn't they look out after you and Gay? How did they let her be taken from you?"

"Awwgh," Max answered, "that's only part of my story. Come on now, we gotta be gettin' ourselves back fa supper."

When we arrived back at the campsite, Tom's wife, whose name I discovered was Fran, was waiting for us with a message. Tom's truck had broken down near Goodooga and he couldn't get back until a new radiator could be sent down from Dirranbandi. Last time it was his rear axle. Took him three months to get back, during which time he got work in the opal fields. But the real message was that on Saturday they were having a *corroboree*—a term that encompasses all ceremonies and rituals that involve singing and dancing—and we were all invited. This particular corroboree was to celebrate the birthdays of Margaret and Matthew, cousins who were born on the same day.

"What can I bring?" Max said, his eyes lighting up. Max was a real social guy.

"Awwgh," Fran said, looking around at our bags piled against the tree, ready to be loaded into the car for the trip back to Sydney, "ya the only one here who can fix a good roo, Max."

"Yeah," he agreed. "Ol' Henry can make a good emu, but he don't know nothin' about roastin' roo." No false modesty for Max. He threw his broad shoulders back and puffed out his robust chest.

"Ya roo are never dried out," Fran said, laying it on.

"Saturday early mornin' we'll go get us one," Max said, with the same satisfied expression Reuel had when I complimented him on his barbecue chicken. "It'd be real good if Tom's back so we can load 'er in the back of the truck."

"We could probably strap it onto the top of my car," I blurted out before kicking myself. All I needed was to have the roof of my rented Holden caved in and dried roo blood dripping down the sides when I returned it to the agent in Dubbo.

"Yeah," Max said, willing to please me. "We could do that awright."

"Ummm, just how heavy is a roo?" I asked, backtracking. But Max and Fran were already onto something else.

"I don't want no grog at the corroboree," Fran said, setting strict limits.

"Ya right," Max agreed. "I'll call a meetin' fa after supper tonight."

No sooner did Max get out those words than Margaret and Chris, followed by half a dozen kids, raced up the road and into Katie's house. Seconds later they emerged with a cold jug of water and a bag of lollies. "Don't go feedin' on all of 'em. Ya haven't had ya evenin' feed!" Katie hollered. The scene was so delightfully familiar.

While Max and Fran continued to make plans for the corroboree, something inside me went click. The second Fran left, I turned to Max and said, "I need your help getting these duffle bags moved inside. I can't stand living out of bags another moment." I was ready suddenly to ease up and enjoy.

Max broke out into his gap-toothed grin. "We'll get ya set up over 'ere in that abandoned house next door to Katie," he said, heaving a duffle bag onto each shoulder. I followed Max, loaded down with two grocery bags, Chris's schoolbag, and my laptop.

And so that evening, while Max led a family meeting to discuss no drinking at the corroboree, I sat by a campfire and watched the sun slide down behind the western horizon, sending out spray paints of orange, pink, purple, and blue. When the light show was over, I stared into the fire. How life had changed in twelve short hours. Early morning, I had woken with one thought in mind: leaving Enngonia. Now, wild horses couldn't drag me back home. And the moment my attitude changed, so did the attitude of those around me. Shortly after Katie watched Max and me bring our bags inside, she sauntered over. I was separating our clean clothes from those that needed to be washed. Tentatively, she said, "I guess ya youn' bloke got himself some new mates."

"He sure is having a good time," I said, treading gingerly.

"They in the scrub now with the big ball. Little Mitchell's tryin' to take it away from ya youngin." She smiled so quickly I wasn't sure if it was really a smile.

"Chris said that he wanted to teach them how to play basketball," I said. "It's real popular in America."

"Yeah?" Katie said with a serious expression. "I heard somethin' about that."

I thought about telling her how all the really great basketball players in the U.S. were black, but then I thought better of it and said nothing.

"Henry got a big emu fa tonight's feed," Katie then offered, speaking to the chipped, water-stained ceiling.

Was this an invitation? I wasn't sure how to respond, so once again I said nothing, remembering Sister Pat's warning that Aborigines consider direct eye contact with strangers to be rude.

A few moments later Katie said, "He's diggin' the pit right now."

I forced myself to keep my mouth shut. I went about separating the clothes.

Katie shifted her eyes from the ceiling to the linoleum floor. "Ya ever tasted emu?"

My heart quickened. "No," I said, still avoiding eye contact.

That's when Katie turned to Max, who had been sweeping sheep droppings out of the hallway. "Max," she said, "bring ya white friend an' the little fulla over fa emu."

Max's face lightened up the dark hallway. "Ya haven't tasted nothin' till ya had Henry's emu!" he proclaimed—taking an enthusiastic sweep with the homemade broom. A half second later, dozens of what looked like chocolate-covered raisins shot through the hallway, out the front door, and onto the red clay. "I'll make damper," he said.

In the excitement of the moment, I broke my first rule of protocol. "Katie," I called out, "please call me Liz." Not supposed to call someone by name, dummy.

"So I'll see ya tonight, Liz," Katie said. She turned and headed back home.

The following morning Henry came around for a cup of coffee and to drop off his recipe for emu that he had promised me after I gushed about how wonderful it was. The truth of the matter: I didn't take one bite of the huge, unattractive bird that can't fly. The wild meat sat on my plate oozing grease and a pungent odor of strong herbs that made me light-headed and nauseous. Several times I attempted a tiny taste, but I couldn't get the dark meat past my lips. Fortunately, the village did not lack stray dogs in search of tucker. Chris and I made some new animal friends that night, and later—in private—we embarrassedly devoured our entire stash of crackers with peanut butter and a full bag of chocolate chip cookies.

The following is the emu recipe that I typed on my laptop computer with Henry sitting next to me:

### HENRY'S EMU

Dig a pit near emu feeding ground
Cover pit with branches
Stick spear into bottom of pit—bird can't jump out
Pluck and gut
Prepare pit for roasting
Stuff bird with herbs and hot stones
To keep the flies away, toss guts about thirty feet away and the
flies will have tucker, too.
When hind leg is cut and bird juice runs clear, bird is done.


When I finished typing, Henry wanted to try my computer. So I immediately set it on his lap and told him to type in whatever he wanted.

"I can't read or write too good," Henry said apologetically.

"That's okay. Just find the A," I said to the short, wiry man, probably in his late thirties or early forties.

Slowly and methodically, Henry ran his brown bony, scarred fingers the length of the keyboard. A minute or so later, he called out, "Hoooo! 'Ere it is! I got A."

"Perfect. Now press down."

Henry pressed down and kept pressing, causing the letter to repeat a dozen times.

"Ohhh! I forgot to say just tap down light and quickly."

Henry immediately lifted his finger.

"Look up at the screen, Henry."

"Awwwwgh!" he said, with pure delight. "All them As. I'll find the B." He pressed down and muttered to himself, "Light an' quick."

By the time Henry got to the G, half of the village was hovering over his shoulder, helping him hunt and peck for the next letter. Their interest, however, was short-lived. Not so with Henry. He wasn't about to quit until he got to Z. And when he did, he let out such a burst that it once again drew a crowd.

"Does ya machine take words?" Henry asked.

"Oh yes," I said. "You can write entire books on this thing."

"Yeah? How?"

"You got me. I'm really stupid about computers, but I do know that there's a little tiny chip inside that does all the work. Don't ask me anything more," I laughed.

Henry laughed, too. "Same like magic?"

"To me it's like magic," I said. "I'll save what you've done and tomorrow you can write some more."

"Yeah?"

"Absolutely," I said. "Maybe tomorrow you can write words?"

Henry's smile faded. "I know a lot a words," he said. "But I don't know 'ow ya write 'em."

"That's no problem. I can help you."

Henry looked at me. "Ya went to high school?"

"Yep."

"Well," he said, deep in thought, "I gotta be goin' into Bourke in the mornin'. I'll be 'round afta that."

"You'll have your first lesson tomorrow. Let's set a time."

"Yeah, we'll set a time."

"What time's good for you?" I asked, forgetting about the unique Aborigine clock.

"Whenever I get here's good fa me," Henry said, totally sincere.

"Great," I said, reprimanding myself for being so uptight, especially out here. "So whenever you can get here, we'll get started."

"We'll get started," Henry repeated. He got up from where he had been sitting crossed-legged on the red, dusty earth, lit a cigarette, and walked back over to Katie's backyard where the men had gathered to watch Max get a haircut from Charlie.

The following few days were bustling with preparations for Saturday's corroboree. The menu was meticulously planned. Nothing seemed left to chance. Katie was making the Australian bread, damper. Max's niece Dorothy was bringing yam salad. Lou was on for potato salad. Lydia for bean salad. Max, of course, was supplying the roo. Squeaky said that the boogalie would be running. Flo was making a chocolate cake with white icing, and her sister Tam was making a vanilla cake with chocolate icing and decorating it with birthday candles—if the Aborigine store ever got them in. And, oh yes, Henry was writing a birthday message to Margaret and Mitchell on the computer.

While the adults were busying themselves with preparations, little Margaret was consumed with what she was going to wear.

Early Friday morning, while I was on my way into the abandoned house for a shower, Margaret walked up to me. "Liz, can ya come over and 'ave a look at two of my jumpers."

"Absolutely," I said. "And maybe later *you* can help me pick out something to wear?"

"What are ya goin' do with that hair?" she asked as she walked alongside me, eyeing my dried-out blond mop with deep concern.

"I'm going to wash it and put some conditioner on," I said, stopping for a moment to run my fingers through Margaret's full head of soft, wavy brown hair with golden highlights. "It'll never be as nice as yours, but," I added, "it'll be better than it is right now."

Margaret looked very serious. "Well," she said, "I suppose I can do ya hair fa ya."

"You will?"

Margaret scrunched her nose up and nodded that that might be my only hope. "Are ya goin' t'wear makeup?"

"I didn't bring any," I apologized. "Ohhh, wait a minute. I have some colored lip gloss in my bag."

"That's all ya got?"

"I'm afraid so. But if I had known I was going to be invited to a special birthday party, I would have brought a party dress and full makeup."

"You don't 'ave ya-self a party dress?" Margaret said, miffed.

"I have a nice pair of brown shorts and—"

"Shorts?" Margaret was stunned. She stopped dead in her tracks, horrified. How could I even think of coming to her party in shorts.

"Come to think of it, Margaret, I do have a sarong. I wear it over my bathing suit."

"Sarong?" There was hope for me.

"Let's go inside and I'll show you."

With Margaret in tow, I gingerly picked my way around sheep droppings that dotted the hallway. Fortunately there was a door to our bedroom that kept the massive unsheared sheep and all the other critters from entering.

"How come ya an' Chris sleep outside an' not in 'ere?" Margaret asked, looking around the bedroom. The only furniture was a soiled mattress pushed up against the wall. The windows were bare and there was no lightbulb in the ceiling fixture.

"We really love sleeping outside."

Margaret pinched her nose. "It's not very nice in 'ere," she said, cutting to the core.

Before she checked out my wardrobe, she darted down the long, narrow hallway to a back bedroom. "I'll be right back wit-cha," she said.

When Margaret returned, she said her Uncle Bampu, who was in the back bedroom, wanted to meet me after he had his bath and a feed. I would like that very much, I said, but wondered why Max had never before mentioned anything about him. Maybe he had, and I missed it. Whatever the case, Margaret and I got busy trying to find a decent outfit for me to wear. We pored over absolutely everything I had. Margaret decided that definitely I would look best in the red sarong with a black T-shirt. She would give me a pair of earrings with dangling red berries and take me out into the bush for lipstick and eyeliner.

That settled, Margaret turned to matters of the heart.

"Are ya an' Uncle Max gettin' married?" she asked, pressing the wrinkles out of the sarong with the palm of her small hand.

"What?"

"Everybody's talkin' about ya an' Uncle Max bein' in love," Margaret confided, girl-to-girl.

"They are?"

"My aunts say that's why ya come 'ere."

"Margaret," I said, bowled over by what I had just heard, "your Uncle Max is just wonderful, but we are *not* getting married. We're not boyfriend and girlfriend. I'm already married." I showed her my ring. She gave it only a cursory glance.

After a bout of uncomfortable silence, she said, "Where's ya man?"

"Back in America."

"He should be 'ere with ya."

"You know, Margaret, my mother told me the same thing."

Later that night, Lila, Margaret's best friend, came up to me and reported that Margaret had made up the whole story about Max and me being in love, because Margaret wanted me to stay in Enngonia so that she could marry Chris! I did not share this information with Chris.

I did, however, tell Max.

Who enjoyed it thoroughly. He let loose with a rip-roaring belly laugh. "Awwww Margaret, she's a magger awright. Ya never know what she's goin' get herself into." He wiped tears from his eyes. "Did she take ya over yet an' see the orange groove?"

"Not yet," I said, "but later she wants to take me over to meet Uncle Bampu."

"She's takin' ya t'do what?" Max said, as if he wasn't sure what he had heard.

"To see the relative in the back bedroom."

"Nawww," Max said, shaking his head, "I don't want ya goin' 'ere."

He gave no reason. There was something in his expression and the tone of his voice that told me to ask no questions.

———

That night I had a vivid mix of disturbing dreams. At some point, I must have let out a bloodcurdling scream, because the next thing I knew Max was shaking my arm.

"Ya awright?" he asked, his blue eyes inches away from mine.

I sat bolt upright. "What time is it?"

Max looked up at the stars. "Just after two."

"I guess I was having a nightmare."

"I thought maybe ya seen somethin'."

"Huh?"

"Yeah," Max said, "earlier in the evenin' when I was down at the cemetery visitin' my mudda, I din't have any matches to smoke the bad spirits away. Some bad spirits followed me back 'ere."

"Are you serious?"

"I'm feelin' the hair on the back of my neck stand up right now. An' you screamin' in ya sleep. That's a sure sign ya got some no-good spirits 'round."

"Oh Jesus," I gasped.

"What did ya do with the matches?" he asked. "I gotta smoke 'em away."

"They're in my knapsack. Over by you."

Our little campfire had burned completely out, making it impossible to find anything.

"I can't find nothin' 'ere," Max said, fumbling around.

"Oh noooo," I cried. "I think I left it in the house."

"That's awright," Max said. "I'll go get it."

"Not without me," I said, getting up and grateful that Chris had been invited to sleep over with Ian, his new buddy.

As we stepped into the abandoned house where our belongings were, the sheep stepped out. Then I heard, or thought I heard, a humming or chanting coming from down the pitch-black hallway.

"What's that?" I asked, clutching Max's arm.

"Bampu," Max said.

I opened the door to the bedroom. "Is he okay?"

Max didn't answer. I grabbed my knapsack. In moments we were back outside.

On a moonless night in the Outback, dark takes on a whole new meaning. We walked toward the cemetery in silence. It was eerily quiet. The only sound was the flip-flopping of my sandals on the parched, cracked earth and Max's heavy breathing.

A bit weak in the knees, I followed Max down a path of scrub and cactus to where I became aware of a fence beside us. Max stopped. Then I noticed the tiny cemetery. I was so spooked that I realized I was humming "Mary Had a Little Lamb"—the nursery rhyme I used to sing to Chris to lull him to sleep.

Max struck a match. "I'm smokin' ya away," he proclaimed to the balmy night air. "We've had enough of ya followin' us 'round! Ya keep ya-selves right 'ere!"

My heart was pounding as loud as Max was talking. "Are they still here?" I asked, afraid to look anywhere but at Max's profile.

Max lit another match.

Then he blew it out, fast and hard. " 'Ey're gone now," he said with total confidence. "We're not gonna be bothered by any more bad spirits."

"You're sure?" I said, getting up the courage to look around. All I could see were a few spindly white sticks marking various stone graves.

Before we turned to leave, Max lingered for a moment. Then he spoke to his mother. "Ya have a good rest, Mudda. I gotta get up real early to go roo huntin' fa the corroboree. So I'll see ya later." Max turned to me. "Ya wanna say somethin'?"

Did I want to say something? I wanted to say, Let's get the hell out of here! "It's real nice to meet you," I said. And then we were on our way.

When we arrived back at the campsite, I was as awake as I had ever been. Daylight was hours off and sleep was not on the horizon. I asked Max how he was doing.

"I'm just lookin' up at the stars," Max said.

So I just looked up at the stars, too. And I got put in my place real quick. The night sky was so resplendent, my only response was to suck my breath in. The vast sky made me feel as insignificant as a flea, and yet, the longer I studied the magnificent and awesome display, the more significant I began to feel. Nothing had been left to chance up there or down here. *I* was part of the harmonious display. And with that thought came an extraordinary sense of comfort that I was beside Max Eulo. In fact, I was so comfortable that I brought up a subject that under normal circumstances, I never in a million years would have. I said, "You know, Max, did you ever hate white people? Were you ever afraid of them?"

Max appeared unfazed by the question that I'm sure appeared to come out of nowhere. "No," he answered, "but my mudda used to be real afraid of white folk. Whenever she'd see 'em comin', she'd tell me and my sisters and bruddas to be gettin' ourselves away from 'em. That's why I wanted to be taken' ya down to be meetin' her, so she'd see ya was a real good white lady."

"Max," I said, "I've never been scared of black people."

He propped himself up on one elbow. "Yeah, why's that?"

I even had to stop for a minute to figure out why that was. "I guess it goes back to when I was a little girl. I used to spend a lot of time with my grandmother, Old Ma. One of the best parts about staying with her was that every Saturday morning, Ted—the black handyman—used to have tea and coffee cake with us. Ted was great. He could blow smoke out of his ears. Make a cigarette disappear. And tap-dance more fancy than Fred Astaire. He taught *me* how to tap-dance. But Old Ma said I couldn't tell anybody. You see, her daughter, my Aunt Ruth, didn't like Ted socializing with us. But Old Ma said that what she didn't know wouldn't hurt her. So Ted kept having tea and cake with us, and I kept getting better and better at tap. I didn't see Ted after I turned, oh, maybe thirteen, fourteen. I got into my teenage years, and stopped spending weekends with Old Ma. But she'd keep me up-to-date on the Saturday morning tea. I was eighteen when Ted got throat cancer. Not long after, he died. I remember it was in the summer. I drove Old Ma to his funeral and we met his wife for the first time. She knew all about Old Ma and me. She knew that I was headed off to Ohio State. She knew Ted taught me how to tap-dance when I was a little girl. She even had my high school graduation photo," I said, my voice trailing off.

I wasn't sure what Max thought about all of this. I couldn't read his expression, especially in the dark. For quite a while, neither of us spoke. Max was lying back again, looking up at the heavens, deep in his own thoughts, and I was deep in mine. One thought in particular stood out: If it hadn't been for Old Ma and all those Saturdays with Ted, maybe I'd never be at Max's side.

"Ya see the Southern Cross?" he asked.

"Where do I look?"

"Right above ya head."

I knew what I was supposed to be looking for. I knew it was what's on the Australian flag. But I couldn't find it.

"Look fa one real bright small star in the groupin'."

When I still couldn't find it, Max came over to where I was lying. He took my face into his hands and positioned my head in the exact location. His hands were gentle and in no way threatening or untoward. They were hands of a friend I trusted and a friend who trusted me enough to know that his gesture would be accepted for exactly what it was.

"It's straight up 'ere," he said, tilting my chin ever so slightly. "Ya see it?"

"I see it! The small bright star."

"It's held 'ere by a spirit," Max said, taking his hands from my face and sitting beside me. "It shines on the heads of all the people who have been hurt by love."

"That's beautiful." For a spell we both sat silent, looking up at that bright star. I thought of how love had wounded me. "I guess it shines on a lot of heads," I said, quietly.

"Yeah."

I got the feeling Max wanted to say more to me, but when he didn't, I couldn't help but ask, "Max," I said, "are you thinking about Gay right now?"

"Yeah," he said, gathering some kindling together and lighting it. "I was thinkin' 'bout her."

"You said that after she left you, you'd go to that special tree."

"That's right. And at night I'd lay there an' look up at that small

139

bright star an' sing to the spirit holdin' it. The star up there would be lookin' right at me, hearin' everything I needed to say. An' I said a lot. A lot of bad things I sung to that star."

"Like what kind of bad things?"

"Awwwgh, one time I said that I was gonna 'ave a bone pointed at her husband."

"What did the star say in return?"

"It'd tell me that if I had a bone pointed, I'd never again be free to run like the water. Wherever I'd walk, the stones would hurt my feet. The wind would always be in front of me, keepin' me in the same place no matter how fast I try to move."

"And you knew that to be true?"

"Yeah, that's what would've happened."

"When did you finally let it go?"

"When my song changed."

"I don't understand."

"As long as ya sing the same song, ya don't go nowhere."

I thought about that for a moment. "But," I said, "how do you get your song to change if you're stuck?"

"Ya go to ya sacred place an' open up every part of ya-self an' listen to what ya supposed to hear."

"How do you hear it?"

"Ya quiet down ya whole body. The birds sing to ya. The water talks to ya. The stars. The animals. They help ya see who ya are and what ya supposed to be doin' with ya life."

"They take the pain away?"

"The pain don't go nowhere. It stays where it's supposed to stay. Right here," Max said, tapping his heart. "The pain that sit right 'ere is what makes ya heart get bigger. Ya never want the hurt to jus' go away. Hurt is what makes ya love. When ya carry aroun' a lotta old hurt, ya carryin' aroun' a lotta love. Without knowin' hurt, ya no bloody good to anybody. An' ya no good to ya-self."

"So what you're saying is that if you don't fight the hurt, maybe it'll start to work for you?"

"Ya right," Max said. "Ya own it. Ya say, that's what happened to me. I'm keepin' it. Then it'll begin to work for ya—not against ya."

"But how do you get that to happen?"

"Ya listen—to the sound of the earth. And when ya do that, ya listenin' to ya-self," Max said. "Once ya learn how to listen to everythin' 'round ya, ya insides open real wide an' ya connect up. And then ya start walkin' the right path. It's not pain that stops ya livin'. It's bein' scared of pain that stops ya in ya tracks. It's the fear."

Suddenly I knew exactly what Max meant. I was full of fear, and the fear was terrible. Yet the pain of John's death was something I had eventually grown to cherish. I'd gotten in touch with something. The hurt made me feel more human, more alive, more compassionate. But the fear was something that still made me run like a scared chicken.

"Max," I said, after some time had passed, "I have a very close friend back home who's dying of AIDS.

"AIDS?"

"You've heard of AIDS, haven't you?"

"Awwgh, AIDS," Max said with sudden recognition in his voice. "That's that real nasty disease."

"Yes," I said. "It's really horrible. My friend's dying really hurts. But in one of the sessions I had with Dwango, I was told I would be led to someone who could give me information that could help Randy. Do you know who that person could be?"

"I don't know," Max said. "I'll sleep on it."

"You mean, you'll ask the spirits to speak through you as you sleep?"

"Ya right." And moments later Max was snoring full force.

When I woke the following morning, Max was gone. It took me a bit to reorient myself and to remember that it was the day of the corroboree. Max was going to leave at the crack of dawn to get the roo. I wouldn't know if the spirits spoke through Max until much later. As I rolled up my sleeping bag, the incredible events of the night began to replay themselves. For a split second, I actually questioned if I had dreamed the whole cemetery and bad spirit thing. But then I looked down at my knapsack. The matches were lying on top of it. The bottom of my rubber flip-flops were coated with sheep droppings from entering the abandoned house in the dark. Everything was very clear. As strange as it was—it all really happened. And more than the spirits and the trip to the cemetery was the simple understanding I had come to, talking with Max just before we fell asleep.

I had traveled halfway around the world to discover that all the pain, loneliness, anxiety, frustration, sorrow, and disappointment that I had balled up inside, that were gnawing away at my vital organs like a tumor, could be turned around. They could be transformed into something positive if I was willing to own my human feelings and stop trying to escape them. The key to all this was simply listening to everything around me, to the birds, ocean, sky, earth. I was so filled with joy and relief with this new revelation that I immediately sat down and began to write to Reuel. I was in the middle of putting this down on paper when Henry showed up for his third computer lesson.

"Hi, Henry," I greeted him. "Do you want to go over to the house and get the computer?"

"Nawww, I'll wait right 'ere fa ya." He dropped to the ground and sat crossed-legged on the red clay, looking exactly as if he were taking his assigned seat in a classroom.

I returned to find Henry with his eyes closed, moving his fingers along an invisible keyboard. On his last lesson, I taught him how to turn the computer on and off and to bring up Microsoft Word. His file name was Henry.

Without wasting a moment, he flipped open the laptop and brought up his file. "I'm ready fa ya," he said.

"That was fast," I said, surprised.

"I've been goin' over and over all night in my head. I got it all up 'ere now." He tapped his temple.

"So what kind of message do you want to write for the kids' birthday?" I asked, plunking down beside him.

"I wanna say fa 'em to have ya-selves a happy birthday."

"That's it?"

Henry looked at me like I was from another planet. "It's their birthday," he said, hunting for the *H*.

"Of course. That's the perfect message."

When the message was finally completed, I printed it out on my small portable printer. Henry examined the sheet of paper carefully. Then he got up—he was going to ask Roland to draw something on it.

"Who's Roland?"

"Awwgh, Roland's my cousin. He come up from Cobar late last night. Roland's a real good artist. 'E's got himself a Holden truck."

"You mean he just came up for the corroboree?"

"Yeah, everybody will be here," Henry said, still studying the sheet of paper.

"You think Tom will be back?"

"Tom's workin' in the opal fields."

"At Lightning Ridge?"

"Ya," Henry said, "that's where he be."

"You mean, he couldn't get the part for his truck?"

Henry gave an uneasy smile, sort of a cover-up smile, sending up a red flag. Did Tom have a little something going on over at Lightning Ridge? In spite of his sixty-plus years, he did have a rather sexy look about him. So maybe that's why Tom kept the old junker truck.

Shortly after ten o'clock Max returned. Chris and I watched from Katie's porch as Max and Roland lifted the freshly killed roo out of the truck. Within minutes, Max took a long knife and began to skin it. At that point Chris, who had been watching the proceedings, grabbed his basketball and took off down the porch steps, screeching at the top of his lungs. This caused Katie to come rushing out of the house, holding her year-old grandson, Matthew.

"Ya fulla's all right?" Katie asked, brushing flies off Matthew's face. She seemed genuinely concerned that Chris might have hurt himself. She didn't even as much as glance over at the carcass that was lying fifty feet away.

"Oh yeah, Chris has just never seen a roo being skinned before," I said, as if I had.

"Ho!" Max called to Katie and me. "Ya think this will be enough tucker?" He was grinning from ear to ear, very proud of himself.

Katie waved her hand dismissively, as if to say just go about your business and quit your bragging. She turned to me. "Matthew's mudda's workin' at the Aborigine store all day today." She swooped up drool from the baby's mouth and added, "Ya wanna ave ya-self a cuppa?"

"I'd love to."

A generous smile broke across her face, and for a brief moment she looked exactly like Max. "Feel like a johnnycake?"

"Oh, I just had a bowl of oatmeal," I said, following her down the hallway and into the kitchen. In spite of the fact that eleven or more people occupied the house at various times of the day, it was surprisingly clean and tidy and bright. The morning sun pouring through the window above the sink created a glare that gave the room a natural whitewash, masking the chipped paint and rough surfaces. Katie placed Matthew atop the kitchen table and asked me to keep an eye on him.

"Sit ya-self right here," Katie instructed. She brushed a few crumbs away and placed a tin box in front of me. "Real tasty biscuits. My son's wife bring 'em last time they come fa a visit. She's a nurse. Real smart lady."

From where I sat on a cushioned metal chair, I could see into the living room. There was a faded brown sofa in front of a large picture window. Opposite the sofa was a small wooden end-table that displayed an array of framed family photographs. On wall-to-wall carpeting were three sheetless mattresses. Somebody I didn't recognize was sprawled across two of them, snoring. Whoever it was, Katie was annoyed with him.

"I found this when I got up," Katie said, irate. She yanked an empty bottle from a brown paper bag.

I knew my place. And my place was to keep my mouth shut. I gave a blank look, and then I plucked up Matthew who was cruising along the edge of the table. I occupied myself talking to him. "Today's your birthday, big guy. Pretty soon you're going to be walking all by yourself. . . ."

"It's pure metho!" Katie barked at the man zonkered on the mattress.

I said nothing. Katie banged utensils around in the kitchen as she boiled up the water for our coffee. I continued to talk to the baby. "Can you put up one finger . . ."

"His family's goin' without no tucker so he can kill himself on the grog. . . ."

I reminded myself that Katie wasn't talking to me.

"A *white* lady an' her youn' bloke 'ave come to visit an' they gonna see ya crazy with the grog. . . ."

I kept up my baby talk. "You and your cousin Margaret are going to get to blow out all the birthday candles. . . ."

"Stinkin' up my house with that stinkin' grog. . . ."

"You wanna play with my watch?" I took off my Timex and dangled it in front of Matthew's huge brown eyes.

" 'Ere ain't gonna be *no* grog at the party. . . ."

I had no idea where Katie was going with the running tirade. Fortunately for all involved, Max and Roland appeared at the front door just as Katie picked up her broom as if it were a loaded shotgun and started toward the living room.

"Ya got some string?" Max called from the front door.

"Come 'ere, Max!" Katie commanded.

"I don't wanna be trackin' blood," Max called back.

"Max!" Katie hollered.

Max and Roland appeared a moment later. Roland looked to be in his early thirties and definitely a Eulo. Both men had blood splashed down the front of their shirts.

"Look over there," Katie pointed with the broom. "He's drunk on metho!"

"Awwghhhh," Max said, shaking his head in total disgust. He went over to the body crashed on the mattress. "Get up an get yaself a shower and 'ave a feed!"

The disheveled man rolled over and drunkenly opened one unfocused eye. On seeing Max looming above him, he rose, steadied himself, and mumbled, "What's goin' on, Uncle Max?"

"What the bloomin' hell ya bringin' metho in here fa? Go get yaself cleaned up!"

Katie's broom was poised for battle. With the soused nephew

stumbling his way down the hall to the bathroom, Katie loosened up. She put down the broom like she was slipping a gun back into her holster. Then she went over to a canvas centered on the wall over the faded sofa. "Here's one of Roland's paintings," she said, a proud smile beginning to emerge.

"That's lovely," I said, turning to Roland. I knew better than to ask any specific questions about the painting that was done in a swirling design of red, brown, black, and white. All Aboriginal art is supposed to have hidden symbolic meaning, clear only to tribe members.

"Roland's fatha died of the grog," Katie said, pushing Roland's hair back affectionately, revealing a prominent brow and a large, fresh-looking scar above his right eyebrow. "I raised this 'ere boy."

"Boomerang," Roland laughed, pointing to the scar.

Max burst out laughing, too. Apparently an inside joke. But then Roland let me in on it: He said that a white lady came into the store where he worked and seeing the "nasty" cut, asked if a boomerang was the cause—more laughter all around.

"Ya have boomerangs in California?" Roland grinned.

"Oh, I'm not from California," I said. "I'm from Connecticut."

"Ca-net?"

"Co-net-ti-cut."

"Ca-net-eee-cat," he repeated. "Ya have movie stars there?" His brown eyes twinkled with anticipation.

"They're mostly in California," I said, surprised by the question. "But, yes, we do have some."

"Who ya have?"

"Did you ever hear of Paul Newman?"

A look of utter delight flashed across Roland's bright face.

"You know him?" I asked.

"*Butch Cassidy and the Sundance Kid*," he spouted as if he were a contestant on a game show. His expression told me that he had waited a lifetime for just this opportunity.

Roland nodded toward his aunt and uncle for their appreciation. "Who else ya got?"

"Ever hear of Robert Redford?"

Roland slapped his hand down, hitting the *Jeopardy!* button. *"Butch Cassidy and the Sundance Kid."*

"Let's see," I said. "How about someone who's no longer living."

"Gowon," Roland said, lighting a cigarette, defying me to stump him. Katie and Max looked on at our game, pleased and yet somewhat baffled by their nephew's worldliness.

"Did you ever hear of Bette Davis?"

Roland took a drag off his cigarette and said, cool and confident, *"What Ever Happened to Baby Jane?"*

Okay, I was impressed. I snapped my fingers, "Marilyn Monroe?"

Roland snapped his fingers back. *"Some Like It Hot."*

We went at it a little longer, and then I told Roland my *Me and Jezebel* story. I told him how I had actually performed in the play.

"Ya an actress?" Roland said, sitting up and looking at me as if I was Jane Fonda.

"Ohhh, I'm not really an actress."

"This white lady here's an actress." Roland turned to Max and Katie, registering the magnitude of what wasn't true at all.

Oh Jesus, I felt like a pompous ass. "I wouldn't call myself an actress."

"An actress," he said, throwing his head back and letting out a gigantic puff of smoke. It was obvious that he really wanted me to be an actress, and at that moment I really didn't want to disappoint him.

"Okay, for a short time I was an actress."

"Ya goin' do somethin' fa us tonight?" Roland asked.

"Huh?"

"At the corroboree."

"What would I do?"

"Whatever ya wanna do," Roland said.

I didn't know what to say, so I put it back onto him. "What are *you* going to do?"

"He better not throw anymore of 'em boomerangs," Max said, getting into the act.

"You know," I said, "Christopher is dying to learn how to throw one."

"Where's ya fulla?" Roland asked.

"He's with Ian. They're helping Squeaky make a new basketball hoop."

That, for some reason, made Max chuckle.

"I'll go borrow one from Henry," Roland said, "an' show him how ya throw one."

"I hope it doesn't come back," I said, now worried.

"If it doesn't, I didn't teach him right," Roland said, rubbing his scar and laughing some more with Max. Then the two men knocked down the rest of their tea and got up to finish off skinning the roo.

"Ya watch that youn' bloke with a boomerang!" Katie cautioned on their way out the door. I nodded gratefully to her. For a brief moment, Katie's blue eyes fixed on mine. There were no words, but I heard her loud and clear. "Soooo, whites care about their children just like us."

The rest of the morning and early afternoon was taken up with party preparations. And then just after four, Margaret emerged from her house as arrogant as Scarlett O'Hara. She was dressed to kill in a red jumper with large white dots. Her shiny hair was pulled into a pony-tail and decorated with tiny white wildflowers. On her wrist was a plastic bracelet with dangling hearts that Max and I picked out on a trip into Bourke two days earlier. She wore new red rubber flip-flops, and her toenails and fingernails were painted bright red, tying the whole outfit together. Her mother Dorothy was at her side, fuss-ing with the flowers in Margaret's hair while carrying a large covered bowl. The scene was so un-*National Geographic*.

I had the special honor of walking down to Fran's house with Katie, Dorothy, and Margaret. Her father Hal had made a last-minute trip into Bourke to pick up cousins who had come up all the way from Mundadoo. One of them, I was told, played the didgeridoo.

We were halfway down the block when Margaret casually in-quired, "Where's ya fulla?"

"The last I saw Chris he and Ian were trading basketball cards. They'll be along shortly."

Margaret shrugged her shoulders in a devil-may-care way. She turned her attention to the wrapped gifts I was carrying on top of a bowl of beans that Matthew's mother had made.

"I bet I can guess what ya got fa me," she said.

"You can guess, but I'm not telling."

She felt the flat, soft package. "A sarong?"

"Nope."

"It's somethin' to wear."

"Could be."

"A jumper?"

"Give up, Margaret," I said. She would just have to wait for the bright gold Banana Republic sweatshirt that fortunately I had never worn. In fact, it still had the tags on. I scratched out the price but left the tag on to prove that it was new and purchased in the United States.

"I know what ya 'ave fa Mitchell," Margaret teased, flashing bright white teeth.

"You do?"

"A toy boat," she said. "Ya wind it up an' it races 'round ya bathtub making a whistlin'."

"Hey, who told you?"

"It was at the Aborigine store in the mornin', an' then afta ya left, it was gone. An' I went up—"

"Yeah, I guess Ol' Tom's back at the opal field over Lightning Ridge way," Dorothy cut in on her detective daughter. She fixed her eyes straight ahead.

"That's what Henry told me," I said, wondering if Dorothy knew anything more.

"Not the first time he be gone fa a corroboree." There was heavy judgment in her tone.

I played dumb. "I guess parts for his truck are hard to come by all the way up there."

Hearing that, she twisted her mouth and threw me a glance sideways. It was the universal expression for "We'll talk."

Fran's house was distinguished from all the others by a freshly painted bright blue front door and a lawn dominated by several orange trees plucked free of oranges.

"All the ripe oranges are in the punch," Margaret reported. "I helped squeeze 'em."

"You're truly amazing, Margaret," I said. "You had time to make punch, braid my hair, do my makeup, and still look fabulous yourself."

Margaret tossed off the compliment and led me along the side of the house to the festive-looking backyard. Picnic tables had been set up and a large pit dug for the campfire. Balloons donated by Chris and me decorated a dozen or so aluminum fold-up chairs. As I set the gifts down, I recognized the old lady whom Chris and I had seen that first evening we had pulled into the village. Fran came over and introduced her as Ama, Max and Katie's aunt. I tried to say hello but she refused eye contact, which was fine with me. In the few seconds that I was standing before her, she hollered at Fran for not having her arthritis remedy and when Fran said that she had it in the house, the ornery old lady shook her fist at several of the kids who were grabbing snacks off the table. As I backed away from her, I suddenly recalled my great-aunt Rosa, another crotchety old battle-ax. Whenever we'd visit, she'd grumble and threaten my brother and me with the same kind of body language. "You kids no-a play inna da St. Francis bird-a-bath—you unnerstanna! Seconds later Gary and I would race each other outside and climb all over St. Francis's head and arms and splash water on each other until we were soaked—or until Aunt Rosa came hobbling toward us, gargantuan bosoms undulating beneath her black mourning dress. "You-a-kids-no-a-good! You-a need a good-a beatin'!" Gary and I would brazenly shake our fists back. "Pasta fa-zool!" My father would have to intervene and order us into the back of our 1955 Buick, where we'd remain until Aunt Rosa cooled off—which usually took a few belts of my grandfather's dago red.

While Margaret circulated, greeting everybody who arrived, I helped Fran arrange the salads and damper on the table. Our conversation was so familiar that I had to keep reminding myself that I was with Aborigines deep in the Outback and not with my family at a Cleveland Heights picnic.

"Yeah, this here bean salad will go real fast," Fran said, pushing it slightly behind the yam salad.

"I stole a taste when I carried it over," I said.

Fran tried some herself. "It's real good, ain't it?"

"Fantastic."

"Ya had Katie's johnnycakes yet?" Fran asked, tearing off a piece and passing it to me.

"Twice. She's going to give me her recipe."

"She don't cook them long enough," Fran whispered, looking around for Katie. "I'll make ya some of mine."

"I'd like that," I said, undercovering a plastic bowl of objects that looked like blackened Chee•tos. "Hey Fran, what are all these things?"

"Awwgh, them's witchetty grub. Have ya-self one."

Oh Jesus, this was the part of the picnic I dreaded.

"Real tasty they are," she coaxed me on.

My fingers moved agonizingly slow toward the charred delicacy, but before they made contact, I eased them back. "Ohh, I'd better save my appetite."

Fran's eyes at half-mast told me that she didn't buy my excuse at all, but she didn't press the issue either.

"So ya been takin' the medicine Tom made fa ya?" she asked, graciously changing the subject.

"Twice a day."

"Ya feel better?"

"No more watery, scratchy eyes," I answered truthfully. In fact, I would definitely have to take some of that concoction back home for our pollen-infested Connecticut summers. "How long do you think it'll last?"

"When Tom gets his-self back, he'll make some more fa ya."

"Great," I said, though I had my doubts when that was going to be.

"Yeah, the part fa the truck is comin' up from Dubbo way any day now. Couldn't get the part nowhere's else."

I thought, Doesn't she know what everybody knows? That he was back working in the opal fields?

"He's not happy 'bout missin' this 'ere corroboree," Fran said, shaking her head in sympathy for her poor, exhausted, stranded husband.

I guess she didn't know. Then again, maybe there wasn't anything to know. Maybe it was my own suspicious mind that had him shacked up somewhere with another woman. Whatever the case, the intrigue was fascinating. But it was nowhere near as fascinating as the next thing that was to happen.

# NINE

About an hour into the corroboree and with Chris still nowhere to be seen, I headed toward Katie's house to find out what he and Ian were up to. I had gotten halfway there when a woman—somewhat ample, in a blue-and-yellow flowered dress—drew near with two small children. I said hi. She said hi back. And then she asked where the corroboree was. I told her that it was at Fran's, and I pointed down the road to the corner house with the blue door. She didn't seem to be in any great hurry to get there and looked around as if she was sizing up the village. I didn't want to walk away rudely, so I, too, looked around at the various houses, and then I smiled at the children who were staring at me as if they had seen a ghost. I didn't think it would be appropriate to introduce myself. The woman may have felt pressured to introduce herself back, and according to Aborigine protocol you don't ask personal questions. After a few moments of neither of us speaking, I said that I was on my way down the road to look for my son. It would only take a few minutes to find him. If she wanted, she could wait and then we could walk over to Fran's house together. She widened her eyes and smiled, half shy, half warm, transforming what I originally took to be a rather ordinary face into one that was quite lovely. Her eyes were deep blue, so deep that they almost passed for brown. She had prominent cheekbones separated by a full nose that gave her an exotic, somewhat Tahitian look that was unlike any other face in the village. I couldn't determine her age, but I felt she was probably in her middle years.

I found Christopher and Ian at Katie's kitchen table in a shouting match over something to do with a basketball card. "Margaret is wondering where you guys are," I said, very motherlike. Ian looked up and said in perfect Chris Fuller, "Who gives!"

"*I* give!" I snapped back at the baby-faced twelve-year-old wearing Chris's Orlando Magic baseball cap. "You guys have five minutes to put the basketball cards away and get over to Katie's. Now hustle!" I waited until they took off and then I rushed back to where the woman and the two children were still standing, and together we walked to the corroboree.

I was relieved to see Chris, Ian, and Margaret gathered around the snack table, but my relief was short-lived. Margaret proceeded to get after the boys for showing up late and then having the nerve to hog all the potato chips.

"Take a hike!" Chris said to the ponytailed brunette. "My mom bought these chips."

"Take ya-self a long hike, Margey, farkey!" Ian added.

Infuriated at the treatment she was receiving at the corroboree in *her* honor, Margaret bellowed, "Ya fullas are low as shark shit!" With that, she pivoted on her new red flip-flops and stormed off for solace to her Uncle Max, who was at the roasting pit with a half-dozen other men. From my vantage point, it looked like she had found a sympathetic ear.

I found an empty chair and offered it to my new friend. Then I brought her and the children punch and a dish with witchetty grub, pretzels, and some kind of roasted nut that looked like almonds but smelled like gasoline. As I passed the tin plate to her, I thought how unlikely this scene was. Me in the role of host for an Aborigine woman I had just met. Several times I started to walk away, but her eyes told me that she didn't want to be left alone. In fact, it appeared that she didn't even want to be seen. The children were sitting on her lap, one on each knee, blinding her view of everyone and everyone's view of her.

"Your children are beautiful," I said, squatting beside her kids.

"My daughter's children," she said, gently stroking each child's head in turn.

"Where do you live?"

"Cunnamulla," she responded.

"Cunnamulla," I repeated, trying to remember why that place sounded so familiar. "Could we have passed your town on the way up here from Sydney?"

"No, it's about a hundred an' twenty kilometers north of 'ere. Up on Warrego River." She looked at me curiously. "Ya know it?"

"Rings a bell."

"Maybe ya heard 'bout the *yapunyah* tree in our town center?"

I shook my head, no.

We sat for a moment not speaking. Then she asked, "Maybe ya heard of Robber's Tree?"

"Not really." I was tempted to lie to make things easier.

"Big sheep station 'ere."

Hearing sheep station, I connected everything. "Ohhh, Cunnamulla!" I told her how one of the guy's at Sylvia's café told Chris and me that our new bush hats looked like Cunnamulla cartwheels on our heads.

"Cunnamulla cartwheels on ya heads?" she laughed, revealing an overbite that was not unattractive.

"Do you know what they meant by that?"

She shook her head. "No, but every August we have the Cunnamulla-Eulo Opal Festival, a big parade an' fancy ball, and maybe—"

"Did you say Eulo?"

"Yeah."

"That's Max's name, and that's where his people are from origi-nally," I said.

An uncomfortable look flashed across her face. I didn't want to pry, so I changed the subject. "Doesn't little Margaret over there look just adorable?"

"Margaret?" she asked, crunching down on a witchetty grub.

The plot was thickening. "The girl with the ponytail and flowers in her hair," I said, catching Margaret's eye. "Margaret," I called out, "come here a minute. I want you to meet somebody."

Margaret skipped over with baby Mitchell bouncing on her slim hip. "I know who ya are," Margaret said, saucy.

The woman jolted her head back and opened her eyes as if saying, How do you know who I am?

"An' I know why ya come 'ere," Margaret went on, *very* saucy now.

The woman dropped her lids, as if dreading Margaret's next words.

I jumped to the woman's rescue. "The corroboree," I said, "is for both Margaret and baby Mitchell."

"Ahhh." The woman nodded.

"Ya come all the way down 'ere from Cunnamulla way?" Margaret asked.

The woman did not appear to be enamored of Margaret's all-knowingness.

"The youngins have to go to the toilet," the woman replied, scooting the children off her lap.

"I'll take yuz there," Margaret offered. She plopped cousin Mitchell down on the red earth so fast he almost bounced back up.

"Oh, that's okay, Margaret," I said, picking up startled Mitchell. "I'll take them. You take the baby."

The woman looked relieved when Margaret skipped off with Mitchell back on her hip. I took them into the house and then I went back outside and cornered the birthday girl.

"Margaret," I said, "who's that woman I introduced you to?"

"What woman?"

"The woman who just went into the house to use the toilet."

Margaret twisted her forefinger coyly around her ponytail.

"Tell me, Margaret," I demanded.

"I'm supposed to keep my mouth shut."

"Says who?"

"My aunts."

"Why?"

Margaret looked around and then she stood on her tiptoes and whispered in my ear, "That woman's Uncle Max's old girlfriend."

"What did you say?" I couldn't have heard correctly.

She mustered up all the sassiness of a girl turning twelve and said, "I jus' said that woman's Uncle Max's old girlfriend."

"Gay?"

"Her name's Thaalangay," Margaret corrected me.

I wasn't so sure I should believe her. Margaret, I knew, could weave some big ones. "Is that the truth?"

Margaret raised her hand as if to swear on a stack of Bibles. "Fair dinkum," she said, her red fingernails flashing before my eyes. I didn't believe Margaret's "fair dinkum," but I did believe it was Gay.

I looked over toward the pit. Max was poking the roo with a long forked stick. He seemed so cool and controlled—so into his roo. Was that just a macho cover? What was going on? Did *he* invite her? Why didn't Gay seem to know anybody at the party? And if she did know folks, why wasn't she talking to them? Or why didn't anybody come over? And why wasn't she talking to Max? How did she even get here? I couldn't stand the suspense, and so when the mysterious woman and her grandchildren came back outside, I situated them at a chair beside crabby old Ama—it was the only vacant chair around, no surprise.

"I'll be back in five minutes," I said, holding up five fingers.

"Five minutes?" she confirmed, also holding up five fingers.

"Not even," I said.

I darted over to the roo pit where now more than a dozen men had congregated and were engaged in some pretty animated cigarette smoking. "Max"—I motioned—"I need to talk to you."

Max passed the forked stick that he was using to test the roo to Roland. "Watch her close," Max instructed his nephew.

On seeing me, Roland took the forked stick and held it like a gun. "*True Grit*," he growled.

"John Wayne," I growled back to a great outburst of laughter from the men.

Max and I walked around to the front of the house where we were alone. "Gay's here," I said, practically breathless.

"Yeah, I know that."

"Who invited her?"

"I did."

"You did!" It took several seconds to register the meaning of it. "Max, why didn't you tell me?"

"I'm tellin' ya right now," he said, too casual for words.

"Aren't you going to go over and talk to her? She's all alone. Everybody's ignoring her."

"Ya not ignorin' her."

The logic was flying right over my head.

"Ya given' her an' the kids somethin' to drink?"

"Of course."

Max tossed out a hand as if to say, So what's the problem?

"Max, when was the last time you saw Gay?"

"Eighteen years," he said without hesitation.

"Why now?"

Max had a sudden thousand-mile stare.

"Max," I pressed, "why now?"

"Ya remember last evening we was lookin' up at the bright star?"

"I remember."

"I told ya how I used to sing to the spirit holdin' that star after Gay married another fulla?"

"Yes."

"An' ya remember how ya told me that ya friend had some real bad disease?"

"AIDS," I said. "And I told you that Dwango was going to lead me to someone with information that could help Randy. I asked you if you knew who that person could be."

"Ya right. An' I said that I'd sleep on it."

"Did you sleep on it?"

"Yeah, I slept on it awright."

"And?"

"The spirit said that I should be talkin' to Thaalangay."

"To help Randy?"

"To help myself," Max said. "So I got up this mornin', rolled up me night swagger an' went out to get the roo. But before I did that, I dropped myself in at the Oasis Pub. Had a cuppa with the owner, Annie. My eye caught the telephone. It was lookin' right at me. I had me another cuppa an' a piece of cheese toast. While I'm feedin', I start thinkin' about how I wanna tell Thaalangay about my white lady friend an' her youn' bloke. I wanna tell her how ya come into our Aborigine village an' ya don't have ya nose all up in the air. Ya treat us real good. My people are not scared of ya. Ya don't look like us, but ya one of us. Thinkin' about ya, I pick up the phone an' call aroun' till I found 'er."

"But what about Gay's husband?"

"Dead fifteen years. I told her that we was havin' this here big corroboree an' I asked her if she wanted to come on down from Cunnamulla an' be part of it. She says that she din't think anybody would wanna be seein' her. I say that my white lady friend from America was gonna be real happy to see her and ya was gonna be real nice."

"So because of *me*, Gay is here?"

" 'Cause of the spirit," Max set the record straight. "They the ones that sent ya to my village an' send Gay 'ere."

"Max," I blurted out, "why am I here?"

"Ya not happy 'ere?" Max said with a disturbed look on his face.

"I *love* being here." I meant it.

"Well, that's why ya 'ere," he said, walking back to the roo pit.

"Wait a minute. When are you going to go over and talk to Gay?"

"Go over?"

"That's right. She's waiting for you to say hello."

He took off his bush hat, ran his fingers through a thick head of gray wavy hair. "How do ya know that?"

"I'm a woman, Max. Women always know what other women are thinking when it comes to men."

He mulled that one over. "Whaddya think she's thinkin' 'bout me?"

Underneath the cowboy getup, Max was like every other guy I ever met. "She's probably thinking that you're a real nice guy."

"Yeah?" He grinned. I thought I could see pink tonsils. "Ya think she thinks I'm an awright bloke?"

"Oh brother," I said, "I feel like I'm back in high school."

"Ya went to high school?"

"Max," I said, "stop trying to change the subject. You're scared to go over to her. Aren't you?"

"Yeah, I'm scared awright."

"I'll walk over with you."

Max started to walk with me, but then stopped cold in his tracks. "Last time I saw her wasn't good."

"Why's that?"

"Grog had me."

"Well, you're not on the grog now."

"Tell her when the roo's done cookin', I'll be over," Max said, heading back to the pit.

"You want *me* to be the go-between?"

"Go-between?"

"Never mind."

I walked back to the picnic table. Gay was no longer sitting beside the old lady. She had moved to a bench about twenty feet away. She was listening to Max's great-nephew, Greg, playing the didgeridoo. When she saw me, she scooted over. "Come," she said, patting the seat beside her.

As I joined her, she reached into a plastic shopping bag by her feet and took out a pack of cigarettes. "Smoke?"

"Oh thanks, but I don't smoke"

She continued to hold one out for me with such eagerness that I had a change of heart. "Why not," I said, helping myself to the mentholated cigarette.

"How long ya gonna be here in Enngonia?"

"I'm not sure," I said, sucking in the first drag of a cigarette I had had in years.

She blew out the match. "Maybe ya can come up to Cunnamulla?"

"I'd like that," I said, coughing.

For a while we sat silent, puffing away on our cigarettes and clearly enjoying each other's strange new company. "Ya married?" she asked.

"A year and a half now. My husband came to visit for five weeks. But now he's back in America."

"Ya only married a year an' half?" she said, surprised.

"My first husband, my son's father, died four years ago. I'm now married for the second time."

"Awwgh, my first husband dead fifteen years."

"I'm sorry."

She took a long satisfying drag. "He was old," she said, telling the whole story in those three words.

"Ohh."

"He was real old."

"Ummm," I said, groping for neutral chitchat.

"America's fa away." Apparently neutrality was on her mind, too.

"Fifteen thousand miles away."

"Whewwwwwww, farthest I've ever been is the Alice."

"Alice Springs?"

"Yeah." She nodded. "Ya feel homesick?"

"I don't feel homesick, but I miss my husband a lot. And I miss talking to my mother on the phone."

She gave a double take. "Ya got a telephone where ya live?"

"Yes," I said. I hoped that I didn't sound boastful.

"Me too," she said, finding another thing in common. She crushed out her cigarette with the toe of her orange flats. "Max rang me up this mornin' on the telephone. Told me 'bout ya."

I feigned surprise. "Told you about *me*?"

She turned away. "He says yuz a real good white lady."

Not to appear brazen, I, too, turned away. "Max told me that you're pretty terrific yourself," I said.

Slowly she turned back to me. A faint smile came over her well-proportioned face. "I know him a long, long time," she replied, almost making eye contact.

I didn't dare let on that I knew about their past. "Oh yeah?"

"I know him before he ever joined up with that boxin' troupe."

This was news! "Did you say Max was in a boxing troupe?"

"He din't tell ya about all that?"

That explained the deeply scarred nose and missing front teeth. "No, he never mentioned a word."

"Only heard about it secondhand myself," Gay said. She smoothed her blue-black hair that was pulled tightly at the nape of her neck and fastened with a hand-painted clip. "Word around town was that he was an awright boxer," she said.

"I'll have to get him to tell me about it." I wondered if she dyed her hair.

"Ya can tell him that I'd like to be hearin' about it, too." Gay smiled, just as Max called out that the roo was done.

So that evening I had my first roo meal. I came close to taking a pass, but Max slapped a thick slice on my plate and insisted that I try it in front of him. Of course, he was looking for praise, and praise he got. It was quite delicious. It looked like beef, but tasted more like lamb. I put some on Chris's plate and told him it was beef and he went back for seconds.

After the roo was plucked clean of meat, we gathered around the campfire and Max regaled us with a "yarn" about his boxing days. Although he was talking to all of us, he was speaking to only one.

"It was my first fight fa Roy Bell," Max said, cross-legged on the red earth, sitting directly opposite Gay and me. "I was a youn' fulla. About twenty. I was a stockman. But it was dry time. An' we were back at Enngonia makin' a few bob skinnin' roos. Wasn't much other work about." He took a glance at Gay, whom he still hadn't spoken a word to.

"I remember Roy Bell drivin' into town," Max went on, pretending that he was at the wheel. "He was comin' down Queensland way. In a big white truck with bright painted pictures all over it—of fighters in bright-colored shorts. They was all shapin' up ready to fight. There was Aborigine fullas and white fullas. Roy Bell pulled up just across the dusty road. We all stopped an' stared. It was the first time we'd ever seen a boxin' troupe come through. He had all the fighters in the big covered truck with him. A little Holden fa his missus, an' four or five other cars followin', with a tucker wagon to feed everyone.

"Roy Bell was a tall, tough-lookin' bloke." Max leaped to his feet and threw out his chest as he assumed the part of Roy Bell. "Roy walked over to us fullas." He took giant steps around the campfire. "I could see his hair was gray. He had a mean fighter's face." Max scrunched up his face and mugged, making us all laugh. But as all good storytellers, Max didn't laugh at his own story. He was as serious and as animated as I had ever seen him.

"Roy Bell had a flattened nose an' cauliflower ears." Max took the

162

palm of his hand and pushed in his nose and wiggled his ears, causing the kids to scream with laughter. "It was Friday mornin'. So he seen this big mob of us 'ere skinnin' roos. We was puttin' the roo meat into plastic bags. Some fullas was skinnin'. Some was bonin'. There was about ten of us, bruddas an' cousins. We was workin' fa a roo shooter, Ron Marr. He used to pay us fa skinnin' the roos his blokes shot the night before. There'd be a few hundred roos at a time fa us to skin. Afta we skinned 'em, we'd pass the bones on an' another fulla bone 'em."

"Gross!" Chris screeched, which caused Margaret to bop him on the head for his impertinence.

"But this one mornin', Roy come over an' said, 'Anyone like to be travelin' around with me an' do a bit of boxin'?'"

"Straightaway I threw my knife down." Max demonstrated with his arm. "I said, real quick, 'Look here, I'll go with ya!'

"All the other fullas was thinkin' about it. But I thought right away, It'll be real good. I needed to be gettin' far out of town," Max said, dropping his gravel voice and shifting for another quick but penetrating glance at Gay. He took a sip of punch, keeping us in suspense and then went on, "I used to do a bit of knuckle fightin' an' that, an' I knew I was awright. I could see Roy Bell had a lot of other Aborigine fullas with him. So I would be joinin' up with them, and they'd be me mates if we had a bit of a jam in the street."

"What's a jam in the street?" Chris asked Max.

Margaret answered. "Sometimes white fullas can give black fullas a hard time," she volunteered, giving Chris another token bop on the head. This time for the stupid question.

"So I grabbed me a couple a blankets an' put on a clean shirt an' trousers. I didn't worry 'bout packin' up anythin' else. I was that excited. I knew that I'd get paid along the way. I didn't even care what he was payin'. I was just real happy to be joinin' a boxin' troupe. I thought my life could take a good turn. I'd been through a lot of sufferin'." Max's voice dropped, and he avoided Gay's eyes. "But I knew that sometimes when ya sufferin' ya can be at ya best."

My turn to steal a side glance at Gay. She was biting her lower lip.

"About an hour later, we was pullin' onto the Mitchell Highway on the way to Bourke. All my cousins an' bruddas was waving."

At this point, all the men around the campfire began to wave, perfectly choreographed. I gathered that Max's story had been performed a few times before.

"I was already shakin' hands with the fighters in the truck, an startin' to get to know them right away. Some was from Sydney. Other ones from Narrabri, Moree, Coonamble. Some of them looked like they'd done a lot of boxin', 'cause they had knocked-around noses, an' no front teeth. Like I got now," Max said, showing his battle scars. Then he wiped beads of sweat from his forehead with the back of his hand and looked over at Gay, checking to see her reaction to these revelations. Gay's face was animated with interest, but she didn't seem to have any other reaction.

"Two days later we pulled into Condobolin," Max picked up the story. "We stood up on a platform over the entrance of our boxin' tent. I had red boxin' trunks an' I had to play a big drum." Squeaky made a drum sound, which started all the kids thumping.

"The platform was all painted up with all the ol'-time top fighters: Les Darcy, Jimmy Cutherers, an' the Aborigine boxers, the Sand bruddas. Roy had trained them all. One other little Aborigine fulla was ringin' the bell." Squeaky led the kids with "*ding-ding-ding*."

"I was banging the drum," Max went on, "an' Roy was spruckin'. . . ."

"What's spruckin'?" Chris interrupted.

Before Margaret had a chance to bop Chris on the head yet again, Katie leaned over and whispered, "Spruckin' means callin' the crowd." She patted his back.

"Roy was a good sprucker awright. He'd pull a big mob away from some other side tent—Tex Morton, or some other sideshow. 'Roll up, roll up, anyone want to fight?' he'd spruck. 'Anyone that can go three rounds with me blokes will get twenty pound!'

"That was a lot of money in them days. An' Roy would be doin' his act on the platform an' really draw the crowd. Blokes would start swarming in the door to get tickets. I was gettin' real excited seein' all 'em blokes crowd around—an' a bit nervous, too." Max began to wring his hands theatrically. "Then one fulla put his hand up an' said, 'I'll fight the little black fulla playin' the drum!' An' Roy says, 'Why you call him black fulla? I call him Snow White!'

"That was the first time I'd heard the name. I laugh about it now. But I didn't like it then. I knew I was real black. An' it was makin' a bit of a joke on me. But the name stuck. I got used to it after we'd been to a few towns—even me best mates started to call me Snow White an' I let 'em get away with it. . . ."

Gay said quietly to me, "I heard he had that nickname."

"The big tent was packed out that day in Condobolin. There was a few of the other boys on before me; then I heard me name called out fa the next fight. I was thinkin', This is a lively lookin' little bloke that's got me. An' I thought I'm going to be in fa a real hidin'."

"Hey, Snow White, ya could 'ave seen yer last gum tree," Squeaky called out, and we all laughed.

"Ya right," Max chuckled. He adjusted his bush hat and went on, "But Roy'd been coachin' us as we went along the road. He'd taught us how to straight right, a short jab, left rip, an' how to get in close an' block." He gave a lively demonstration of each move. "So, when I got in the ring with this local bloke, I went three quick rounds." Now he performed a boxer's dance while he punched his invisible opponent into oblivion. "Then I knocked 'em down fa ten." Max let go with a powerful left hook that finished the poor bloke off and punctuated the drama.

"Roy Bell held up my arm." Henry leapt up from beside me and lifted Max's arm high into the cool night air.

"I'd won the fight! It was the first fight I had with gloves on, an' my first fight in front of a big crowd. I felt real good. I was a winner!" Max cried.

What delivery! I thought. I turned to see Gay's reaction. I wasn't sure, but her eyes might have welled with tears.

"Yeah," Max said, looking straight at Gay now, "that was a long time ago."

"Cool story," Chris piped up. "Would you ever fight again?"

"Too old fa that now."

"Not a cushie job," Henry added.

"Mike Tyson makes ten million for *one* fight!" Chris said.

"I don't care about makin' a lot of money," Max said, facing Gay directly. "I got other more important things to do."

Gay looked away. I could feel the tension in the air, but my sensitivity to the moment was shattered when Roland called out, "Liza, it's ya turn to do something!"

"My turn?" I said, both surprised and amused by my new theatrical name.

"Sing!" Henry chimed in.

"I can't sing," I said. "Henry, *you* do something."

That was all the encouragement Henry needed. Without a moment's lag, he pulled a folded sheet from his back pocket and stood up. He looked into his rapt audience and read, "Dear Margaret and Mitchell, Have yourselves a real happy birthday." He looked up from the sheet of manuscript paper, gestured toward me, and said, "I wrote this 'ere on our good white lady friend's IBM ThinkPad. An' Roland drew this 'ere picture." Henry then held up a drawing of small animals done in an earth-toned design that seemed typical of Aborigine art.

"That's real nice work, fullas," Katie said. She turned to me and nodded her appreciation. And then Margaret marched right up and accepted the sheet of paper. She was wearing the gold Banana Republic sweatshirt, which hung down literally to her knees.

Out of nowhere Squeaky appeared at Henry's side. He had a guitar strapped over his shoulder. And together, like Simon and Garfunkel, they burst into song. It was about a turtle quarreling with a fish. Angry, the fish heaves a flat rock at the turtle. The rock sticks to the turtle's back, and that's how the turtle got its shell. While they sang this to a tune that sounded ever so slightly like "Puff the Magic Dragon," a dozen or more kids acted out the words. From tots to teens, they crawled on the ground, hurled invisible objects into the night air, leapt, strutted—even Chris got into the act. When the song was over, the kids scampered back to the campfire and waited anxiously for the next performance to begin.

Roland had no intention of letting me off the hook. "Liza's turn! Liza's turn!" he cheered. Everyone joined in the chorus.

Just the thought of standing before my new friends and risking making a complete ass of myself was not something I cared to do. I stood up, threw out my hands like an umpire, and said determinedly, "No-way!"

Startled, hurt faces looked back. "Let her be," I heard Max say. "She don't need to be takin' part in this here corroboree."

Hearing that, I felt awful, but not awful enough to change my mind. I plopped back down onto the ground. The earth seemed harder—the night air cooler—the sky blacker, the stars dimmer. I wrapped my arms around my body, tucking myself into a cocoon not so much for warmth, but for escape. While Henry and Squeaky began to sing a ballad with Aborigne words, I sat staring into the blazing fire, huddled into myself like an isolated island.

The next thing that happened was Max came over. He sat between Gay and me. He took her hand in one and mine in the other and then together Gay and Max began to sing along with Henry and Squeaky. And as they did, I became aware of a subtle tingling that started in my head, ran down my neck and shoulders, into my arms and hands, and finally on down through my legs and into my toes. Thinking that one of my legs had fallen asleep, I changed sitting positions. But nothing had fallen asleep. It was quite the opposite.

Every part of me was just waking up. I could feel in Max's gentle touch the strength of life. I could hear in the pure voices of my Aborigine friends a resonance of perfect harmony. I could feel in myself a surge of energy and an indescribable connection to the earth. I found myself unfolding to the fullness of life as a flower to the sun. As the voices of song continued to ring out, my soul seemed effortlessly and gracefully to extend across a vast ocean, bridging me in my isolation to the tranquil, sweet warmth of new friends near me.

When the song was over, Max released my hand. And as he did, tears streamed down my cheeks. I wanted the song to go on forever, and I told this to him.

"You'll be right," Max whispered.

"What happened to me?"

"We sang the song into ya heart."

I sat there and cried through the warmth and exhilaration and clarity. I felt a fearlessness and trust. I looked around at the faces looking back at me and at once surrendered myself to my friends. Only minutes earlier I had been so afraid of being vulnerable. And now I had the vision to see that when you're the most vulnerable you're sharing the most—you're loving the most. How different everybody now looked from the time Chris and I first pulled into the village. How different my own son looked. How spontaneous he was. How uncomplicated and real he was. Why hadn't I seen that before? How could I have spent so much time looking for what he wasn't? How fortunate I was to be here, surrounded by people so real that for the first time in my life, I felt so real, so uncomplicated, so nonjudgmental, so unafraid of failure.

All those feelings poured into me such a sense of pure fun that I jumped to my feet and announced, "Okay, you guys, I'm going to do a skit from my show in New York."

"Go, Liza!" Roland yelled.

"Awright," Max added, still clutching Gay's hand. "We're waitin'."

I heard Max whisper to Gay that I was an actress. I didn't correct him. I looked out into the eager group and gave a somewhat lengthy explanation that I would be doing an imitation of a famous actress, Bette Davis, portraying the character Mildred, in a famous movie, *Of Human Bondage*. I went on to explain that when Bette Davis had stayed in my house, I had performed this skit for her and she wasn't at all amused by my very poor acting. In the skit, Mildred was giving a man, who was deeply in love with her, a royal tongue-lashing. Once I was sure—well, sort of sure—that they knew this was supposed to be amusing, because it would be very, very overacted, I took a deep breath and gave the performance of my lifetime.

"You cad!" I spat out to the still audience. "You dirt-ty swine! I never cared for you, not once. Ya bored me stiff! I only kissed ya, 'cause ya begged me! Ya hounded me! Ya drove me crazy!" I was enunciating like crazy, clutching my head and shaking it in a violent manner as if I were truly out of my mind. Surprised that nobody laughed at my bad acting, I became even more hyper. "And every time ya kissed me, I would wipe my mouth!" I took the back of my hand and made a gigantic pass across my mouth, fingers fully extended, in an attempt to elicit a chuckle or two from the tough house. "Wipe my mouth!" I repeated to the perfectly confused faces. I took another deep breath and bulled ahead: "But I got even with ya. I laughed at ya. Ha! Ha! Ha!" I gave three big fake laughs that never failed to get a few yuks in New York. But here in the Outback, nothing. You could hear a pin drop. I wrapped up the skit drawing on all the twitchy drama of Bette Davis herself: "You were a mug! A mug! A mug!" And then I took a little bow.

"That's it?" Henry asked.

"Pretty much," I said, thinking that nobody back home would ever believe what I had just done.

"What did the bloke say back at her?" Squeaky wanted to know.

"Was she on the grog?" Fran called.

I was shocked at how they were getting so deeply into this whole thing. I worried that they had misunderstood. This was not some sacred story with a deep, profound meaning. This was supposed to be funny.

"I think Leslie Howard felt real hurt. He really loved Mildred. And Mildred never really loved him back. But it was just a movie," I stressed.

"Did they ever get themselves straight?" Max asked, shaking his head in sympathy for the unrequited love.

"How do you mean?"

"They ever get themselves back together?" Squeaky asked.

"Ohhh," I said, looking over at Max and Gay, who were looking at me eagerly awaiting the end of the story—as if the movie's outcome would have some bearing on their own outcome.

I didn't want to put a downer on the evening by telling them that Leslie Howard came to his senses and dumped her, and a short time later Mildred ended up dying alone and miserable, so I threw up my hands, shrugged my shoulders, and said, "You know, I really can't remember how the movie ends."

"I think I saw that movie an' they got themselves married," Roland said, putting a happy ending on the corroboree.

# TEN

*D*uring the following two weeks, while Max and Gay rekindled their love, I found myself spending more and more time with Chris. For the first time in years, we were not at each other's throats, ready to pounce for the least thing said or inferred. With my new clearer vision, I was able to see that what my son needed to grow into a man was my stepping back and allowing him to discover his path, knowing that it need not lead to my destination. Letting go was something all very new to me. And in letting go, Chris and I began to live our separate lives together, which was much different from what we had previously been doing—living our *inseparate* lives apart.

With this new awareness, I felt as if I had taken a hundred-pound knapsack off my back. I had released myself from the burden of carrying around my heavy will. I became free to explore. I began to alter my perception not only of myself but of the world around me. When that happened, I began to concentrate on the moment. I stopped allowing myself to regret the past because regrets would distract me from living in the present. And the more I lived in the present, the less I thought of the past—about John's death, the shock of learning Randy had AIDS, and all the things I wished that I had done or said. Living in the present created its own healing energy. I felt it. And Chris felt it.

"Mom," Chris said to me one afternoon down at the watering hole, "it's pretty cool that you met Reuel."

"Why do you say that?" I asked.

"Because you're so happy now." He took a drink of water out of cupped hands, "You're over Dad dying."

"I've got him right here in my heart," I said, tapping my chest. "Dad's memory is allowing me to live more fully right now. You know what I mean, honey?"

Chris scrunched up his still-chubby cheeks. "I think so," he said. He seemed to be in deep thought. "Mom, it's like a few months after Dad died you took me to Disney World. Remember how we laughed so much on all the rides. I think it was because we were so happy that we weren't crying anymore. I think I never laughed so much in my life."

"That's exactly what I mean."

I stretched out on top of a blanket of delicate purple and yellow wildflowers that had miraculously sprung up out of the dry, parched earth in the past few days. I lay back breathing in a sweet vanilla fragrance, cherishing my son's feelings that ran as deep as the watering hole and his spirit that bubbled as effervescent as the spring. How appropriate, I thought, that we were talking about all of this beside this sacred watering spot.

"I feel like we're in paradise," I said to Chris.

"Or Gilligan's Island," Chris said as he dove into the blue water, sending up a gentle mist that sprayed the wildflowers and me. He surfaced a moment later with large gray-green eyes peeking through a mop of wet sandy blond hair. "I'm going to be a professional golfer when I grow up," he declared.

"That's your dream?"

In one swift move, Chris hopped out of the water and onto a sandy ledge. "Dad said that if I dedicate myself to that goal, it could happen."

And as Chris spoke words, I heard in my head as clear as a bell: What you say at the moment, affects the future's outcome.

"Yes," I said, "I believe Dad's absolutely right. Live that dream."

Chris beamed. "Mom, what was your dream when you were my age?"

"You know, Chris, you're the first person to ever ask me that question."

Chris wrapped his suntanned arms around his knees and waited for my answer.

"Let's see, when I was your age, I dreamed of one day going out to Hollywood."

"To see Bette Davis?"

"That's right, with your great-grandmother—"

"You mean, Old Ma?"

"Yep. Old Ma and I used to fantasize about one day going out there together. We were very close. We both adored movies and movie stars."

Chris gave a no-big-deal shrug. "So why didn't you just go there?"

"We didn't have the money.

"It's cheap to fly out there."

"Well for us back then, it was a lot of money." A bittersweet memory came back to me. "You know, we'd actually light candles in church so that we might go one day. Half the time Old Ma would light the candles without even dropping a dime in through the metal slot. She said she was saving every penny for our trip."

Chris started laughing. "Cool, I wish I knew Old Ma."

"You would have been good friends," I said, convinced that if Old Ma were anywhere, she was here with us, delighting in the story.

"So tell me more."

"Well, we used to write Bette Davis fan letters and then collect the autographed postcards that she'd send back."

"Just like I do with Michael Jordan?"

"Exactly!"

Chris moved from the sandy ledge beside me. "Did you ever get to Hollywood, Mom?"

"Eventually. But unfortunately, Old Ma was too frail to go. I brought her back postcards, souvenirs, and photos. Her favorite was a photo of me in front of Graumann's Chinese Theater. I was standing behind Bette Davis's footprint, posing like her with a cigarette between my fingers."

"Was Old Ma real sick?"

"She had a stroke, but her mind remained sharp till the end."

I could tell Chris was thinking about his dad's last days. "How'd you feel when she died?"

"Awful," I said, pulling Chris near to me. "I was living in Min-

172

neapolis when I got the call, and I flew back to Cleveland that night. After the funeral, we went back to Aunt Ruth's house where she was living. I went into her bedroom, and Scotch-taped to her dresser mirror was that photo of me taken in front of Graumann's Chinese Theater. The Scotch tape was all brown and curled at the edges. And inside a little cedar box that I bought at the gift shop at Warner Brothers, was our stash of postcards autographed by Bette Davis."

For a few moments Chris and I sat silent and close.

"Wouldn't it have been cool if Old Ma was alive when Bette Davis actually came to live in our house."

"I think Old Ma knew."

Chris pulled away. "How?"

"Well, I'll tell you. A few days before Old Ma died, she whispered into the phone, 'Honey, when I get to heaven I'm going to send you a message that I'm still around.'"

"Wow! Do you think Old Ma sent you Bette Davis?"

"It's crazy, but I think she did."

Chris's eyes misted over. "Do you still miss her?"

"She's right here in my heart."

"Next to Dad?"

"That's right," I said. "Next to Dad."

"Do you think Randy's going to be in our hearts?"

"I think he's in our hearts now," I said, holding back tears.

"Mom, I want to write Randy when we get back to the camp."

"Good idea," I said. "We'll both write to him."

"Let's send him some of this red dirt," Chris said, sifting the clay through his fingers.

We arrived back at the campsite to find Margaret on the warpath.

"Ya missed basketball practice!" she exploded at Chris. "Roland don't know no rules! He just know movies. Ol' Henry and Squeaky they think they writin' a book! Uncle Max is too lovesick to be any good to anybody except Thaalangay!"

"Put a sock in it!" Chris snapped at her. "The play-off isn't till next Saturday when Ian gets back!" He grabbed the basketball out from Margaret's arm and together they took off down the road to the hoop, leaving me free to write Reuel and Randy. "Don't forget to send Randy some of the dirt!" Chris hollered back.

Squeaky and Henry were sitting on Katie's front porch, hunched over the computer, thoroughly engrossed. When they saw me coming, they yanked the lid down, covering up what they had written on the screen.

"Yeah," Henry said, "we all done writin' fa today. I'll just save it, and it's all yours."

I guess they trusted me enough not to bring up Henry's file.

"Katie's been lookin' fa ya," Squeaky said, lighting up a cigarette. "Mail come while ya was havin' a swim."

I had been anxious for a letter from Reuel. "When did it come?"

"Jus' a little while ago," Henry replied. He passed his cigarette to Squeaky so that he had two hands to save their secretive work. "Ya got a big package of somethin' sittin' in there on Katie's kitchen table."

Sure enough, there was a large brown manila envelope for me from Gladys. I immediately sat down at Katie's table and began to sift through the dozen or so envelopes. A folded piece of paper dropped out from between two bills. It was a note from Gladys:

Dear Liz,

I hope your visit is going well. Down here we've had nothing but bloody rain. I've been watching the telly and it says that up north where you are it's dry as a bone. I think at this point, I'd rather have the flies and dust. Talked to my cousin out near Perth over the weekend—eight years now and no rain. I put Chris's Boogie Board right in your hallway. With all the wind we've had, it was flopping around in the garden.

Liz, I have some unpleasant news. I wasn't going to write this but maybe you can talk to Chris about it before you return to Manly. Soften the blow. Yesterday, when I was collecting your mail and tidying up your garden, my eye caught a white lump by your back window. I walked over and saw that it was a cockatoo. I suspect it was Chris's bird, Prince Charles, because it was so near where he always perched during his visit on your back deck. I

174

hope I'm mistaken, but I think not. Tell Chris that I buried his little friend beside the rose pergola. I planted a eucalyptus sapling to mark the spot.

Well, Liz, remember to pay the bloody utility company on time. They'll shut you off as soon as look at you. Sometimes I think that the only ones who make out here are the dole bludgers. I'll keep sending up your mail until I hear otherwise. It's awfully quiet down here without my Yankee mates.

Gladys, affectionately

Learning about Prince Charles was a definite downer. To add to this, there was no letter from Reuel. And then to make matters even worse, I went over to the Oasis and placed a call home and got only our answering machine. I calculated that it was three o'clock in the morning. For the following three days, I called home only to hear Reuel's recorded voice.

On the sixth day and still unable to get in touch with Reuel, I phoned his son, Gerald, at the University of Richmond. Gerald said that he had spoken to his father and that he was going out on an overseas flying mission, but he didn't say where. Gerald's next words sent me into a state of complete panic. "Don't worry, Liz, but I saw on CNN this morning that two of our planes got shot up in Bosnia. I don't think they were the type he flies. Dad's fine. He's one of the best pilots the Air Force has," Gerald said with all the optimism of a twenty-one-year-old about to receive his diploma.

I hung up, called home, and left a desperate message on the machine: "Reuel, please leave a message telling me what's up. I'm a wreck. Are you okay? I'll call till I get you. I love you."

Over the next twenty-four hours, I was plagued by horrible thoughts. I became certain that Prince Charles's death was some sort of ominous sign of worse things to come. All my exalted feelings of the past week were ancient history. Max tried to calm me down. There was no reasoning with me.

By the following afternoon, I was beside myself. "Max," I said, "take me to the watering hole"

"Ya know where it is," he said, annoyed.

"I need you to come with me."

"I'm goin' to get an emu fa the night feed."

"Max," I begged, "don't leave me."

Max started to walk away and then he turned back. "Katie says ya canceled ya trip into Bourke with her this mornin'. She was really lookin' forward to goin' there with ya."

"Yes," I said, avoiding his eyes. "I explained to Katie that I needed to stay close by. You know—today's mail day. I gotta be here to—"

Max cut me off. "Did you see the bird?" he asked.

"What?"

"The bird. Did ya see it?"

"I don't know what you're talking about."

He shook his head in a combination of pity and disgust.

"Max," I said, "I can't shake this awful feeling that something terrible has happened to Reuel."

"In your condition, ya can't feel anythin' that's real."

"Huh?"

"Awwgh, go have ya-self a rest."

How could I rest? How could Max be so insensitive? I began to conjure up the most graphic images of Reuel being shot down. By the time Max returned, dragging a limp, lifeless emu, I was non-functioning. I told Max that we had to head back to Sydney. Immediately.

He chopped off the bird's head and tossed it to salivating dogs. "Why?"

"Why! Something's terribly wrong! I'm packing and loading the car." I burst into a flood of tears.

Cool and controlled, Max said, "Go pick up some gum leaves fa the stuffin'."

"Gum leaves?"

"Gum leaves!" Max barked so loud that I actually flinched. My tears were instantly replaced with indignation. Who did this guy think he was, shouting out orders like General Patton. I turned to walk toward the abandoned house and begin packing, but before I took one step in that direction, I turned back toward him. I was about to let him know in no uncertain words that I didn't appreciate his ordering me around like I was in boot camp. But when I turned back, there was something so commanding and powerful about his presence that without saying a word, I walked off in search of gum leaves.

I looked high and low for gum leaves. With no eucalyptus trees in sight, I sat down on a large red rock and began to wallow in my misery. Deep in self-pity, I rubbed my eyes, whereupon they started to sting like hell and then swell and then shut. I had gotten some sort of leaf pollen in my eyes, bringing on an immediate allergic reaction. The bitter irony of this allergy did not escape me. I don't know how long I remained on the rock in that pathetic state. But the next thing I knew, I heard my name being called. Max had sensed that something was wrong and had sent Squeaky to get me. Before we returned, Squeaky took me to the watering hole and washed out my eyes.

Back at camp, I approached Max timidly. He was at the roasting pit, peacefully basting his emu with dark, pungent herbs in a glass canning jar. He didn't even look up to acknowledge my presence— or to see how thoroughly exhausted I was, how my eyes were swollen, how my denim shirt was ripped. He gave me nothing.

"Max," I said, "I'm really sorry, but I couldn't find the leaves."

"No leaves?" Max said. With his bare hands, he smeared the herbal concoction over the hind legs and breast of the emu.

"I see you made a real good smelling marinade," I said. For a moment, I thought I was going to puke.

"Couldn't find no leaves," Max said.

"Believe me, I looked everywhere."

"Ya looked everywhere?" He scooped out the last of the herbs with his fingertips and applied the goo like an artist putting the finishing touch on a canvas.

"I went down to the river," I told him. "Near where that disgusting kangaroo carcass was. By the way there's nothing left of it. Just a skeleton." I wasn't sure if he was on a slow boil or what. I continued to tell him how hard I looked. "Max, I even went all the way downriver to where we got those terrific plums that melt in your mouth. There's a lot more ripe ones now. If I had a bag, I would have brought some back for dessert."

Max stuck a forked stick into the bird's enormous chest cavity. Seconds later greasy liquid oozed over the browned skin and dripped into the fire. "So the gum leaves are gone," he said barely audible.

I made a weak attempt to change the subject. "Hey, remember last week when we took a shortcut to the watering hole and I stumbled over the roots of that kempeana bush and I thought that I had tripped over a snake? Remember how I panicked and started screaming that I saw a snake slither under the bushes?" I gave a few quick chuckles and went on, "And you pulled out your pocketknife and were ready to make a cross in my foot and suck out the venom. But you couldn't find a mark anywhere on my foot. And then you noticed a six-inch root sticking up out of the ground and we both burst out laughing? Remember that day, Max?"

Uninterested in my trip down memory lane, Max put the metal lid back onto the empty glass jar, tightened it, and said, deadpan, "There are no gum leaves 'ere."

"What?"

"There are no gum leaves 'ere," he said. He tore a loose piece of skin from the bird and passed it to me to sample.

"No thanks." I fleetingly thought of my father, who did the same thing with our Thanksgiving turkey, and which I always accepted.

"Max, for a second I thought I heard you say that there are no gum leaves in this village."

He popped the crispy skin into his mouth. "That's what I said."

What the hell was this all about? Furious with the warped little game Max had played on me, I blew up. "Max, you sent me out to find gum leaves when you knew there were no gum leaves?"

"An' ya wanted to send me a-packin' fa Sydney when ya knew nothin' happened to ya husband!"

Max didn't speak to me the rest of the evening. The following morning he broke his silence. "Yeah," he said, "I slept real good last night."

"So did I," I said. I had already been up for an hour. I'd had two cups of coffee and I was just waiting for Max to stir. There was a lot I needed to say. I started off by telling him that I was sorry.

Max shook the red earth from a horse blanket. "What are ya sorry 'bout?"

"My flipping out the past few days."

"Yeah?" Max said. He folded the blanket and then shook out a second horse blanket that he slept on for more cushion.

"You know, old mean Ama talked to me last night," I said.

He tucked the bedroll underneath his arm. "What she say to ya?"

"She told me to get out of her chair."

Max burst into laughter. "That's our Ama awright."

"Max," I said, "she's not a mean old lady. She's a scared old lady. When she ordered me out of her chair, I was really mad at her. Boy, I wanted to give her a piece of my mind. But then I looked over at her, and the way the fire was reflected on her face, I suddenly saw her differently. She seemed so vulnerable, if that makes any sense. So later when it started to get chilly, I mustered up all my courage and went over and draped my sweater around her. And she let me do that. Then I sat down beside her, with all of you chatting away."

"Yeah?" Max smiled. He put the blankets down and sat on them, giving me his undivided attention. "I'm real happy fa ya."

"Remember when I told you about all those mystical revelations I had at the watering hole, about how I had seen Dwango's reflection and felt joined with a light and all that stuff?"

Max nodded. "I remember hearin' all about that."

"Well, all that peace and good feeling went right out the window the second I didn't get a letter from Reuel."

"Ya was like a possum up a gum tree awright."

"But the minute I got out of myself and did something for somebody else, I felt my mind getting rid of a lot of clutter, and when that happened, I knew that Reuel was not in any danger. Max, if you hadn't sent me on that wild-goose chase for those damn gum leaves, I would have run back to Sydney and missed out on last night."

"It woulda been real hard fa ya to drive with ya eyes all closed up." Max laughed.

Max got up and headed into the abandoned house for a shower, but before he even reached the road he came back. "Awwgh, last night me an' Squeaky walked Ama home. She give me the sweater ya let her wear. It's over on top of my bag," Max said, pointing to his brown satchel. "She says she wants me to be bringin' ya 'round later today fa a cuppa."

I was so moved by this news that I threw my arms around Max's bearlike body and gave him a hug only to hear two pixie voices approach, singing, "We tellin' Thaalangay. . . . We tellin' Thaalangay. . . . We tellin' Thaalangay. . . ."

It was Margaret and her best friend Lila.

Max teased right back: "Thaalangay will be up on Saturday fa the big playoff. Ya better not let her down. We all countin' on the Suns and the Kicks."

"Hey!" Lila cried. "It's the *Knicks*."

"Awwgh, Uncle Max, ya don't know B-ball at all," Margaret got her digs in. A few moments later, she spotted Chris on Katie's front porch having a bowl of cereal and she ran over to join him. I watched Chris duck into the house as soon as he caught sight of Margaret crossing the road.

With Margaret safely out of hearing range, Lila was bursting with new gossip: Margaret was planning to get engaged to Chris before he left. She wouldn't hear of marriage before she was fifteen. She didn't want kids until she was at least sixteen. She would never go live in "Canecktigot." Chris would have to live in Enngonia and pay for everything Margaret wanted. I was tickled but thought I'd withhold this information from Chris too—at least until we were on our way home.

Max and I were enjoying every juicy morsel of gossip when Margaret skipped back from Katie's. She was waving a large manila envelope. "Liz, this come to Katie's yesterday!" It was my mail from Gladys.

I had been so exhausted from yesterday's search for gum leaves that when I finally returned to the campsite, I had forgotten it was mail day. Reuel was safe! And he'd sent me an oversized postcard of a topless Hawaiian woman! "Guess where I am, Lizzy?" Reuel had scribbled. "You are taking major chances not getting back home. Hawaiian girls love aging pilots! Our plane broke down at Hickam Air Force Base three days ago and we're waiting for parts to be flown in. . . ."

I was so happy to hear from him. The card also came with the distinct smell of Hawaiian Tropic suntan lotion.

"Yeah, this 'ere card smells like coconut awright," Max said, checking out the babes. He added with a devilish grin, "If I was you, I'd be more worried about my husband bein' on that beach than bein' shot down."

Saturday was supposed to be the big basketball game for the kids, and Max had invited Gay down. He was driving up to Cunnamulla to get her and asked if I wanted to go up for the ride.

"I'd love to," I said. "You going to send a bird to tell when we're coming?"

"Naw. Gay gotta phone. We can call her from the Oasis an' grab us a sandwich at the same time," Max said. "Annie makes up some real good steak sandwiches.

"Y'know," Max went on, "while Henry was workin' on ya writin' machine yesterday mornin', a white cockatoo was flyin' all 'round it. Ya don't see cockatoos 'round 'ere much. Henry jus' watch the bird an' think the bird got some sort of message fa ya."

That was a coincidence. I told Max about Gladys saying she had buried Prince Charles. Did he think the bird Henry saw was some sort of spirit bird?

"I wasn't 'round. Ya 'ave to ask Henry what he seen."

Unlike me, Max was not blown away by what I thought was a sure sign. He turned his attention to the dinner menu. "Boogalie's runnin' real good this mornin'," he said, whetting both of our appetites for the delicious miniature prawns. "Let's get over there now. We can stop on the way back an' get us some of Annie's steak sandwiches fa lunch an' I'll ring up Gay an' tell her we'll be up."

"And we gotta get to Ama's house later too."

"We be in real trouble, we don't get us over to old Ama's."

It was a twenty-minute walk down to the river. The morning was bright, crystal clear, and hot. Directly ahead of us, the river sparkled in the morning sun. Max didn't say much. Max never said much when he was walking. Although he was willing to talk, I was the one who initiated most of the conversation. A few times I told him to be sure to tell me when I was talking too much. "Yeah," he'd say, grinning from ear to ear, "my white lady friend 'ere sure can talk awright."

Regardless of how he teased me, Max seemed to enjoy my crazy stories about home. Whenever I was quiet, he'd look at me and say, "Ya right?" I'd tell him that I was trying to become more like an Aborigine. "Ya stay the way ya are," he'd say. Max especially liked hearing about how I had been a flight attendant yet was scared to death of flying. "That'd be like me a cowboy an' scared to get on a horse," he laughed.

When we neared the riverbank, Max pointed to a flattened area about fifty feet from the bank. "I wanna show ya somethin'," he said, leading me up a small rocky incline. When we got to the top, he turned to me, clutched my arm, and said, "Ya not scared up this high, are ya?" He could be funny.

"Right straight in front of ya is where my family's humpie used to be."

"Humpie?"

"Our house," Max explained.

"What was it made out of?"

"Awwgh, stringy bark," Max said. "Paperbark. Tin. The roof was smeared with clay. Kept us dry, summer an' winter. Yeah, it was a real good humpie."

He moved to its exact location, squatted down, and inspected the earth. "I slept right here," he said, scraping away some soil, almost like he was looking for a buried artifact to confirm this.

"Did you help build it?" I didn't move too close for fear that it was a sacred site.

"My grandfatha an' fatha build the humpie," Max said, still squatting, still looking for something.

"Awwgh, here it is." He pulled a small object out of the earth.

He brushed off soil to reveal a rather ordinary-looking stone. "Gay an' me bury it the night of the corroboree," he said. "Yeah, Gay remembered this 'ere humpie real well. She was sittin' right 'ere the night they come to take her away."

"You mean when they took her away to marry the older man?"

Max nodded. "I gave her this here stone to take with her."

"All those years she kept it?"

"That's right."

"She must really care deeply about you," I said.

"Listen real good," Max said, changing the subject. "Ya can hear the boogalie from 'ere."

I stood very still, but the only thing I could discern was the sound of the river. "I can't hear the boogalie, but I love the sound of the river," I said. "Back home in Connecticut, we live on a river. The Saugatuck River—it's named after a tribe of Indians who once lived there."

"Ya got some good fish in ya river?"

"Trout."

"Good tucker?"

"Real good."

"I bet ya got fish in America, I never seen before," Max said, with a sudden faraway gaze. "Yeah, it's real different up 'ere, ain't it?"

"Max," I said, suddenly curious, "what do you think America's like?"

"Awwgh, let's see," Max said. He wiped his forehead and pushed his hair back at the same time. "Ya got lotsa buildings like Sydney. But ya got a lot more of them. An' ya cities are a lot bigger than Sydney. Ya probably got more people too."

"A lot more people," I said. "You've got sixteen million people. We've got over two hundred million."

"Yeah?"

"And we're roughly the same size. In fact, if you turn the map of the United States upside down, it looks like Australia."

"Yeah?" Max said.

"But most all of your people live along the coast and there's absolutely *nothing* in the middle of your country."

"Nothin' in the middle of my country?"

"Ohh, I mean in the way we have major cities in the middle of the country. There's Chicago and Cleveland and Detroit and Kansas City. I'm originally from Cleveland. The land is really boring. Flat. Very uninteresting. But now the city—in the last twenty years—is really coming along."

"Comin' along?"

"Yeah. There's a new stadium. And we have the Rock 'n' Roll Hall of Fame—with an *Elvis* collection. And there's—"

Max jumped in, "Where do all ya big cities sit themselves on top of?"

"What do you mean?"

"What are all ya cities sittin' on?"

"Land," I said.

"If ya didn't 'ave the land, where would ya big cities be?"

"Well, I guess we wouldn't have any big cities."

"Ya gotta respect that land in the middle of ya country," Max said. "It's sacred land. Ya supposed to take good care of it."

As Max went on to speak about the special relationship between a person's soul and the site of his birth, a collage of scenes from my life flashed before me. I was playing in our backyard in Cleveland Heights. I was helping my grandfather pick tomatoes. "Widda this tomato," he'd say in his thick Italian accent, "I make-a da best sauce in da whole-a world." I was plucking up dandelion greens for salad. My mother and I were weaving dandelion bracelets. I was crying over Old Ma as she was lowered into the ground.

At that moment, I wondered how I could have lived all these years and not realized the connection between my land and me. I had once loved my small backyard with a fresh vegetable garden and rusted-out red swing-set. And then I grew into a teenager and believed that my only chance for true happiness would be to get as far away from Cleveland Heights as possible. And yet, it was in Cleveland Heights, where I grew up, where I took love and gave love—where I had the best friends of my life and the worst enemies of my life, who later became best friends again. It was in Middle America where I experienced the depths of sadness and the heights of joy and the wonderful tranquility in between.

"Max," I said, "a land where you draw your strength—isn't that sacred land?"

Max passed the stone to me. "Whaddya feel?" he said, seeming to disregard my question.

I clutched the stone and closed my eyes. A few moments later I passed it back. "I felt a cool, smooth stone," I said.

"Yeah," Max said. "But it feels real warm to me. Lotsa feelings here." He took the stone and put it back into the ground.

As I watched him bury it, I said, "I'd give anything right now to have a stone from the backyard where I grew up."

"Next time ya go fa a visit, why don't ya get ya-self one?"

We walked down to the river and filled two big plastic bags with prawns. And then it was off to the Oasis.

Annie's steak sandwiches reminded me of White Castle hamburgers, square pieces of meat smothered in grilled onions tucked inside a hamburger bun. They were everything Max cracked them up to be. But the best part about lunch at the Oasis wasn't the steak sandwiches. It was sitting at the bar, listening to the jukebox while chatting with Annie, a large, handsome, no-nonsense white Australian woman who had an enviable Wild West air about her. It was apparent that Annie wouldn't want to be anywhere else in the world. She had found her bliss as owner and operator of the Oasis Hotel and Pub.

"Annie's a real good woman," Max had said to me on the way in. "I tell her that if any of my bruddas get outta hand, she's to let me know. I don't want nobody givin' Annie trouble."

There was a mutual respect between Annie and Max. When Max got up to phone Gay, Annie leaned over and said, "Max is the salt of the earth. He keeps his brothers on the straight and narrow. My business suffers when he's in town." She laughed heartily.

I told Annie that Father Ted, Sister Pat, and Sister Dorothy all expressed the same thing about Max. And then I asked, "Annie, why's he so special?"

"The bloke's heart is bigger than anyone's I've ever met in my life," Annie said in a hushed voice so that the two locals at the end of the bar couldn't hear. "He's had a tough life. You wouldn't know it talking to him. All the Aborigines here have a rough go of it. Most all of them are on the dole. Nothing but menial jobs around Enngonia."

I was beginning to tell Annie how I met Max when he returned to us. He was beaming from ear to ear. "Yeah," he said, hopping back onto the barstool with a seventeen-year-old's spring in his step. "Gay will be waitin' fa us Saturday morn."

"Who's Gay?" Annie asked, wiping down the counter.

"Awwgh, Gay's an old lady friend of mine," Max said, still on cloud nine.

"An old lady!" Annie hooted. "She's probably younger than me."

Max laughed. Then he pulled out his wallet. "What do I owe ya, Annie?"

I reached for my money. "It's my treat," I said.

"Ya money's no good 'ere," Max said. He passed Annie a five-dollar bill before I could intervene. "We gotta get these things cleaned," he said, holding up two plastic bags of prawns as we headed out.

Just then, the jukebox started, almost magically, to play "She's Got Bette Davis Eyes."

"Hey, listen to this. Did you play this for me?"

"*I* played it fa ya." Roland suddenly appeared out of the side room where there was a larger bar, a small dance floor, and billiard table. "Ya can't leave till the song's over," he said, blocking the door. He had a pool cue in one hand and a cigarette in the other. As Kim Carnes sang, Roland brought his cigarette up to his mouth. With his hand moving like a window washer and his eyes practically popping out of his head, he belted out the lyrics: "She'll love ya . . . She'll leave ya . . . She's got those Bette Davis eyes."

"Roland," I screamed above everybody's uncontrolled laughter, "you got the part."

And with those words I had a brilliant idea. I would call Randy. It would be the middle of the night, but I was sure he wouldn't mind. Besides, chances were that Randy would be up watching an old movie or *I Love Lucy* reruns. He picked up on the first ring.

"Randy," I said, motioning Max and Roland to the phone, "you sound like you're next door."

"Let me turn the TV down," Randy said. I heard him mumble in the background, "Where's the goddamn remote." A few seconds later he said, "Liz, are you home?"

"I'm in the Outback. In a pub called the Oasis. I'm with Aborigine friends. One of them just did a fantastic imitation of Bette Davis."

"What?"

"Roland, a full-blood Aborigine, can do *Bette Davis!*"

"Should I be worried?" Randy said with a snippiness that instantly told me that he was feeling pretty good. Then he said, "Okay, put him on. I'll be the judge."

I passed the phone to Roland. "Roland," I said, "do Bette Davis for my friend in Philadelphia."

But Roland apparently had a better idea. *"You dirty rat,"* he said, and handed the phone back to me.

"Tell James Cagney not to give up his day job," Randy chuckled. "Liz, when are you coming home?"

"Ask the man who brought me here," I said, passing the phone to Max now.

Max placed the palm of his hand against the mouthpiece. "Is this ya real sick mate?"

I nodded.

"I'm thinkin' a lot about ya, brudda," Max said to Randy. "I'd like to be 'ere with ya."

My first reaction was to grab the phone. This was supposed to be a phone call to cheer Randy up, not remind him how sick he was.

"Can ya walk in the sun with ya loved ones?"

"Yes," I could hear Randy say.

"Brudda, I'm goin' be walkin' in the sun with my people an' askin' the spirits to walk next to ya." There was a long pause where neither Randy nor Max spoke. Max wiped a tear from his eye. "Ya take real good care of ya-self, brudda," Max said, finally giving the phone back to me.

Randy had tears in his voice. "Thanks, honey," he said.

# ELEVEN

A ma lived with her nephew Henry in a front bedroom. She liked the large window beside her twin-size bed. She could lie on the patched mattress and keep an eye on the goings-on up and down the road. If she sat straight up in bed, she could see the kids playing ball in the scrub. She used to sleep in a back bedroom where she had a bird's-eye view of her sister-in-law's kitchen, which was dirty. When Ama wasn't in the room she shared with her niece, she was sitting on the front porch in her metal rocking chair that had foam rubber cushions covered in red plaid corduroy. The cushions were made in New Zealand. Henry had gotten them for her birthday. She had bad arthritis in her fingers, neck, and hips. But thanks to Tom's medicine she didn't suffer much.

Children, according to Ama, were not anywhere as well behaved as when she was a girl growing up in Eulo. "Youngins have too much today." Margaret was out of line with all the jumpers she had and the way she marched around the village "spruckin' off." Maybe she could learn a thing or two from the little white fulla with the cap and metal teeth. He always stopped by on his way to the hoop and had something nice to say.

I was quite taken aback by this news. Chris had never mentioned a word about visiting Ama.

" 'E give me this 'ere yesterday," Ama said. She lifted her wrist and proudly showed off a red-and-yellow-woven cotton surfer's bracelet that Chris had gotten free when I bought him the Boogie Board in Manly.

Max inspected Chris's gift. "Ya got ya-self a real good bracelet 'ere, Ama. Them bright colors look real nice on ya skin."

"Come all the way from America," Ama said, admiring the cotton.

"Actually," I said, "it was bought . . ." I caught myself. "Yep, it's from America all right."

"Ya fulla show ya what I give 'em?" Ama asked, rubbing her neck and grimacing. When she did that, her face became distorted, giving her a spooky appearance. "No, he didn't," I said, feeling very warm toward her.

"What I give 'em come by wurekker."

"Wurekker?"

"She says that she give fulla somethin' that come by messenger," Max interpreted.

"Did it come by mail?"

"Awgggggghhhh," Ama sputtered, annoyed. She pointed her disfigured forefinger to the sky. "Bird!"

"Bird?"

Ama rattled off something in Aborigine to Max, and then Max said to me, "Remember when I tell ya about the cockatoo Henry see yesterday flyin' 'round ya writin' machine?"

"Yeah."

"Ama says that she see the bird an' the bird dropped an old clamshell onto her lap. She know in her head that the bird's from Sydney area an' that the clamshell be a message fa ya. Ya fulla put it in his pocket."

This was all the confirmation I needed: The bird had been sent by the spirit world. I was without words, perhaps for the first time, which caused Max a bit of concern.

"Ya right?" Max asked. He clutched my elbow and looked into my eyes as if he were preparing to give me CPR.

"I'm fine," I said. I would have given anything for Reuel to be here with me to hear this one. I would have given anything to have a glass of merlot.

"Ya don't look too good to me," Max said. "Drink ya tea."

I sipped the greenish-brown tea Ama had waiting for us when we arrived. Ama proceeded to reprimand us for having kept her waiting all afternoon, then told me that the tea would be good for my eyes. Floating around in the tea was a tiny golden flower about the size of a pea. When we were done drinking the tea, we should eat the flower. This would allow us to see the spirits that walk at our sides. All this via Max, who translated for Ama.

"Have ya-self a piece of this 'ere sugar cake," Max said. He helped himself to a chunk oozing orange butter icing, and then he held out the tin tray for me.

"It's okay to eat both the cake and this yellow flower floating around in my tea?" I asked. I hoped I didn't sound like a wise-ass. More than that, I hoped the flower wasn't like a psychedelic mushroom.

"Ya be right." Ama waved. She, too, helped herself to the cake. "Oranges outta the grove," Ama said, frosting dripping down her chin and onto an otherwise clean brown dress. A drawback of no teeth.

After my last sip of tea, I scooped the tiny flower from the bottom of my mug and with my fingers unceremoniously ate it. It tasted like one of those edible flowers that sometimes adorn your dish in fancy restaurants. For the next ten or so minutes, as we walked back, I checked my side, half anticipating spirits, half spooked. Nothing. By the time the sun had set, I had all but forgotten about the flower. But I did remember to ask Chris about the old clamshell Ama had given him.

"It's right here," Chris said, digging it out from his pants pocket.

I examined the shell. It looked exactly like the petrified shell Prince Charles had dropped on my computer. "Did she mention how she got it?"

"I don't understand anything she says, Mom."

"But you've been visiting her?"

"When I see her on the porch, I go say hi," he said, adjusting his baseball cap on backward. "I only first went over because Margaret dared me to."

"She dared you?"

Chris gave an evil grin. "Mom, Margaret said she eats kids and her bedroom is filled with kids' bones. She keeps the eyeballs and liver in the refrigerator. Margaret said that she had twelve brothers and sisters, and now they're all gone."

"So you went over?"

"Yeah," Chris said. "Margaret and Lila were hiding inside Roland's truck watching me go up to her front porch."

"Were you scared?"

"*Ama* looked really scared. I stood like a foot away and said, 'Hi!' "

"What did she do?"

"She got up out of her chair and told me to sit down."

"She let you sit in her chair?"

"Yeah."

"Then what?"

"Nothing."

"You two just sat there and said *nothing?*"

"There was nothing to say."

"Weren't you a bit uncomfortable?"

"No," Chris said. "She's got a real comfortable chair."

"I mean, weren't you uncomfortable that you two were sitting there and not talking?"

"Why?"

"I see," I said. At that moment, I did see. I saw my son's spirit so delightful that as soon as he left I pulled a small pad of paper from my L. L. Bean money belt and wrote just beneath my shopping list of peanut butter, biscuits, milk, eggs, chips, soda, oranges, toilet paper, the following:

> Today I "saw" Chris's calmness of mind, his quiet eyes, his open heart. And with this sudden awareness of his spiritual gifts my own feel on fire. I have this unbelievable urge to seek only the best from every person I meet. And in return, I will offer only my best. I will admire every person's goodness and I will put no energy whatsoever onto their flaws. I will no longer beat myself up for my flaws. I will spread the narrow and confined boundaries of family love and extend my heart for every living thing I encounter on my journey.

When I was finished writing this very heavy stuff, I tracked down Max and read it to him. In fact, I read it to him twice, making certain that he recognized not only Chris's depth but my depth as well.

Max's response: "Yeah, that's a real handy little pad a paper ya carry 'round with ya."

My thought: Didn't this guy get it? I was just about to read it to him for a third time when he said, "Looks like Chris jumped up an' broke Squeaky's hoop smack off the steel pole."

"What?"

"Ya fulla an' ol' Squeaky got themselves in a bit of a blue over how that hoop is supposed to be attached an' Chris ripped it clear off."

This certainly didn't sound like my kid with the calmness of mind, quiet eyes, and open heart. "Are you saying that Chris got into an argument with Squeaky and ripped off the hoop?"

"I guess. He told ol' Squeaky to fuck off."

Hearing that, my heart sank to the parched earth. I sat silent. I felt so foolish for everything I had just read to Max about Chris.

"Kids are real funny blokes, they are," Max said, drawing out each word. "Just when ya think ya got 'em all figured out, they do somethin' to make a bloody liar outta ya. That's a real right thing 'bout kids. They real good sometimes an' some other times they reeeel bad. Yeah," Max chuckled, "I guess ya wouldn't want to have it any other way."

At the time Max spoke those words, I had been so upset about my son's behavior that I really didn't hear him. The following morning, however, I woke up and blurted out to Max, "It's all about balance, isn't it?"

"Balance?" he asked, half awake.

"That's my lesson!" I exclaimed, loud enough for Henry to stop what he was doing under the hood of Roland's truck and rush over to our campsite, which was only ten or so feet away.

"Did I miss me a writin' lesson?" Henry asked, oil stick in his hand.

"No," I said, "but I almost missed a lesson."

Henry looked bewildered. But Max, although still in a fog, knew exactly what I had meant.

"You guys—all you guys—every Aborigine I've met here has *bal-*

*ance*. It's just part of your whole being. I see it in the way you look at yourselves. How you look at others. How you treat all of those around you—even the dead. Nobody here is all hung up on right and wrong. Just on being the best."

"The best?" Henry asked.

"Yes," I said, "in my country it's all about beating out the next guy. Being better at absolutely everything. Winning. Number one. Happy days. Prozac!"

"Prozac?"

"Prozac. It's a drug that keeps you up all the time. You don't have any down days."

"How do you know when ya down if ya up?" Max said, sincerely wanting an answer.

"You're never down with Prozac."

"Where does the down go?" Max asked, a more profound question than he realized.

"I guess it gets all covered up," I said. "Just like yesterday at the Oasis when we were on the phone with Randy. I wanted the conversation to be idle chitchat because that was safe. Nobody would get hurt. The fact was, nobody would get any better either. But you spoke from the heart. And when I hung up the phone, I felt so light. So hopeful. I felt so connected." I paused, then went on to say, "I realized all this in a moment's flash when I woke up this morning."

Max shook his head. "Ya realized that 'cause the spirit spoke to ya last night."

"Huh?"

"Yeah, the spirit come spoke to me too."

I had come a long way in accepting the reality of the spirit world, but each time Max or somebody mentioned spirits roaming the village the hair on my arms stood up.

Max turned to Henry. "Ama give us the yellow flower yesterday in our cuppa."

"Awgggh," Henry said, as if everything now made perfect sense.

"Yeah," Max said, "the spirit that come visit me last night says that I have some place to take ya later."

Up went the hair on my arm. "To the watering hole?" I asked. I always felt safe and good there.

"Nawww, some other place."

"Where's that?"

But Max was back onto the here and now. He pointed to the oil stick Henry was holding. "What are ya cookin'?"

Henry and I laughed. "Ol' Max know as much about fixin' trucks as ol' Squeaky know about fixin' hoops."

"Speaking of hoops," I said, glancing at my son's empty sleeping bag, "have you seen my Chris?"

"He down with Squeaky right now makin' a new hoop," Henry said.

I was relieved to hear that they had patched up their little feud. "What are they using for a hoop this time?"

"Somethin' Tom bring back from Tinnenburra way."

"Medicine Tom's back!" I yelped, shocked practically off my bed-roll.

"Yeah, two o'clock this mornin' he pull his truck in. New wind-shield. New headlight. She's all fixed up real nice."

"How come he's back?"

"He lives here," Henry said, giving me a look as if I were incapable of making obvious connections.

"So he'll be around for a while?" I said, anxious to say hello, anxious to get more allergy medicine, anxious to ask him about the yellow flower Ama gave Max and me.

" 'E's not goin' nowheres, 'cept on Friday."

"Where's he going on Friday?" I asked.

"Friday we're headin' down Bourke way to pick up Greg an' a few fullas fa Saturday B-ball play-off."

"Who all's in this play-off?" I asked, amused at how Henry had rolled the word B-ball off his lips as if he had been saying it his whole life.

Henry shrugged. "Whoever show up."

It was clear Henry would never make it as a coach for the Weston Middle School. "What time will it be?" I asked.

"When everybody gets 'ere," Henry said, moseying back to Roland's truck, leaving me to luxuriate in my newfound world of no-pressure timelessness. I took off my waterproof Timex with calendar and indigo light and dropped it into my duffle bag.

While Henry went about changing Roland's oil and Max boiled up water for our coffee, I took out my little notepad and wrote in bold print across the gobbledygook I had read to Max: "TODAY'S LESSON: LIGHTEN UP, LIZ!"

But I was a time junkie. Without my watch, I was totally out of whack. Physically, I felt unbalanced. I didn't know if I should be hungry or tired. I couldn't be positive if it was Tuesday or Thursday. April or May. The fourteenth or the twenty-fourth. I didn't know if it was the time of the day when I always dragged or the time of day when I got my second wind. I wasn't sure if I had a taste for coffee or chardonnay.

By the following morning, I had grown horrified at just how much I had relied on that $39.95 hunk of stainless steel and rubber strap. At one point, I had to laugh thinking about all the uses it served. Without my watch, how was I going to check to see if I had a hearing loss? And in thinking about hearing loss, I began to think over all my neurotic behavior. How often I would check myself for symptoms of some dread disease. Breast cancer ranked right up there. I was forever feeling around for lumps. It didn't much matter where I'd perform this self-examination—escalators, lunch with friends, driving in the car. Of course I'd be discreet. A year earlier, I had been convinced I had MS, and then I discovered that the shoes I was wearing were just too pointed, and they were causing me to trip. I was worse when it came to imagining illnesses with my son and parents. There wasn't a night that went by without my worrying I'd get a call that one of my parents had died. In thinking about all of this, I tracked Max down on Katie's front porch—his usual perch—and asked him if he ever worried about getting sick. Max immediately jumped to the erroneous conclusion that I was telling him that he looked sick.

"Not at all," I corrected him. "I just wondered if you ever *worried* about coming down with something when you're *not* sick."

Max furrowed his brow. He brought his hand to his chin. "If I'm feelin' good, why would I worry 'bout feelin' bad?"

"That's a very good point."

Max sat unflinching as he waited for me to explain why I had asked him such an inane question. But I didn't explain myself. I was too stuck in the fact that here was a man who truly wasn't afraid of getting sick. "So you're never afraid that you're going to come down with some awful disease?"

Max's expression suddenly shifted from concern for my sanity to one of concern for my health. "Ya got somethin'?" he asked, moving in closer, not farther away.

"Oh, no," I laughed. "I'm perfectly healthy. At least I think I am."

Max looked puzzled. "Ya don't know if ya are?"

"How do you know for sure?"

"Ya jus' know," Max said, helping himself to a chocolate biscuit that I had brought over to go with our coffee. Carefully, he separated the biscuit, which looked like an elongated Oreo, and licked the vanilla cream filling.

"Hey, I do the same thing."

"What do ya do?"

"Lick the cream filling out before I eat it."

Max burst out laughing.

I loved to get Max laughing. He had the most wonderful, expressive, no-holds-barred laugh. Most of the Aborigines I had met really knew the art of a rich, from-the-guts belly laugh. Sometimes, when we were all laughing, it reminded me of my Italian and Irish relatives during a family gathering. It seemed that people who had hard lives could give the greatest laughs. My grandmother, for instance. She raised four kids during the Depression, working as a waitress in a corner luncheonette. "I brought home seven dollars a week. Sometimes we'd just eat onions," she'd say with a faint Irish lilt. Whenever Old Ma reminisced, she did so with a wistful yearning that made those times seem like good old days. Anyway, she could laugh. We used to crack each other up so much that we'd literally fall to the pink shag carpeting in my bedroom, holding our sides. She'd always say, "If ya can't laugh, you may as well lay down and die."

"These here biscuits are the same ones we bring with us?" Max asked, savoring each bite.

"Yep," I said. "When they're gone, it's time to go."

Max's smile disappeared. "Ya wanna be leavin'?"

This was the first time since my little episode over Reuel's safety that the issue of leaving had come up. I knew, however, that the question was in the back of both of our minds. But I didn't want to think about leaving at the moment. I had a nagging feeling that there was some unfinished business. I just didn't know what that unfinished business was.

I turned the table. "Are *you* ready to leave?"

Max turned the table right back. "When ya ready to go, ya let me know."

Perfect, I thought. No pressure to either stay or leave. And with all pressure lifted, I sat back alongside Max and reveled in the moment—until Max said, "So ya scared of gettin' ya-self sick 'ere?"

"Ohh, I'm not scared of getting sick *here*. Just sick in general."

"Awwwgh," Max said, shaking his head. I couldn't get a reading on what he was thinking.

"Max," I said, "do Aborigines know when they're going to die?"

He dipped his third biscuit into the coffee. "Yeah, ya know."

"How?"

"Ya feel that 'ere's a lotta space between ya body an' ya soul," he said, tapping his chest.

I had never heard of death explained that way. But it all made perfect sense. "I'm going to write that down, Max," I said.

He smiled and helped himself to yet another biscuit. "Can't stop eatin' these 'ere sweets," Max said, adding, "They no good fa ya teeth."

"Max, you're not afraid to die, are you?"

"I jus' never think 'bout dyin'."

"That's good. That means that you're not obsessed or anything."

"Obsessed?"

"You know, worried, really worried about dying."

"Ya right," he said, crossing one short, thin leg over the other. "I'm not scared a dyin'."

"That's not just a macho, Aborigine cowboy thing to say, is it Max? You're telling me the truth. You have no fear of death."

Max smiled with such serenity that I suddenly felt foolish for questioning him. "I can see that you have no fear of death," I said. "I can see it in everything you do. I see it in your eyes. I see it in—"

Max cut in. "I used to be afraid of dyin'," he admitted. "When I was on the grog. I told ya 'ow I rolled into the fire one night an' got all burned up. Got the scars right 'ere to prove it." He lifted his shirt. I winced at the horribly scarred chest and back, made even more grisly by the fact that his skin was so black and the scar so white. "Yeah, I almost died back then. When I wasn't livin' right, I was real scared a dyin'. Everythin' changed when I got me off the grog."

"Max," I said, "I'm not on the grog. I was never on the grog. But I'm still scared of dying."

"Yeah?" He appeared surprised.

"I'm terrified that somebody close to me, like Chris, Reuel, Randy, my parents, are going to die. I don't want them to die. I want everything to go on peacefully just the way it is."

He jerked his head back. "Everything to go on jus' the way it is?"

"That's right."

"Ya wanna go on livin' bein' scared a dyin'?"

"Oh no," I said, "I want everything to continue the way it is, *except* for me being scared of death."

"That's what I thought ya jus' say."

"Max, *what* did you think I said?"

Max set down his coffee cup, shooing away a stray cat. "In my mind when ya scared a dyin', it means that ya scared a livin'."

He found my button. "Max," I snapped. "I'm certainly *not* scared of living," I said, giving a bitter laugh into the oppressive afternoon heat. "That's a real joke."

Max crossed his arms, rested his chin in his hand, and sat observing me like he was Sigmund Freud and I was some pathetic patient.

"I think a woman who travels halfway around the world with her son is in my mind not scared of living," I said in as cocky a tone as I could muster.

Still no expression or comment from Max. It always drove me

crazy when people didn't respond—when I didn't know exactly where I stood in their eyes. Max's "wise" passiveness triggered in me the urge to expound on my zest for life. "If I was so scared of living, you think for one second I'd be here? I doubt that!"

With that, Freud rose. My forty-five minutes were up and he was calmly showing me the door.

"So I'll see you later," I called to Max just before he disappeared down the dusty path toward town. As miffed as I was, I didn't want to take any chances on alienating this five-foot-five Aborigine who seemed to hold some key for something—even if I didn't know what that something was.

I didn't see Max for the rest of the day. That evening as I sat around Henry's campfire listening to one of Katie's old stories about how the river came to be, Max took me by the arm. "Come with me," he said.

"Where we going?" I asked.

Max didn't answer but the sounds of the Outback did. The howling of a distant dingo and the cry of a bandicoot in chorus with nearby crickets beckoned me along.

"I bet you're taking me somewhere very special," I said, envisioning a precarious hike through the prickly grassland to a magnificent sacred site—to a Shangri-la. Yes, I thought, everything I had said earlier to Max about my fear of dying had sunk into his head and he was now taking me to a magical spot where I might once and for all wash away fear. Soon I would arrive at a place where I could drink sacred water or roll in the red soil or pluck a wildflower and in doing so my soul would be untied from the constant never-ending fear of sickness and death. After all, that's what I was here for in the first place.

"Should I change into my sneakers?" I asked, with an edge of excitement.

"You'll be right," Max said, low-key, not tipping me off.

As I walked at his side, I suddenly felt guilty for having overreacted earlier in the day and I told Max so. Max didn't respond. He didn't talk much when he walked. "Walkin' without talkin'," he once told me, "lets ya see jus' where ya supposed to be goin'. When ya real quiet, ya learnin' things that ya suppose to learn fa today. Everythin' that ya learn back yesterday takes up a lotta space in ya mind."

When he had first told me that, I asked him if when he walked quietly, he meditated. Max didn't know what meditation was so I explained it to him as best I could: "It's all in the breathing. You close your left nostril with your finger. Breathe deeply through the right nostril and hold the breath for a moment. Then close the right nostril with your finger and exhale slowly through the left nostril. Equally important, you have to empty your mind of all thoughts. Think about nothingness."

"Too much fa me to remember to do," he said, adding, "I don't know why ya'd wanna be thinkin' about nothiness?"

I told Max that clearing my mind of all thoughts was the hardest thing for me to do. In fact, it had been *impossible* for me to do. Then I asked him what he thought about during his long, silent walks.

"Aborigines jus' let their minds go where they're supposed to go. We find our path an' walk in it."

I was thinking about all of this when Max came to a stop in front of the abandoned house. "Wait 'ere," he said. "I'll be right back with ya."

My first thought was that Max needed to use the bathroom. Three weeks earlier Max and I had gone in and given the bathroom a scrubbing like it had never seen before. Our cleanser, of all things, was the red soil mixed with a bottle of metho Katie had confiscated from one of her nephews. Max and I had come up with that idea together. To clean the toilet, I had devised a johnny mop out of a stick and rag. I soaked the rag in a generous amount of cleaning goop and handed it to Max. While Max swirled the johnny mop around the black bowl until it was almost restored to toilet white, I got down on my hands and knees and scoured the gummy, hairy, moldy shower until it would have passed even my mother's inspection. I was only able to attack this job after smearing Noxzema skin cleanser underneath my nose so that I couldn't smell anything, except the camphor. It was a little trick I had learned from an emergency medical technician for entering a house where somebody had been dead a while, sort of like the leaf Medicine Tom gave me by the rotting roo carcass. When Max and I were finally finished scrubbing, I hung a small wreath of orange blossoms on the mirror and put all my little hotel soaps in a decorative tin that had held hard candy. The final touch was the photo display above the light switch. I hung three photographs of Max, Chris, and me at Manly Beach. Max and I spent the rest of the day giving guided tours. Max reminded everybody who expressed a desire to use the bathroom to bring their own soap and towels and to clean up after themselves. I suddenly hoped that I wasn't turning Max into a Cleveland Heights housewife.

Now, as I waited outside the abandoned house, I thought I could hear voices inside. Oh yes, I thought, Max had stopped off to see Bampu. There was always a lot of action in and out of Bampu's back room. I just had never been part of that action. From the sound of his weird moaning, I felt lucky. I had been spared the agony of having to visit a sick old man who was probably off his rocker.

"Ho!" Max called from the doorway. "Come on in."

As I walked up the path, I felt that Max had stuck a pin in my celestial balloon. A trip to see Bampu was *not* a trip to Shangri-la. "What's up?" I stammered.

"Bampu wants to be meetin' ya now," Max said in a servantlike tone—as if the master of the house were ready to receive me.

"Really?" I said, stalling for time, hoping that Max would sense my trepidation and decide to forget it.

"Yeah," Max said. He motioned me inside.

I walked through the door, heard the didgeridoo echoing from down the hallway, and got instant willies. I told Max that I needed to use the bathroom. A safe haven.

"When ya finished, come on down to the last room," he said.

I watched Max enter Bampu's sanctuary and then I went into the bathroom to gather my thoughts—to think of a graceful way to get out of this one. My thoughts, however, were temporarily distracted by a pile of Chris's dirty clothes plunked in the middle of the floor. What a slob the kid was. I plucked them up and shoved them into a plastic bag that hung on the door handle. Chris would be hearing about this one. Other than for the dirty clothes and glops of Chris's bubble-gum-flavored toothpaste smeared on the washbasin, the bathroom looked and smelled pristine, thanks to Max and me. We shared latrine duty. Well, that wasn't quite accurate. We started rotating responsibilities, but after the third day, Max lost interest. Typical man.

Now, as I washed my hands, I looked into the mirror and rehearsed how I was going to beg off seeing Bampu. "Katie's meat pie's coming back at me," I'd say. I tried that one out in the mirror and decided that it wouldn't be nice to blame poor Katie—even though her meat pie had been swimming in lard. I'd go with the old standard: "It's been a long day and I'm bushed."

That settled, I splashed water on my parched, cracked face and watched it make its way over and around the gentle grooves and valleys of my forty-plus face and finally into the basin where it left a red dirt residue, reminding me that I was in the Outback, light-years away from my well-stocked medicine cabinet where I had antiaging moisturizing cream, Retin-A, and numerous other products that promised to repair what I was seeing before my eyes. Patting my skin dry, I began to study my face for signs of age—a most unfavorite and neurotic pastime after I hit the Big Four-Oh. How I looked was very important to me. It always had been. I wished I could forget about how I looked to myself and others. I wished I could paw through *Vogue* and not beat myself up for what I was not. What I'd never be. It was such a waste of time, looking for my flaws—real and imagined. Maybe some pharmaceutical company was at this moment developing a potion that allowed you to be satisfied with what you look like.

With that ridiculous thought, I reached for the towel, and as I did a bright intense streak of light flashed before me, literally wiping out my reflection in the mirror. My first thought was that the light bulb had exploded. It hadn't. I closed my eyes tightly, then opened them, trying to refocus. I was *not* in the mirror! Frozen with fear, I fumbled for my face and felt my features as if I had been blinded by acid. Nothing felt different. I looked down at my hands. My wedding band. My arms. My legs. I was there all right. I just wasn't *there*—in the mirror. Maybe the flower from Ama's tea caused this to happen and like people who had taken LSD, I'd end up in a loony bin, shuffling around in paper slippers the rest of my life. With that, I let out a bloodcurdling scream, which caused Max and his relatives to come running.

"Ya awright?!" Max called, banging on the door at the same time he flung it open. Tom was inches behind him, and Greg was behind him.

I clutched onto Max for dear life. "Max, I can't see myself!"

Max held me as if I were a frightened child who had just been awakened by a nightmare.

I buried my head into his chest. "I can't see myself in the mirror," I wailed.

He asked for no explanation. "You'll be right," he said, continuing to hold me near.

Finally, I calmed down enough to tell Max what had happened. He—and Tom and Greg—listened without a word. Then Tom spoke to Max in Aborigine, and then with Tom on one side of me and Max on the other, I was led back to the mirror. Greg had begun to blow into his didgeridoo in the hallway.

I stood before the mirror but dared not look up. I was still shaky. Max turned the water on and began to dab cool water onto my face with his fingertips. "You'll be right," he kept repeating in so soothing a voice that my fear subsided and I could think again.

"Max," I said, "was it Ama's flower?"

"What about it?" Max said.

"Remember, Ama told us that if I ate the flower, I would be able to see spirits at my side."

"Did ya see any spirits at ya side?"

"Maybe." Still looking down, trying to be clearheaded, I recounted for Max the several incidents of light since this Outback journey began. First, the ball of light on the Mitchell Highway on our way to Enngonia. Then the light at the sacred watering hole that seemed to lift me up. Then this. "Do you think Dwango had anything to do with it?"

"Did ya see Dwango here?"

"No," I said, "but I just feel he might be here."

While Max and Tom talked, I cautiously lifted my head toward the mirror. The first thing I saw was the crown of my head. A green light wavering just above it. Mesmerized by the soft emerald radiance, I lifted my head a bit higher until my eyes came into view. They were so clear, so bright, that for a brief moment I didn't recognize them as mine. But the longer I looked, the more I connected to them. I had seen my eyes look that way only once before. In a photo of my brother and me on our red swing set. I was five. Gary was six. I loved that photo. I loved the way my eyes shone, wide and free and uncomplicated, so untouched by the tragedies of life. Seeing those same childlike eyes now, I broke out into a joyous smile so big and spontaneous that I surprised myself. And on seeing this innocent and trusting smile reflected back at me, I knew that I had seen it before too. In another photo, one my parents kept on their dresser. I was standing outside the church in my First Holy Communion dress. I was so happy. Communion—the connection of one being to All. I was only seven, but I knew even then that I was connected. I knew as I walked down the aisle, hands pressed together, veiled head bowed, wafer melting on my tongue, my mother and father, Uncle Bud, Aunt Betty, and Old Ma watching with tears in their eyes, that I was part of the Whole Big Deal.

Standing before the mirror, recalling my First Holy Communion Day, I remembered the communion only weeks earlier at St. Vincent's in Redfern. As I received the sacrament from Father Ted, I had prayed for guidance. "Please God, what do I do? Do I stay here or go home? Do I communicate with the spirit? Is there really a spirit? Am I out of my mind? Lead me wherever I'm supposed to go." Just before, I had turned to the pew behind me and met Max. "Peace be with you," we said, shaking hands—connecting.

Here we were, still connected—connected in a way that I had never dreamed possible.

"Bampu's waitin' to see ya," Max said, turning off the water and arousing me from my reverie. He straightened his cowboy hat in the mirror.

I followed him out of the bathroom and down the hallway—a

seven-year-old girl in my pearl and satiny communion dress walking without effort or fear—to the accompaniment of Greg's didgeridoo.

The moon shining in through Bampu's window illuminated his face, allowing me to see at once that Max's uncle was indeed a very sick man. When Bampu turned his sunken face toward the doorway where I waited for my cue to enter, I recognized the same faraway look that my husband had had just before he died. Suddenly the memory of John's death—something I had fought for years—came flooding back.

Chris and I were with John the evening he died. He left us at 5:40 P.M. I'll never forget that time. Because at five o'clock, after drifting in and out of consciousness all day, he opened his eyes, searched the room for Chris, and motioned for the nurse to take off his oxygen mask.

"Come here, Scooter," he said, his voice faint but audible.

Scooter was a long-forgotten nickname John had given Chris as a toddler.

Chris, frightened but brave, went to his dad's bedside. Then with an energy that came from some divine source, John began to sing a song he had sung the first time he held Christopher. It was Cole Porter's "You're the Top." Over the years, it went on to become "their" song.

"You're the top!" John sang through parched lips. "You're the Colosseum. You're the top! You're the Louvre Museum. . . . You're the smile on the Mona Lisa . . ."

Chris gently stroked his father's bruised and thin arm as he waited to sing his favorite part.

John nodded to Chris, cuing him.

"You're Mickey Mouse!" Chris belted out just as he had in his father's better days.

I, on the other hand, was too frightened even to hold my dying husband's hand. I stood ten feet away and watched with despair and horror as John struggled with his last few breaths.

Now, as I walked to Bampu's bedside, deep in the Outback, twelve thousand miles from Weston, Connecticut, and face-to-face with a full-blood Aborigine who had the same blue, blue eyes and black,

black skin as Max, we connected. And without a second thought, I took Bampu's paper-thin hand into mine as if he were a beloved relative. As I did so, I knew beyond a shadow of a doubt that I was touching an evolved soul and that Bampu's soul was in touch with other souls and that the room was filled with spirits. And as much as I ever felt anything in my life, I felt John on one side of me and my grandmother on the other. They were showering me with the energy of their love that was all so familiar and yet all so new. I was so utterly convinced of their presence that I spoke aloud. "You're here," I said, stroking Bampu's twisted fingers, but speaking to John and Old Ma. And with Bampu's next breath, I "heard" as clear as a bell: "Darling, you are here."

I understood. I was here, within. I, the real me, was *here*. Me—the kid with the shiny, nonjudging eyes and trusting smile—was here. I was here without the fear of death. I was here with the full mindfulness that Randy would die—like John and Old Ma—and yet would continue on and be able to communicate with the living. I was here with the full knowledge that the next world is not a change of place but a change of consciousness and in order to bridge the gap we must transcend the boundaries of our awareness. Or as Max had said so many weeks earlier when I asked him why the spirit doctor Dwango chose to speak through me: "Sometimes spirits talk to those who will listen."

As I continued to hold Bampu's hand and listen to his choppy but seemingly painless breathing, I suddenly had the clarity and understanding to know that when you are truly here—in the present—you are there, too. Being here allowed me to step around the iron fence of the material world into the fullness of existence where suddenly the world appeared to be one great thought rather than one great machine.

We stayed with Bampu for a while—I had no idea of the time—before Max said that we'd better be on our way. Before we left, I said to Bampu, "I feel as if we've known each other for a long, long time."

Bampu squeezed my hand, gentle but strong. "A very long time," he responded.

Embraced by John and Old Ma, I said, "My relatives are here with us now."

"Yes," Bampu replied, "mine are here too. If you invite them, they will walk with you."

"Your family will walk with me?"

Bampu nodded, yes.

"Will they walk with a very good friend of mine who is dying?"

"If they are asked."

Tears streamed down my cheeks. "Thank you. Oh, thank you so much. I had been scared to come in before."

Bampu studied my face, which now seemed to have no weight to it—if that can make any sense. "I saw that you were frightened," he said, kindly.

"May I come back?"

"As often as you like," he said, and he turned his head toward the window and shut his eyes.

With that Greg stopped playing the didgeridoo, and Tom dabbed some sort of leaf mixture onto Bampu's closed eyes.

"Tom's medicine is real soothin' fa blind eyes," Max whispered.

Startled by this revelation, I said, "Bampu's not blind."

"Blind fa almost twenty years."

"But— but he definitely was able to see me."

"Yeah, he can see ya awright," Tom said as he pressed green goop onto Bampu's eyelids. "He's jus' not lookin' at ya with his eyes."

"Deaf too," Greg said.

"But he answered me. He said as clear as anything that his spirit relatives will walk with me. They'll walk with Randy."

"Aborigines don't need to be havin' to look through their eyes and hearin' with their ears to be talkin' with ya," Max said. "Come on now, we gotta get on our way. Tomorrow's a real big day fa everybody."

# TWELVE

T he following morning, I wrote in my journal:

Today. Sometime Saturday morning. May something. My watch remains in the bottom of my duffle bag. I am liberated from the tyranny of time! Right now, the sun is beating down on Katie's tin roof with vengeance. The flies are trying to get into my mouth and up my nose as I eat some of Chris's sickening sweet cereal that we bought in Bourke the other day. I wish I had bought one of those bush hats with the corks hanging down on strings that swish the flies away. I'm on Katie's front porch, in her metal rocker, waiting for Max to finish his shower so we can pick up Gay for the big basketball play-off later.

Last night's visit with Bampu is very much alive inside of me. When I close my eyes, I can still feel Bampu's blue eyes clamped on mine. I feel the veins on the back of his hands embedded on my fingertips. I feel the warmth of his soul pressed on my soul. The flies, heat, sweat, and red dusty earth tell me that this place is not Shangri-la, but I'm still not convinced. I'm at home here. I feel completely at one with myself and these people, who at times are bigger than life and at other times subject to the same frailties as the rest of the world.

Chris and Ian are sprawled out sound asleep on the floor in Katie's living room. Greg, Roland, and two others I've never seen before are also crashed on the floor, flophouse style. I've come a long way. I'm not even paranoid about Chris getting bugs from the mattress. My mother would die if she could see her grandson now. I just peeked in on him and had to chuckle. The scene reminds me of *The Jerk,* where Steve Martin plays a white kid adopted by a poor black family in the South.

I can hear Katie in the kitchen carrying on about the empty booze bottles she found on the front porch. I know she's trying so hard for everything to be ideal for Chris and me. It's not perfect here. Maybe that's why I love it so much. I see Max coming now. He looks very serious. More later . . ."

Max had every reason to look serious. "We're not gonna go up Cunnamulla way," he said as I made my way to the car.

That got my undivided attention. "*What* did you say?"

"I says: 'We ain't gonna be gettin' Gay.'"

I felt like I had just been hit in the face with a cream pie. "I see."

Max nodded and gave me a look that said, Finally she got it.

I opened the car door and tossed the map and car keys onto the seat and then slammed the car door shut. "Why aren't we going?"

Max took off his bush hat, fixed the jaunty little feather that stuck in the brim, and said, "Ya hungry?"

How long was he going to keep me up in the air? "I could go for a cup of coffee."

"We'll go on down to the milk bar an' get us Dorothy's egg plate."

How could he be hungry? "Should we drive?"

"I feel like walkin'."

It was his macho pride. She must have dumped him. "I feel like walking, too," I said.

The heat and the windlessness made our walk feel unusually long. But as usual, Max walked without talking. He seemed to be in some sort of trance. I stole glances sideways. At one point, I thought I saw a tear stream down his cheek, but it could have just as easily been sweat. It was so hot I was tasting my own. I was practically running to keep pace.

Halfway there, Max finally spoke. "Fresh dingo tracks," he said, squatting down for a closer look. I could barely see the paw prints in the earth. I asked Max how he could tell that it wasn't just a stray dog. "Ya jus' know."

This was so like Max, answering practically everything with "Ya jus' know." Well, every other time, it didn't bother me, but it did right now and I let him know it.

"*How* do I just know, Max?"

Max didn't break his stride. "Awwgh, *ya* wouldn't know," he said. "*Aborigine* know."

What a cocky little answer. He was taking his disappointment over Gay out on me. Okay, so he felt close enough to me to act like a wise guy and not be afraid of jeopardizing our friendship. I was perversely pleased.

"I heard the dingo last night," I said, filling in the dead air.

"Ya din't hear no dingo," Max said, in the same tone Reuel used whenever I'd tell him I heard a burglar downstairs.

"I heard a dingo," I said, holding my ground.

"Ya hear bandicoot."

Men. They love to tell you what you heard and saw. "I know what I heard, Max. It was a dingo."

"Bandicoot."

We were worse than Chris and Margaret. "Dingo!"

"Bandicoot!"

This was getting ridiculous. It was no longer fun and I purposely let slip a private thought. "You're an asshole, Max."

Max didn't flinch. "You'll be right," he said, pressing ahead like Napoleon leading his troops to the Russian Steppes.

"What the hell does 'you'll be right' mean?"

"It means, 'you'll be right.' "

"It means gibberish to me."

Without breaking pace, Max attacked right back. "The trouble with ya is that ya speak fancy an' ya can't understand plain talk."

"What!" I said, tugging his shirt sleeve, slowing his stride down. "*I* speak fancy?"

"Yeah, sometimes ya do."

"I just called you an asshole."

Max stopped dead in his tracks. He looked at me as if he were seeing the devil incarnate. I didn't know what he was going to do or say. His mouth had narrowed to an alien slit. I folded my arms and scrutinized his tight face right back, daring him to deny the hard, cold fact. The heat coming from Max's retinas made the Outback sun seem like a joke. Slowly, very slowly, his eyes widened, loosening his set jaw.

"Good on yer," Max mumbled, breaking into a grin, then into a chuckle, and finally into unleashed laughter that brought us both to the red soil, practically splitting our guts like two goofy kids. I hadn't laughed like that since Old Ma was alive. It was a pee-in-your-pants, best friend, insane laughing episode that might have been, in retrospect, the turning point in my journey.

As we devoured Dorothy's unbelievable fried eggs and bacon at the Aborigine milk bar, Max said to me, "Ya a real funny white lady."

"Me? What makes me so funny?" First fancy, now funny.

Max put enough butter on his toast to clog every artery. "Ya don't hold back what ya thinkin'."

I wondered for a minute if he was being sarcastic. "That's good?" I asked.

"Reeeel good," Max said. He called over to Dorothy to bring us another cuppa. "Yeah, Gay wants me to tell ya that she really enjoyed meetin' ya. An' if ya ever get up Cunnamulla way she be wantin' to see ya."

I took a sip of the strong coffee and forced out my next words. "So it's over with you and Gay, isn't it?"

Max dumped three packs of sugar in his coffee. "Whaddya mean, it's over?" he asked with such a penetrating look that I thought that there was a good chance I had just overstepped my boundary.

I backpedaled. "I guess, what I mean is, since we didn't go get her this morning that maybe you and—you know—you and Gay may have decided to cool it a little."

Max was not cutting me any slack. "Go on, whaddya mean 'cool it'?"

I was saved by the bell, Dorothy coming over and joining us. And after a few minutes of chat a sixteen-wheel rig pulled up in front of the store, and that meant three, four, possibly five, trucks would follow in a road train, all hauling sheep. A Crocodile Dundee character in jeans, a khaki shirt with the sleeves lopped off at the armpit, and a bush hat covering a mop of blond hair leapt out of the cab. He entered the tidy, spic-and-span milk bar looking worn, sexy, and starved. Dorothy, who apparently knew the bloke, called over, "We all outta tucker 'ere, Lester!"

Lester helped himself to a pack of cigarettes behind the counter and yelled back, "Turn it up, mate. Don't kid me!"

Before Dorothy headed for the kitchen, she turned to Max and me, but mostly just to me. "Too bad ol' Tom's not gonna be back fa the B-ball game."

"Medicine Tom's leaving again?" I asked, immediately thinking the obvious.

An exquisitely sly look came over Dorothy's balloon-round face. "His truck broke itself down again. This time near Brewarrina way." She flashed one of her confidential-but-anything-but looks. With that shared, she got up, retied a white apron splattered with grease, and headed off to the griddle to whip up some bangers and bum-nuts—sausage and eggs, as Max translated.

Max picked up where we'd left off. "Yeah," he said, "if ya never had come up 'ere, I wouldn't ever seen Gay."

Max had told me that once before. But I called him on it, now. "Did you *really* get in touch with Gay because you wanted her to meet *me?*"

"Ya right," he answered without a second's hesitation.

"I'm flattered."

"Flattered?"

"You know, that you thought so much of me that you wanted me to meet a very important woman in your life." I hoped that I didn't sound fancy *or* funny.

"Yeah." He swilled the rest of his coffee and turned to the window. "Lotsa sheep in 'ere," he said, escaping to safe ground. His eyes were moist.

I didn't know what to say and so I tried something different—kept my mouth shut.

"Yeah," Max said, "them sheep know where 'eyre headed awright. They real nervous."

"Max," I said, charting new territory, "do you know where you're headed?"

There was a long bout of silence. Finally Max turned to me and said, "Where I'm headed is right where I'm supposed to be goin'."

"Where's that?"

"Back to Redfern," Max said, with no trace of reluctance, "to work with Fatha Ted, Sister Pat, and Sister Dorothy helpin' my bruddas."

"You mean, Gay wanted you to go live in Cunnamulla?"

"I'm most good to my bruddas when I'm free," Max said. He pointed to the rig outside and with a devilish expression added, "Them sheep aren't free an' look where they off to."

"Okay," I said, thinking his light mood had given me carte blanche to be brutally frank, "so you're saying it's over with Gay?"

Max gave a look of incredulity. "How can a person ya love real deep be over with?" He paused a bit. "Where does the 'over with' go? Thaalangay's right 'ere," Max said, tapping his heart. "I'm walk-ing with all that love I'm feelin'. I'm jus' not walkin' Back o'Bourke fa now an' she's not walkin' in Redfern fa now."

"I like that."

"Whaddya like?"

"That you're taking all the love you feel and walking with it," I said. "And I like the 'walkin' for now' part. The way I figured it, you're either together or apart. And if you're apart, well, then it's over. I think I like your way better."

Max nodded. "Yeah, if I wasn't walkin' in Redfern, I wouldn't ever met ya in Fatha Ted's church, an' ya a reeel important person in my life. I never met an American lady before. When ya not thinkin' ya-self to death, ya real full of the earth. Yeah," he said, "ya reeel far away an' reeel close in. Jus' like the stars. Ya'll be in my heart fa as long as I'm walkin'."

I was so moved by this, that I leaned over and gave Max a hug. I didn't care that Lester had just sat down at the table next to us and gave a snicker and headshake in response to our embrace. Nor did I care that Max, sensing Lester's cynical eyes on us, eased out of my clutch, turned to his fellow countryman. " 'Ow's it goin', mate?" he said. To which Lester responded, "Not bad, mite."

While the men were doing their male thing, I went up to the counter to gossip with Dorothy. I was hoping to find out more about Medicine Tom. Instead, she said, matter-of-factly, "I see ya brung white folk in 'ere with ya."

"I brought *who* in?" I thought I had misunderstood her.

Dorothy sliced off a dark spot on one of the oranges. She took the rind and rubbed it along a grease burn on her wrist. "A man an' a lady followed ya in 'ere," she said.

"No, we came in alone," I corrected her. But a moment later, I realized that Dorothy might have been referring to something else. The hair on my arm stood up once again. "Are you telling me you saw white *spirits?*" I whispered, my eyes glued to the candy bars on the counter acting like Cadbury chocolate was my touchstone for reality.

"Right. A real tall man an' a real short lady—they was both real, real white," Dorothy said undramatically.

I took in a deep breath of wafting sausage grease—as if that was going to make the moment normal. Could it have been John and Old Ma? What did they look like? Why didn't I see them? Did they try to get my attention? Were they in *street* clothes? Was there a message? Would I have fainted if I had seen them? Ever since talking with Bampu at his bedside, I felt them near.

Guardedly I looked around. "Dorothy"—I hesitated—"are they still here?"

She gave a cursory glance around the store. "Don't see nobody now."

I didn't know if I was pleased or not. This, again, was new ground for me. Irreverently, I thought of Topper. I was disbelieving, scared, and delighted all at the same time. Did they know that I think about them every day? Did I blow the chance to tell them this?

It was probably inappropriate, but I asked anyway: "Dorothy, why can Aborigines see spirits and white people can't?"

Dorothy stopped examining the oranges momentarily. She looked at me with eyes that seemed to reflect unlimited knowledge of the spirit world. "Aborigines see with eyes behind their eyes," she said.

I didn't want to sound impertinent, but I needed to know more. "Can I learn how to do that?"

Her response was immediate: "Jus' look."

There, I had my answer, and a reprimand for my stubborn refusal to see what was already there.

"How do I just look?" I pressed.

"From the bottom up," Dorothy said. "From the inside out."

On our way back, a meat pie for Katie in hand, Max asked if we might detour down to the river where the family's humpie once stood. For most of the way, we walked without saying a word. I was practicing Aborigine "thought walking," and from all outward appearances, Max was doing the same. But just as we decended a low sandy, scrubby hill festooned with anthills and black, stocky roots, a lizard darted out from beneath a grass tree. I nearly tripped. Thinking it was a poisonous snake, I screamed.

"Awwgh, goanna," Max said, closing up his pocketknife. He scooped his hand down, claw-style, and plucked up the six-inch lizard. For a brief moment, I wondered if this was going to be dinner.

"Will he bite?" I asked, inching away from the scaly reptile.

"Real nice animals," Max said, petting it, and holding it out for me to do the same.

I was never much of a nature woman. "Nice," I said with my arms pasted to my side.

"Yeah, he was right in ya path, comin' to see ya." He smiled and stroked the contented goanna.

For Max's sake, I forced myself to run two timid fingers along the critter's back. It felt just like my mother's alligator handbag that my brother used to chase me around the house with when we were little. "I almost stepped on you, little fella," I said, worrying that I was going to get warts.

"He likes ya," Max chuckled. He was totally into that lizard.

"Hey," I said, "why don't we take him back for Chris?"

"What fa?"

"For a pet."

"He belongs right 'ere," Max said in a scolding tone. He gingerly set it down, and the lizard scampered back under the grass tree and down a hole.

And in that moment Dwango's words spoken through me in our Manly basement came rushing back: "When the lizard appears, you will know that you're on the right path. Stay close to the ground and follow the source. Open yourself to the earth and look to the sky."

"Max," I said as we continued on our way, "how do I open myself up to the earth?"

A look came over Max's face that I hadn't seen before. It was a look that a teacher might use for a student who just doesn't quite get it, but desperately wants to. "Ya take a long journey deep inside ya-self. On ya journey, respect everything aroun' ya. The earth, the trees, rocks, flowers, birds, goannas, snakes, small children, old sick, dyin' people. Ya listen to them. They're all singin' songs aroun' ya. An' waitin' fa ya to sing with them."

Everything Max said sounded so simple and so easy and so right, but I still wasn't grasping the concept. "How does a white lady hear them?"

"Same way Aborigine hear them," Max said. "With ears behind ya ears."

"How do you know when you've heard them?"

"When ya feel lighter in ya step. Ya heart feels real big. Laughin' an' cryin' is easy. An' sayin' good-bye's easy."

I felt a jolt. "Saying good-bye? That can be easy?"

"When ya feel free inside ya-self."

"You're free inside yourself, Max," I said. "I can see it in everything you do."

"I'm not thinkin' about what happened yesterday," Max said, reaching for a leaf from the *cunjevoi* tree that would reduce the pain in Ama's joints.

"You know, Max, for the first time in my life, I think I'm actually happy with who I am."

"That's real nice," Max said, " 'cause when ya bein' ya-self, that's when ya livin' the most."

"Max," I said, "I want to walk in the sunshine every day. Even when I go back to Connecticut and it's pouring rain or in a snowstorm, I'm going to be out walking. I want to go back to where I grew up and take a rock from our garden."

"That's what ya say the last time I brung ya here," Max said. He surprised me that he remembered. "I remember everythin' ya say to me. It's all 'ere in my heart. Yeah, ya made my heart bigger bein' with ya."

Hearing Max speak those words, I could feel my own heart begin to expand to places it had never been before. "Max," I said, looking deep into his eyes, "I suddenly feel like there's no space between us."

"Awwgh," Max said, slinging his arm around my shoulder in a gesture that went far beyond anything physical, "now you're talkin' like an Aborigine."

"I feel like I've learned a lot about Aborigine ways."

"Yeah?" Max chuckled as we walked arm in arm toward the river. "That's a real good way fa ya to feel."

When we arrived at our destination, Max removed the buried stone from where his family's humpie had once stood. We then walked a short distance over to the sacred watering hole. Ceremoniously, Max threw the stone into the middle of the spring. As the ripples spread to the edges of the pool, thousands of teardrops cascaded gracefully back down, creating an incandescent halo above where the stone entered the water.

When he completed this ritual, he asked me if I wanted to have a swim. I told him that I did. Of course, I did. He said that he would wait for me under "his" tree, off in the distance. As he did the first time he brought me here.

"Take as long as ya need," he said with an expression of enlightened tranquility that one would expect from a Buddhist monk. "I might have me a little snooze."

I took off my clothes and dove into the clear, cool, blue spring. The moment the pure water embraced me, I knew that I was part of

Max's ritual. I *understood* the Aborigine words he had chanted after he had thrown the stone. The words had bubbled up from the depths of the pool. "It's time to return to ya place," I heard with ears behind my ears.

And I knew that just as the tree which Max was now snoozing under and the watering hole where I was swimming in were joined by some larger design, Max's soul and my soul were also connected and we would always be "lookin' out fa each other."

# THIRTEEN

*L*ate afternoon, the adults were summoned to the field for the long-awaited B-ball play-off. Ama and Fran arrived first. They were followed by Dorothy, Pat, Lou, Roland, Greg, and a gang of people I was meeting for the first time. Ama was more chipper than I had ever seen her. There was a reason. It seems that the cunjevoi leaf had done its job on Ama's arthritic joints. As far as she was concerned, Medicine Tom and his truck could rot in Brewarrina. Apparently Ama suspected what everybody else in town suspected. Fran, on the other hand, seemed to buy the broken truck routine. "He's goin' be real sad missin' this 'ere game," she said, shaking her head in sympathy over her poor husband's bad fortune. Of course it did occur to me that Fran, like many women whose husbands have affairs, was just glad to get rid of him for a while.

Aborigine children were like American kids. They performed much better with a cheering crowd, and so Chris, the young impresario, instructed us to cheer loud and long. Once he was certain that we got the hang of what to call out, he separated the audience into Home and Visitors. That was a scene in itself. Nobody could make up his mind what side he wanted to be on—nobody, that is, except Ama. She was staying right where she put her chair, under the only shade tree. Finally we were evenly divided on opposite sides of the field, and Chris proceeded to announce the starting lineup. Moments later, these micro New York Knicks and Phoenix Suns bolted out of the tall scrub and onto the red dirt court. Ian was leading the pack. He was wearing Chris's Michael Jordan shorts. Margaret was swimming in an Orlando Magic T-shirt; little Henry was scooting around in Chris's Pumps basketball sneakers. Fred had on my son's Knicks baseball cap. From the looks of the gang, Chris didn't have a stitch of clothes left in his backpack.

Henry and Squeaky were the coaches who doubled as referees. Henry had THE KNICKS boldly painted across his bare chest and back. Squeaky had the same with THE SUNS. Each wore a reed whistle. Neither was shy about using it. I knew very little about the official rules of basketball, but I did know that both sides don't cheer at the same time for the same thing. In fact, this was the most charming and telling thing about this Aborigine game. Nobody would take sides. Each time a kid missed a basket, both sides mournfully lowered their heads and muttered, "Awwww, air ball." And whenever any of the kids made a basket, *both* Home and Visitors fans jumped up with fists in the air, and ran around in a circle cheering, in chorus: "Yeah! Yeah! Yuh the Man! Yuh the Man!" Even Ama raised her arthritic fist high into the afternoon sky. "Yuh the man!" she called out loud and long.

The game dragged on well past sunset. On the way back to Katie's for meat pie and damper, I caught up with Chris. "Hey," I said to my bedraggled son, "great game. You really did a super job teaching everyone how to play."

"Thanks, Mom," he said, giving me a quick, sweaty kiss. "Hey, did you see the awesome slam dunk Fred made tying the game?"

Uncertain of the rules, I asked, "Can basketball end in a tie?"

"Only Aborigine basketball," Chris said, fully embracing the rule. Then he said, "Mom, don't get mad, but I told the kids that they could keep the clothes."

I wasn't sure that I had heard correctly. Chris's basketball shorts and jersey and caps had been so important to him that he refused to leave them in the house in Manly for fear that somebody would break in and steal them. And now he was going to just give them away? I must have misunderstood. "You're giving *what* away?"

"Please don't be mad," Chris begged. "They're so happy with the stuff."

Registering those words, I was unable to speak. There were so many different emotions coursing through me. I dropped the plastic bag filled with empty soda cans, took Chris into my arms, and held him close. Feeling his young heart beating furiously against mine, I drew in a strength and delight that made me want to plunge into this life with even more sense of vitality and enthusiasm.

"Yuh the man," I whispered.

"You're the mom," he said back.

As I watched Chris run up and join his mates, I knew that I had made a final leap in my journey. My inner voice spoke: The most precious gifts of life are the ones that are seen in the radiant faces of our children—their love that bursts forth spontaneously is no different from a bird that sings, a flower that blooms, and the wind that blows. I must remember always to let my son be free to explore. And I must continue to fearlessly walk my own path.

After the meat pie and damper, we sat around Katie's campfire and the customary singing and storytelling began. While I was making a mental list of everything that needed to be done for our early morning departure back to Dubbo, Katie related something from the Dreamtime. This was about the crocodile and the owl arguing over who was the better hunter. Katie used so many Aborigine words that I only got the general idea and the end of the story where owl tracks could still be seen at the bottom of the river and crocodile teeth could sometimes be seen hanging inside the acacia tree.

I was deep in thought about how I was going to get splotches of emu blood out of the trunk before I returned the rental car, when Roland called out, "Liza, do ya Bette Davis fa us!"

"Yeah, that's real good," I heard Dorothy say. She was undoubtedly referring to the last time I performed that insane skit. Although I didn't feel like being clownish, I did want to share myself with my friends—friends, I realized, that I might never see again. I grabbed Roland's cigarette and was on the verge of becoming Bette Davis when I had a change of heart. I handed Roland back his cigarette and without a moment's rehearsal, I said what was really in my heart.

"I'd like to tell you one of my own personal stories," I began. I didn't have a clue where I was going with this. "It's about a lady who traveled halfway around the world with her young son to visit very special people deep in the Outback. But on her arrival, she and her son were so frightened by the people she was seeing for the first time that they didn't even want to get out of the car. And now just the thought of getting in the car and leaving troubles her a lot. Each person this woman met along her journey made her step lighter and heart bigger and taught her that the only thing that matters in life is walking in the sunshine with the people you love. She had taken a journey to a faraway land without her husband so that she could return to journey with him, free from limited attachments, free from a confined view of the world, free to allow all our passions to flourish.

"She learned from these people how to love, laugh, share, live— and die. She learned that when you respect what's around you— everyone and everything—you gain an inner respect and vitality that allows you to connect to all that's around you. She met children. Old people. Sick people. Dying people. All were angels of light. While in the beautiful red earth village, the Unknown became the Known. The After Life became the Now Life. My friend, Randy, who is in America right now sick and dying, is more alive right now in my heart than ever. Last night I phoned him from the Oasis to say that I'll be home in a week's time, and he asked me to tell all of you that he feels the love you've been sending."

A chorus of "Ahhhhhhhhh" reverberated in the balmy night air.

I went on, "Because of each person here, I know how to hear better and see clearer. Every soul I'm looking at is a precious jewel in my heart that will shine with me for as long as I'm walkin'." With those words, I sat back down.

The only sound was the crackling of the fire. Then I heard Max mutter something to Lou, who got up and went off for something.

"Max," I said, looking at only his profile in the flickering light, "all through my stay, I kept asking you to lead me to someone who could help Randy."

"That's right," Max said, his eyes fixed on the flames.

"And now I know that you did."

"Yeah?" Max turned full face, his deep blue eyes no longer reflecting any secrets.

"Max, you led me to myself."

Max smiled, and Greg picked up his didgeridoo to play. The next thing I knew, Lou was back from wherever she had gone and was at my side. "This is fa you," she said, handing me an elaborately carved emu egg.

Wordless, I accepted the gift. I held the delicate object in both hands, as Max told me the story behind it. Six months before I arrived, Lou had awakened one morning very early and walked deep into the scrub where she was led to the egg. She picked it up, and sitting on a rock, she began to carve onto the egg the face of a spirit doctor who had lived many, many years earlier. When it was complete, she rotated the egg so the carved image was upside down, and guided by the spirit, she continued carving. It was the face of a woman with features far different from those of anyone she knew. At the right moment, the spirit told her, she would present the egg to the person whose face she had carved.

"Bring it to the light," Max said, leading me to the fire.

As I held the egg near the flame, there was no mistaking the face Lou had carved. It was Dwango. I had seen him in the house in Manly and then again at the sacred watering hole.

Lou came over to me and turned the egg so Dwango's face was upside down. "See," she said, "it's ya face. Yuz the fair bush princess."

My image was instantly clear. I looked around the campfire. Everyone looked back at me as if Lou's pronouncement had suddenly made me special. Feeling a bit awkward, I asked, "When did you know to give this to me?"

"That first evenin' that ya pull ya car into our village," Lou replied.

Everyone nodded their heads in agreement. "You knew back then?"

"That's right. But we had to wait to give it to ya."

"Wait?"

"Back when ya first got here, ya was lookin at us, but ya wasn't seein' us," Dorothy said.

"I didn't know how to," I said.

"We had to wait until ya learned things that ya needed to learn," Max said. "Ya can't jus' go givin' somebody somethin' until they're ready to have it."

Those words released tears, which released laughter, which released dancing. And while Roland strummed the guitar and Henry and Squeaky sang out, Max and I danced. We danced on the red soil under the star-filled sky. I felt as close to earth and heaven as I could get. "Max," I said, "my soul has roots and wings."

"Now you're an Aborigine," Max whispered, moments before Max felt someone tapping at his arm. "Margaret wants to dance, too."

And that night I danced with everybody. Even Ama gave quite a sprightly two-step around the campfire. But most surprising was to see Chris and Margaret doing the funky chicken to an Aborigine folk song.

Chris later said, "It was only a dance."

# FOURTEEN

At five o'clock the following morning, Max's inner alarm clock went off. "Time to get up." He shook my arm, jolting me from a deep sleep.

For a brief moment, I was confused by the wake-up call. "Huh? What?"

"Ya told me to wake ya at five," Max said, his hand still clutching my arm.

Slowly my eyes adjusted to the darkness. Max was all dressed in his western shirt, red bandana, and bush hat. "Did you sleep in that?" I asked.

"I jus' had me a shower," Max said, perky, anxious to hit the road.

I looked beside me. Chris was nestled into his sleeping bag without a care in the world. Our campfire had burned down to a pile of black ashes. "It's still dark," I grunted.

"It'll be light in about twenty minutes," Max said. He checked the sky as if to verify the exact time. "I'll boil us a cuppa an' we better be headed outta 'ere."

I fumbled my way out of my zippered sleeping bag and stumbled toward the abandoned house for a quick shower. Finally awake, I went back to the campfire, woke Chris, and told him to take his pillow and get in the car. We would stop in Bourke for breakfast.

"But I wanna say good-bye to my friends," Chris said, still half asleep.

I looked up and down the road. "There's not a single light on in any house," I said. "You'll have to write to them when we get back home."

"Can't we stay just one more day," he begged as he snuggled further down into his sleeping bag.

It was a very tempting idea. If we hadn't already changed our train tickets the day before and told the car rental agency to expect us around noon, I might have just given in and stayed.

Once at the car, Max and I took a final bag count. "Do we have enough bottled water?" I asked.

"Three bottles will be good fa us." He squeezed them between two duffle bags.

"Tires okay?" I asked my copilot.

"Greg an' me checked them yesterday. Henry checked ya oil."

"Well, I guess we're out of here," I said. My hand was on the driver's door, half hoping that the car wouldn't start.

Just then, Chris yelled, "Here they come!"

I looked down the road to see a virtual parade of people approaching. I looked up the road. There were more people. The houses were all lighted and doors were opening and closing as if it was three o'clock in the afternoon. There was Roland, Greg, Pat, Fran, Lou, Dorothy, the entire mob of kids; even sleeping baby Matthew arrived on Margaret's hip. Off in the distance, Ama was hobbling toward us, using a long shaved stick to steady her. Henry was at her side and Squeaky was at his side. Tucked underneath Squeaky's arm was something that looked like a book. On closer inspection, I saw it was computer paper. And on still closer inspection, I saw something had been written on it. When everyone was finally gathered at the car, Squeaky passed each person a sheet of the paper.

Then we began the bittersweet agony of saying good-bye. Katie told us to be sure to remember that when you make johnnycakes not to flip more than once on each side. Fran said that she would make certain that Tom sent me more allergy medicine as soon as his truck was fixed. Ian, clutching the basketball Chris left for him, said, "Tell Michael Jordan if he's ever in Australia to come to Enngonia!" Roland said, "Same goes fa Paul Newman!" Greg said that he was going to paint a picture for us and we should have it whenever he finishes it. Ama didn't say anything other than to wave. She was wearing the surfer's bracelet Chris had given to her. Margaret was wearing

Chris's Knicks cap backward. Lila whispered to me that Margaret cried herself to sleep. Chris, overhearing that, went over and said to Margaret, "Hey, let's write to each other and tell each other what we're doing and maybe sometime when I'm grown up, I'll come back to Enngonia and we'll like maybe hang out together." Margaret beamed.

Hugging these gentle people for the last time, I couldn't help but be overwhelmed with tears. "When am I going to see you guys again?" I asked with a plaintive wail.

For a moment, nobody spoke. Then Henry looked up and said, "When ya see the emu in the sky."

And with that Max, Chris, and I got into the car. I turned on the ignition. And as we were about to drive down the red dirt road, a chorus of familiar voices, singing as one, swelled with "America, the Beautiful."